TO PROTECT, CONSERVE, AND ENHANCE

The History of the Pennsylvania Fish & Boat Commission

By Kenneth C. Wolensky, Ed.D.

Editorial and Design by Ted R. Walke

inside front cover photograph by Terry Malloy

The mission of the Pennsylvania Fish & Boat Commission is to protect, conserve, and enhance the Commonwealth's aquatic resources and provide fishing and boating opportunities.

Published by the
Pennsylvania Fish & Boat Commission
P.O. Box 67000
Harrisburg, Pennsylvania 17106-7000

© 2016 Pennsylvania Fish & Boat Commission
All Rights Reserved.
First edition: July 2016
Second printing: August 2016
Printed in the United States of America
22 21 20 19 18 17 16   2 3 4 5

ISBN 978-0-692-70778-4
Library of Congress Control Number: 2016940620

www.GoneFishingPa.com
www.fishandboat.com

photo-Art Michaels, PFBC

Table of Contents

Foreword  .... *iv*

Introduction .... *xxi*

Chapter One:
The Common"wealth" of Natural Resources *2*

Chapter Two:
The Board of Fishery Commissioners is Born *14*

Chapter Three:
The Progressive Era  *40*

Chapter Four:
The Great Depression  *62*

Chapter Five:
From the Post-War Era to Earth Day  *108*

Chapter Six:
Earth Day to the End of the Twentieth Century  *156*

Chapter Seven:
2000–2015 .... *264*

Conclusion *316*

Notes: 325 • Appendix: 332 • Index: 361

Foreword

John A. Arway, *Executive Director*
Pennsylvania Fish & Boat Commission

On March 30, 2016, the Pennsylvania Fish & Boat Commission (PFBC) commemorated the 150th anniversary of our founding in 1866. A convention was held in Harrisburg in 1866 to investigate water pollution being caused by the wholesale logging of Pennsylvania's forests and the impacts caused by sedimentation of our mountain lakes and streams. There were also serious concerns about the reduction of American Shad runs in the Susquehanna River. This discussion resulted in Governor Andrew Curtin signing the law, Act of March 30, 1866 (P.L. 370, No. 336), that named James Worrall as Pennsylvania's first Commissioner of Fisheries. In 1925, Act 1925-263 established the Board of Fish Commissioners. Then, in 1949, Act 1949-180 officially established the Pennsylvania Fish Commission as an agency and described its powers and duties. The Commission appointed Charles A. French as its first Executive Director in 1949, and in 1991 under Act 1991-39, the Pennsylvania Fish Commission (PFC) became the Pennsylvania Fish & Boat Commission (PFBC).

Through its history, the Commission has evolved from a one-man operation funded solely by the General Fund to an agency with a complement of 432 staff funded by anglers and boaters through license and registration fees and the federal excise taxes on fishing and boating

Circa 1900, Susquehanna flats, Maryland.

equipment. Our mission has broadened a bit from our original one, but we are still focused on protecting, conserving, and enhancing our aquatic resources and providing fishing and boating opportunities.

I would like to take this opportunity to highlight some of our major accomplishments from our agency's history and conclude with my optimistic view of our future.

A fishway in the Susquehanna River at Holtwood in 1914.
Image from Pennsylvania Report of State Fish Commissioners of Fisheries 1914.

Susquehanna River Dams

In 1867, the first fishway was constructed at the Columbia (Wrightsville) Dam (built in 1840) on the Susquehanna River as the first attempt to restore anadromous fish runs to the Susquehanna River. Then, along came Conowingo (1929), Holtwood (1910), Safe Harbor (1931), and York Haven (1904) dams, which have been major impediments to migratory fish since they were built. In the 1950s, the resource agencies implemented a program to restore access for migratory fish to the upper Susquehanna River basin, focusing on American Shad. In response to harvest declines that signaled critically low fish-stock levels, fishing for American Shad in the Chesapeake Bay region was closed (Maryland in 1980 and Virginia in 1994).

Although Executive Director Ralph W. Abele (1972–1987) fought passionately to have fish passage installed at these dams and built a shad hatchery at Van Dyke along the Juniata River to assist the restoration process, we continue to fall short of our migratory fish restoration goals of two million American Shad and five million river herring spawning upstream of the York Haven Dam. The American Shad stock in the Susquehanna River improved slowly and made an impressive comeback by 2001, when more than 200,000 adult shad were counted at the Conowingo Dam fish lifts. Recent numbers of American Shad passing the four major downriver dams reveal only 43 American Shad passing York Haven Dam in 2015. The 2010 *Susquehanna River Anadromous Fish Restoration Cooperative (SRAFRC) Migratory Fish Management and Restoration Plan for the Susquehanna River Basin* identifies poor efficiency of fish passage measures and facilities, low hatchery production in recent years, low numbers of spawning fish accessing quality habitat, poor young-of-year recruitment upstream of Conowingo Dam, ocean and Chesapeake Bay mortality, turbine mortality, and predation as the major causes of this decline. In recent years, the Holtwood Dam underwent a $400 million expansion, and the owners committed significant resources towards improving fish passage. At the York Haven Dam, plans are in place for a nature-like fishway to be built, which would be the largest of its kind in the eastern United States to allow shad and other species to freely migrate. A new operating license application is pending at the Conowingo Dam, and the future of shad restoration in the Susquehanna River is dependent upon the improvements to fish passage that may be required. Therefore, there is still work to be done if we ever expect to fulfill the dream of seeing a fishable population of American Shad return to the Pennsylvania portion of the Susquehanna River.

State Fish Hatcheries

In 1870, Thad Norris, a private citizen, purchased 450 bass taken from the Potomac River and relocated them to their new home on the Delaware River near Easton. This action resulted in others doing the same thing on the Susquehanna and Schuylkill rivers and other waters throughout Pennsylvania, creating the naturalized fisheries we still enjoy today. In 1873, the "State Hatching House" was built in Lancaster County near Marietta on Hoover's Spring, which is one of the famous Donegal Springs. John P. Creveling was appointed as superintendent.

Early fish stocking wagon used at Pleasant Gap State Fish Hatchery.

In 1875, the legislature appropriated $5,000 to purchase and build the Western Fish Hatchery in Corry, and William Buller was appointed as superintendent. It was constructed in 1876. The Western Hatchery received the first shipment of Brown Trout eggs from Germany in 1886. Funding to construct other state fish hatcheries followed: Pleasant Gap (1903), Pleasant Mount or Wayne (1903), Union City (1905), Tionesta (1928), Reynoldsdale (1928), Huntsdale (1932), Bellefonte (1933), Linesville (1939), Benner Spring (1952), Tylersville (1963, originally a federal hatchery), Oswayo (1968), and Fairview (1976). Big Spring State Fish Hatchery was constructed in 1970 and closed in 2001. Our system of state fish hatcheries has been upgraded, over time, with state-of-the-art wastewater treatment plants and updated fish culture equipment to produce and stock more than 5.1 million adult and fingerling trout, 1 million steelhead smolts, and more than 50 million juvenile fish of other popular sportfish species for Pennsylvania waters in 2014. In 1879, the United States Commission on Fish and Fisheries provided Pennsylvania Common Carp to culture; but in 1895, the agency abandoned carp culture in favor of black bass. In 1888, Rainbow Trout were first stocked in the Susquehanna River. And, then in 1892, the Commission had the rail car "Susquehanna" built to transport fish around Pennsylvania for stocking. In 1904, more than 90,000 frogs and more than 10.2 million Chain Pickerel were stocked. In 1907, Commission staff experimented

continued on page xi

THE BROOK TROUT.

From Pennsylvania Report of State Fish Commissioners of Fisheries 1900.

THE LAKE TROUT.

From Pennsylvania Report of State Fish Commissioners of Fisheries 1900.

Foreword ix

From Pennsylvania Report of State Fish Commissioners of Fisheries 1900.

THE RAINBOW TROUT.

Early 1900s, Pleasant Mount State Fish Hatchery

with raising freshwater Pearl Mussels and stocked more than 80,000 Coho Salmon in the Lackawaxen Creek drainage. In 1912, the Commission hatched more than 500,000 Muskellunge eggs at Union City and first stocked Muskellunge fry in the waters of Pennsylvania. In 1917, electric lights were installed at fish hatcheries, and in 1928, the Bureau of Research was established. In 1932, the United States Bureau of Fisheries started the Cooperative Nursery Program with 21 sportsmen groups receiving 450,000 Brook Trout eggs and fingerlings. In 1962, PFC took over the program for Pennsylvania and established the Cooperative Nursery Branch in 1965. Peak participation occurred in 1992 with 192 nurseries. Today, there are 162 nurseries actively participating in the program. In 1958, Kokanee Salmon eggs were hatched at Pleasant Mount and stocked experimentally in eight lakes. In 1969, the Soviet Union (Russia) provided the Commission with Amur Pike eggs. These were hatched and grown into fingerlings and subsequently stocked in Glendale Lake, Cambria County, making it the only lake in the United States where anglers could catch this species of fish and Pennsylvania the only place in the world where Muskellunge, Northern Pike, Amur Pike, and three species of pickerel could all be caught.

Education, Information, and Outreach

The Commission participated in the 1893 Chicago World's Fair and 1904 St. Louis World's Fair with live fish displays. The first issue of the *Pennsylvania Angler* magazine was published in December 1931 and cost 50 cents, compared to today's price of $3.00. In 1984, the legislature established the first Fish-for-Free Day, and the first issue of *Boat Pennsylvania* was published. The Commission created a presence on the Internet in 1996 with www.fish.state.pa.us (now, www.fishandboat.com), Twitter in 2010, and Facebook in 2012. In 2001, online (Internet) sales of fishing licenses began, and the sales system was updated to a point-of-sales system in 2006. The Commission was given the authority to sell multi-year and reduced-cost licenses in 2012. This resulted in 3- and 5-year fishing licenses being offered for sale in 2013. A new voluntary youth license to fund youth fishing programs was introduced in 2014, and the first special Mentored Youth Trout Day began in 2013. A metal fishing license button was reintroduced in 2014 as a voluntary license display option. Fishing license prices were reduced by $1.00 for the first time in history as an attempt to increase license sales, and a free FishBoatPA mobile application (app) for mobile devices was introduced in 2015. Additionally, the Save Our Susquehanna (S.O.S.) campaign was initiated in 2015 to increase public awareness and funding for projects to help a declining Smallmouth Bass fishery in the Susquehanna River from Sunbury to York Haven.

The entrance to the Fish Commission's exhibit at the 1893 Chicago World's Fair. Constructed of oak panels, it displayed photos of the Commission's hatcheries and various fish.

The shad hatchery in Bristol, Bucks County. It was established in 1893, along the Delaware River.

Fisheries

In 1907, the *Commodore Perry*, a 70-foot steam tug, was built for the agency's use on Lake Erie, and in 1913, it assisted in raising Perry's flagship *Niagara* from Misery Bay. In 1924, agency staff began performing stream surveys to classify waters to manage fisheries based on scientific principles. Daily creel limits were first set in 1925 for trout (25), bass (10), Walleyes (10), pickerel (15), and Muskellunge (3). Today's general creel limits (consult the current *Pennsylvania Fishing Summary* for sizes and exceptions) are trout (5), bass (6), Walleyes (6), pickerel (4), and Muskellunge (1). Fisherman's Paradise was opened in 1934 and attracted almost 3,000 visitors. The "Paradise" grew in popularity to where it hosted almost 35,000 visitors in 1950 and was then made a Fish-for-Fun area in 1962. In 1946, the Commission acquired a mobile biological laboratory for fisheries research and management. In 1956, uniform fly-fishing-only regulations were established. The *Perca* fisheries research vessel was launched at Lake Erie in 1959, and Governor David L. Lawrence signed Act No. 673, which established the opening day of trout season as the first Saturday after April 11, which continues today. In 1969, the start of the opening day of trout season changed from 5:00 a.m. to 8:00 a.m., due to complaints from landowners. Also, in 1969, the Commission created the Wilderness Trout Stream (WTS) program and added 75 streams in 1972. Today, 105 stream sections are included

Foreword **xiii**

THE PIKE PERCH OR SUSQUEHANNA SALMON.

From Pennsylvania Report of State Fish Commissioners of Fisheries 1900.

in the WTS program, which qualify for the Pennsylvania Department of Environmental Protection's (DEP) Exceptional Value (EV) special protected water use classification, which represents the highest protection status provided by the Commonwealth. In 1970, the Brook Trout was named the official state fish. In 1971, Chinook Salmon smolts were released into Lake Erie tributaries. The Commission received authority for regulating reptiles, amphibians, and aquatic organisms in 1974. The world record Amur Pike was caught from Glendale Lake in 1976, and the Commission promulgated the first regulations for organized snake hunts. The Commission adopted Operation FUTURE (Fisheries Utilization Through User Resource Evaluation) in 1981, and as explained by former Director Abele, "(This) marks a formally declared shift in the philosophy and mission of the Pennsylvania Fish Commission from recreation first to resource first. This truly makes the Pennsylvania Fish Commission a conservation agency." Resource First was adopted by the Board of Commissioners as an agency motto in 1987 and then as an operation philosophy in 2008. An early regional opening day for trout season in southeastern Pennsylvania counties was initiated in 2007.

Law Enforcement

The Act of June 3, 1878, forbade fishing on Sunday, and in 1937, Act 86 made Sunday fishing lawful again. In 1878, Fish Wardens Ludwick, Lowe, and Hoover were paid $50. In 1901, there were 12 Fish Wardens, and in 1902, Special Wardens (now Deputy Waterways

Circa 1930s, a Fish Warden is shown patrolling at Fisherman's Paradise, Centre County.

Conservation Officers (DWCOs)) were created. In 1901, a law (Section 26 of Act of May 25, 1901 (P.L. 302, No. 203)) went into effect that prohibited placing poisonous substances in any waters. And, in 1909, another law was passed forbidding the emptying into any waters of the Commonwealth any waste deleterious to fish. These two laws historically established PFBC as one of the oldest water pollution enforcement agencies, not only in Pennsylvania, but in the entire nation. In 1913, Governor John K. Tenner signed into law the first controls on motorboating requiring motorboats to have mufflers. In 1915, fish wardens and deputies were given arrest powers. In 1919, non-resident fishing licenses were first sold for $5.00 to 50 non-resident anglers. Bradford County Fish Warden William E. Shoemaker was shot and killed on August 25, 1921, and in 1958, Lycoming County Fish Warden Raymond L. Schroll Jr. drowned attempting to rescue his partner. Both were inducted into the National Law Enforcement Officers Memorial in Washington D.C. In 1921, the "Resident Fish License Law" was passed and more than 200,000 licenses were sold to citizens 21 years of age and older (age reduced to 18 in 1923 and then to 16 in 1925) for $1.00 in 1922. This was the beginning of the agency becoming self-dependent on user fees. The first fishing license button was introduced in 1923, and resident license fees were increased to $1.50 in 1928. In

Beginning in the early 1960s, the Fish Commission transported this live fish display truck to various events throughout the state.

1941, trolling was prohibited from a motorboat, which was then changed in 1944 to again allow trolling on rivers. In 1942, a prohibition was added to regulation for operating a motorboat while intoxicated. In 2015, PFBC Waterways Conservation Officers (WCOs) had 91 Boating Under the Influence (BUI) arrests. In 1956, carp fishing with long bow and arrow was legalized. Rules-of-the-road boating regulations were amended to prohibit water-skiing within

the provisions of the 100-foot rule. In 1957, Fish Wardens received the authority to enforce littering. Fish Wardens were retitled Waterways Patrolmen in 1968. In 1980, the Fish and Boat Code codified fishing and boating laws and provided limited police powers to Waterways Patrolmen. Act 1984-66 changed the name of Waterways Patrolman to Waterways Conservation Officers, and in 1984, the first female Waterways Conservation Officer, WCO Sally A. Corl, was hired. A peak law enforcement workforce occurred in 1995 with 106 WCOs and 340 DWCOs. In 2000, operators of personal watercraft (PWC) were required to complete a safe boating course, and in 2003, it became mandatory for all persons born on or after January 1, 1982, to possess a Boat Safety Education Certificate to operate a boat with a motor over 25 horsepower.

WCO Sally A. Corl

Foreword **xvii**

The Future

It is a great time to learn about our agency's contribution to the health of "Penn's Woods and Waters" and celebrate the fact that our 86,000 miles of streams, nearly 4,000 lakes and reservoirs, more than 404,000 acres of wetlands, and 63 miles of Lake Erie shoreline are still home to more than 25,000 species of known plants and animals, and perhaps, many thousands more yet to be identified. These facts demonstrate the enormity and complexity of the challenges that face PFBC as we strive to fulfill our legislative and Constitutional duties to protect, conserve, and enhance our Commonwealth's aquatic resources.

More than 150 species of plants and animals have been lost from Pennsylvania, and 664 others are species of greatest conservation need and are detailed in our State Wildlife Action Plan: 90 birds, 19 mammals, 65 fish, 22 reptiles, 18 amphibians and 450 invertebrates. The major threats have been identified as residential and commercial development (15 percent), energy production and mining (13 percent), pollution (13 percent), invasive and other problematic species, and genes and diseases (12 percent).

We currently have a population of 12,763,536 people which continues to increase on a fixed amount of land, 45,333 square miles. As of 2015, 83,438 miles of streams and rivers, out of a total of 86,000 miles, have been assessed by DEP staff for aquatic life use support, and approximately 19 percent (15,882 miles) do not fully support healthy aquatic communities. Furthermore, some of these waters are still not fishable or swimmable. We have the nation's sixteenth largest river, the Susquehanna River, which drains nearly half of Pennsylvania's land area and has been identified as a major contributor to the impairment of the Chesapeake Bay. The Susquehanna River currently supports a Smallmouth Bass fishery in distress with bacteria infecting young bass producing mortality rates of 10 to 70 percent (2005–2015). Adult bass have been found with cancerous tumors, other open sores and lesions, intersex conditions (male bass with egg precursors and hormones, which should only be found in female bass), and black spots that aren't understood (blotchy bass syndrome or melanosis). There is something wrong with the Susquehanna River, and we need to admit it and begin working on a plan to solve its problems. We also know that 15,882 miles of our streams and rivers and 37,761 acres of our lakes are not attaining their aquatic life uses because of the current and legacy impacts from

The main stem of the Susquehanna River at Harrisburg

photo-Spring Gearhart, PFBC

agriculture and coal mining creating siltation, metals, nutrients, and organic enrichment of our waters.

Aldo Leopold (1887–1948) recognized the importance of land ethic in his writings and teachings; however, our society is still trying to balance the importance of a strong economy with the value of a healthy environment.

> "The land ethic simply enlarges the boundaries of the community to include soils, waters, plants, and animals, or collectively: the land. In short, a land ethic changes the role of *Homo sapiens* from conqueror of the land—community to plain member and citizen of it. It implies respect for his fellow-members, and also respect for the community as such."—*Aldo Leopold*

Our future is bright but not without challenges. We have made substantial progress over the last generation by cleaning up our waters, so that we can now say that we have more waters to fish today than when we were children. However, yesterday's challenges were simple compared to the environmental and natural resource challenges that we face in the future. Today's challenges include cancerous tumors, bacterial infections, black spot, and intersex Smallmouth Bass in the Susquehanna River; rapidly expanding deep natural gas development across Pennsylvania and the uncertainties about fracking; the Brook Trout being compromised by changing climate; aquatic invasive species (AIS) outcompeting native species; our lakes, rivers, and the Chesapeake

Bay clogged with nuisance algae blooms that lower oxygen to dangerous levels for fish and other aquatic life; less people, including our legislators, fishing, boating, and recreating outdoors; and, we can't forget about our obligation to restore American Shad to the mighty Susquehanna River. Unfortunately, I can't promise you the same thing that Executive Director Robert J. Bielo promised anglers in his "Turn of a Century" article in 1966. He was able to promise doubling the acreage of fishable lake waters from 57,000 acres in 1966 to 111,000 acres in 1975 because of a Commonwealth commitment to fund and build new lakes.

Today, we have a similar funding commitment, but it is to repair and maintain those same historic dams, which have since become unsafe and high-hazard. This commitment will ensure that our children and grandchildren will continue to have places to fish in Pennsylvania.

Our new challenges will no longer be at the local scale but will require much different solutions at the watershed, regional, national, and even global scales. We will have to work across disciplines and use the appropriate science to diagnose the problems, apply the engineering skills to develop the solutions, and have the political will to create the laws and provide the funding for the solutions. It won't be easy, but I am confident that our next generation will have the knowledge, skills, abilities, and the guts to get it done right. Perhaps, we will finally come to recognize that a healthy economy and a healthy environment must co-exist, and the adoption of a land ethic will no longer be optional as Leopold professed.

Aldo Leopold

photo-Bob Weber, PFBC

Introduction

This is the history of the Pennsylvania Fish & Boat Commission. The story stretches back to 1866 when the agency was founded just after the end of the American Civil War. As with most institutions, PFBC's history is complex and compelling. It is a history of progress and setbacks, advances in science and hindrances posed by man, the propagation of species and threats to their existence, the appeal of angling and boating to the average Pennsylvanian, and the need to educate them to ensure that laws are obeyed. And, it is a history that demonstrates that some of the environmental problems evident in Pennsylvania during the nineteenth century remain in twenty-first century. Certainly, the history of PFBC is a history worth sharing.

American Shad

The agency was created primarily to restore the American Shad. Restorative efforts occurred contemporaneously with raising public awareness of the growing problem of water pollution caused by the American Industrial Revolution. Moreover, the agency was established to deal with the problems caused by rogue anglers who took large amounts of fish with impunity by using such aberrant means such as using dynamite and oversized fish nets.

Throughout much of nineteenth century, the Commissioners of Fisheries struggled with inadequate funding and human resources. Yet, there were some successes in fish propagation. During the early twentieth century, the agency issued its first fishing license, accepted the responsibility of registering boats, published the first issue of *Pennsylvania Angler*, and increased its efforts to address water pollution problems by enforcing new statutes such as the fish protection laws. But, that wasn't

photo-Art Michaels, PFBC

Shad gill nets at night on the Delaware River. From Pennsylvania Report of State Fish Commissioners of Fisheries 1900.

enough. Water pollution from industrial and human waste continued to plague much of the Commonwealth's streams.

By the mid-twentieth century, the agency had a new name: The Pennsylvania Fish Commission. Its staff developed the Commonwealth's first fisheries management program, expanded its law enforcement and propagation programs, and implemented many outreach and educational initiatives through its publications and by conducting angling and boating workshops at schools and other venues. As these pages explain, the latter half of the twentieth century witnessed a maelstrom of new statutes, programs, initiatives, applications of science and biology, and many other developments. The Commission's history during this era must be understood within the broader framework of major public policy reforms and initiatives when it came to the environment and conservation. Chief among them is Article 1, Section 27 (passed on May 18, 1971) of the Commonwealth's 1968 Constitution, entitled "Natural Resources and the Public Estate" (also known as the Environmental Rights Amendment):

> "The people have a right to clean air, pure water, and to the preservation of the natural, scenic, historic and esthetic values of the environment. Pennsylvania's public natural resources are the common property of all the people, including generations yet to come. As trustee of these resources, the Commonwealth shall conserve and maintain them for the benefit of all the people."

It is during this era that the Commission matured as a true conservation agency, changed its name to the Pennsylvania Fish & Boat Commission, and moved its Harrisburg headquarters to a state-of-the-art facility. In the twenty-first century, PFBC's mission remains clear:

"To protect, conserve, and enhance the Commonwealth's aquatic resources and provide fishing and boating opportunities."

logo design-Ted Walke, PFBC

Introduction **xxiii**

photo-WCO David Kaneski, PFBC

photo-Carl Haensel, PFBC

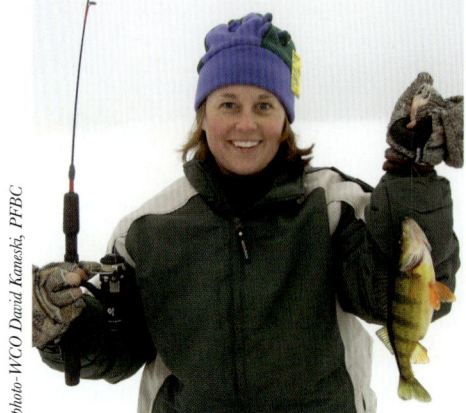

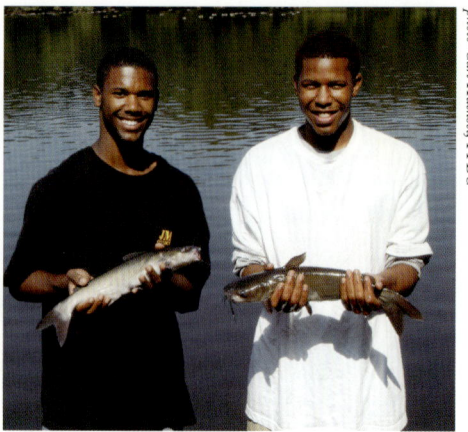

The agency provides the public with opportunities to enjoy some of the best recreational fishing and boating in the United States. This is possible because the Commonwealth's aquatic resources are rich and diverse. Remarkably, there are 86,000 miles of streams in Pennsylvania, 45,000 waterways, and nearly 4,000 lakes, ponds, and reservoirs. More than one thousand species of aquatic insects are found in Pennsylvania, as well as 38 varieties of freshwater mussels. Moreover, 159 species representing 24 families of fishes live in Pennsylvania's waters. Two broad categories exist: non-migratory freshwater fishes of 119 species in 10 families, and 40 species in 14 families categorized as migratory (such as the American Shad) and salt-tolerant fishes (Mummichog) or, essentially, freshwater representatives of marine groups found in the lower Delaware River tidal reaches.

photo-Art Michaels, PFBC

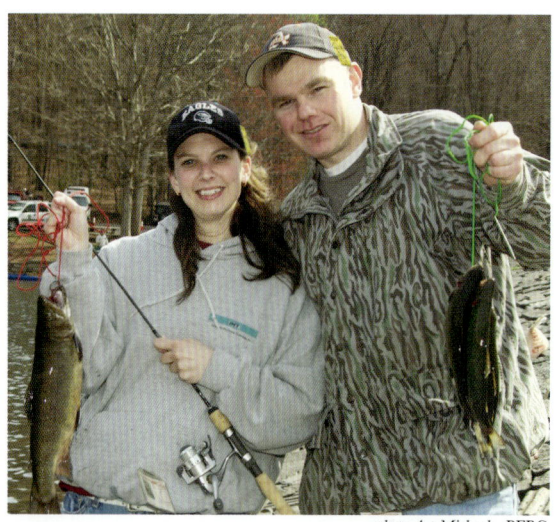

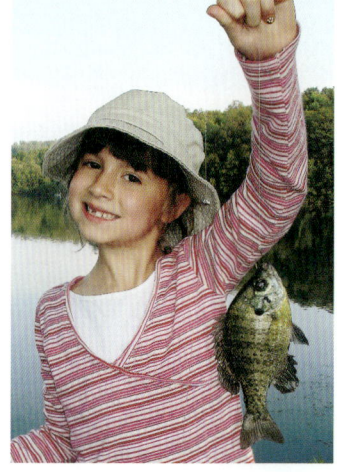

The artwork above and on the page that follows shows the diversity of fish species in Pennsylvania's waters. The art is from PFBC's Pennsylvania Fishes book. A printed version may be purchased from the Commission, and an online version can be found at www.fishandboat.com. Artwork by Ted Walke.

Pennsylvania's streams are home to 81 species, including mudminnows, perch, pike, and suckers, while five other families comprise 38 species endemic to North America such as Bowfin, Trout Perch, and Bullhead Catfishes. There are 38 species of amphibians (salamanders, frogs, and toads) represented by nine families in Pennsylvania. Also, there are 38 species of reptiles (lizards, turtles, and snakes) represented by eight families in the state.

The agency manages and safeguards these resources. According to Executive Director John Arway, "In 2015, PFBC issued more than 887,000 fishing licenses. We have 333,000 registered boats. There are nearly 400,000 members of conservation and sportsmen associations. PFBC conserves and manages the Commonwealth's many aquatic resources and does a great job of educating the public about the importance of conservation. The quality of our staff is second to none, and PFBC is widely respected by the public and public officials not only in Pennsylvania, but across the nation. Telling the story of PFBC's 150-year history is a critical step to further explain our work that reaches back to 1866."[1]

Though it was verbalized more in the latter half of the twentieth century and in the twenty-first century more than ever before, PFBC's mandate and philosophy has been consistent through its history since 1866: to protect, conserve, and enhance. It was best exemplified by former Executive Director Ralph Abele's philosophy of "Resource First." Abele charged the agency's staff with conserving Pennsylvania's aquatic resources. The best interests of the resource(s) were—and are—to be placed first. It wasn't just a slogan. It was a way of life that permeated the agency and still does today.

photo-Alysha B. Trexler, Western Pennsylvania Conservancy

Introduction

Abele's "Thin Green Line," as he referred to the agency's Bureau of Law Enforcement, is charged with ensuring that laws and regulations are obeyed by the public. WCOs are spread across the Commonwealth and may well be PFBC's most publicly visible representatives. But it isn't only about enforcement. Presently, PFBC has numerous programs that implement its work in a variety of ways.

For example, another of the agency's primary functions is to inform and educate the public about recreational angling and boating through its outreach functions. Here, online and social media play a key role. In 1996, PFBC launched its website followed by a Twitter account in 2010 and a Facebook page in 2012. Moreover, agency staff conduct fishing and boating education programs throughout the Commonwealth. Youth are a key part of PFBC's educational outreach. Initiatives such as Mentored Youth Days encourage young people to learn about and enjoy fishing and boating. In honor of Abele, the Ralph W. Abele Conservation Scholarship Fund was created in the early 1990s to encourage young people to pursue a college education in an environmental discipline.

A myriad of written materials are in the agency's outreach toolbox as well. For example, its legendary *Pennsylvania Angler*—changed to *Pennsylvania Angler & Boater* in 1997—was first published in December 1931. Today it has a print and digital readership of more than 50,000. John Arway's "Straight Talk," headlining each issue of *Pennsylvania Angler*

Pennsylvania Angler & Boater:
Since 1931

& *Boater*, discusses key topics of the day, addresses controversial issues, and educates anglers and boaters on a variety of topics. Print materials go back to when James Worrall, first Commissioner of Fisheries, began issuing annual reports in the late 1860s.

PLAY newsletter: Since 1980

When it comes to protecting aquatic resources, the agency's work takes on a life of its own. The Commission's original mission called for the protection and restoration of the American Shad. By the end of the nineteenth century, the agency hatched millions of young shad annually and planted them in major waterways such as the Susquehanna and Delaware rivers. Thanks to the work of Commission staff, the largest shad migration ever recorded in the Delaware River occurred in 1961 and, in the mid-1980s, the shad was given gamefish status and the protection of a creel limit. On the Susquehanna River, a closed season remains in effect on harvesting until greater migratory numbers return.

In the twenty-first century, various species continue to be propagated at PFBC's numerous hatcheries which are spread across Pennsylvania. Staff utilize their professional expertise, as well as state-of-the-art techniques, to produce fish. In addition, various aquatic and terrestrial species and their habitats are managed and protected by PFBC experts. The Commission's protection of other species was legislated at various times throughout its history. For example, a 1974 statute gave it jurisdiction over reptiles, amphibians, and aquatic organisms.

The agency's partnerships are many. All are vital for the Commission to meet its mission to protect, conserve, and enhance the Commonwealth's aquatic resources. PFBC staff regularly work with the

Introduction **xxix**

Stream habitat improvement projects, like this one in Boiling Springs in 2014, are great examples of how PFBC partners with host organizations.

Governor's Office and General Assembly to educate and inform staff and members not only on species and aquatic issues, but to lobby for legislative and regulatory initiatives that are central for the agency to carry out its mission.

PFBC also partners with several Pennsylvania state government agencies. These include the Department of Environmental Protection (DEP), Department of Conservation and Natural Resources (DCNR), and the Pennsylvania Game Commission (PGC). Moreover, the agency works with many federal government agencies, including the U.S. Fish and Wildlife Service, the Environmental Protection Agency, and the U.S. Army Corps of Engineers, to name a few. Partnerships with neighboring states are important as well. Examples of multi-state collaborations in which PFBC is active include the Atlantic States Marine Fisheries Commission, the Chesapeake Bay Commission, the Delaware River Basin Commission, the Great Lakes Fisheries Commission, and the Susquehanna River Basin Commission.

In addition, there are countless non-profit environmental, conservation, and outdoor recreation organizations with which PFBC partners to carry out is mission.

PFBC staff are staunch advocates for species protection and clean water; these are essential for high-quality recreational angling and boating. In recent times, Executive Director John Arway has spoken out regarding pollution in the Susquehanna River and its impact on Smallmouth Bass. And, while numerous studies have been undertaken to merge PFBC with the PGC, PFBC Commissioners and staff have consistently argued that its mission is unique and that fish and aquatic species deserve special attention by properly trained and expert staff and by dedicated funding that won't get muddled in a large bureaucracy. And, as much of the angling and boating public agree, they are better served by a single professional agency dedicated to aquatic resource conservation and recreation. PFBC staff—from the Executive Director to the front-line WCOs to hatchery workers and volunteers—carry out this mission as no other agency can.

Indeed, PFBC's staff believe in the philosophy that the natural resources of the Commonwealth belong to the public, a notion that goes back to William Penn's founding of the colony of Pennsylvania in 1681. As John Arway puts it, PFBC "holds our natural resources in public trust for our anglers, boaters, and conservationists, as well as for the general public and the many generations to come."[2]

Of course, fishing and boating are traditions that stretch back a long way. Native Americans, William Penn's early migrants, colonists, nineteenth- and early-twentieth-century immigrants, workers in urban industrial Pennsylvania, suburbanites in the post–World War II era, environmental activists in the 1960s and 1970s, and today's residents have engaged in fishing and boating for both sustenance and leisure.

Where and why did today's PFBC begin? It is a complicated story that doesn't follow an easy trajectory. It is a history that emerges from the confluence of the abuse of natural resources and responses to such exploitation, the interests of the conservation and environmental movements, collaboration among like-minded natural resource proponents, economics, education, and reactive and proactive public policy. To better understand this convergence, it is important to look to the agency's origins and its evolution in its span of time since its beginning in 1866. It is likewise necessary to discuss Pennsylvania's natural bounty.

Introduction **xxxi**

Acknowledgements

Leading this book project, especially before and during an auspicious anniversary year such as the Commission's 150th in 2016, has been both a very daunting and gratifying experience. The first acknowledgement must go to John Arway, current PFBC Executive Director, and the Ralph W. Abele Conservation Scholarship Fund Board. Without their vision and commitment to spark the process to produce such a chronicle, our website chronology would have continued to be the main history source for our accomplishments. John's reverence for history and his selection of noted Pennsylvania historian Kenneth Wolensky as author gave the book a firm foundation for a building process that spanned more than 18 months until publication of the book you're holding in your hands. Consolidating 150 years within 400 pages during 18 months is a fantastic accomplishment. Ken provided the research and produced an excellent manuscript to be framed with the rich visual content PFBC has in its archives.

Beyond my own efforts with contracts, editorial, design, and image collection tied to this project, acknowledgement must go out to those within my division, the Division of Outreach & Marketing. Spring Gearhart, Media Productions Section Manager, provided skillful proofreading and image retrieval. Andrea Feeney, also within this section, provided the amazing task of extracting approximately 1,500 images I identified from the digital archives of *Pennsylvania Angler* and *Pennsylvania Angler & Boater* magazines. Education Section Manager Carl Richardson provided a thorough review of the educational programming portions of the manuscript. And, many subject-matter experts and those in leadership throughout the Commission provided reviews and commentary on the manuscript. For that, I am deeply appreciative for helping us remain on course with the accuracy of the effort.

As this book is intended to capture the span of time before and during the Commission's existence, it's more of a story about the needs and challenges to protect, conserve, and enhance the Commonwealth's aquatic resources. And, it's about how the agency has met and continues to meet this obligation for not just the present but for future generations.

Ted R. Walke, *Chief*
Division of Outreach & Marketing
June 2016

artwork- Ned Smith, from Pennsylvania Angler, *July 1959.*

TO PROTECT, CONSERVE, AND ENHANCE

The History of the Pennsylvania Fish & Boat Commission

By Kenneth C. Wolensky, Ed.D.
Editorial and Design by Ted R. Walke

Chapter One: The Common "wealth" of Natural Resources

"The wealth of trees and streams has made the state marvelously beautiful. William Penn roamed these forests, learned the Indian tongue, and loved the land for its own sake."
—*Wallace Nutting*, **Pennsylvania Beautiful**[1]

William Penn did, indeed, roam the forests, loved the land, and became familiar with the native cultures that he encountered when he arrived at what he would call Penn's Woods in 1681. Ten thousand years before Penn was born, Native Americans occupied the land. The Lenapes and the Monongahelas were among these cultures. Archaeological evidence suggests that they lived in small settlements. Villages typically consisted of perimeter fencing, small thatched huts, and a central structure used for rituals, preparing foods, and consuming the products of their hunting, fishing, and gathering.

The land and waterways were essential to their survival as were small and large game and fish. Native Americans used bone for fish hooks, nets made of hemp, and constructed pens into which fish were gathered. According to one account:

> "The Delawares had many ways of catching fish. They used fish hooks of dried birds' claws. They used dragnets which had been knitted by the women with thread from the wild hemp. They trapped fish behind dams, catching them there with their bare hands or shooting them with bow and arrow. Sometimes they placed a 'fish basket', or trap, below the sluice and collected the fish as they came through. They also speared by torchlight.[2]"

Archaeologists also suggest that the earliest fishing "rods" in North America can be traced to native cultures who carved them from long tree branches. Far earlier, the ancient Egyptians used long cane poles to

continued on page 6

Images courtesy of The State Museum of Pennsylvania.

The Common"wealth" of Natural Resources

The manner of makinge their boates. XII.

The browyllinge of their fishe over the flame. XIIII.

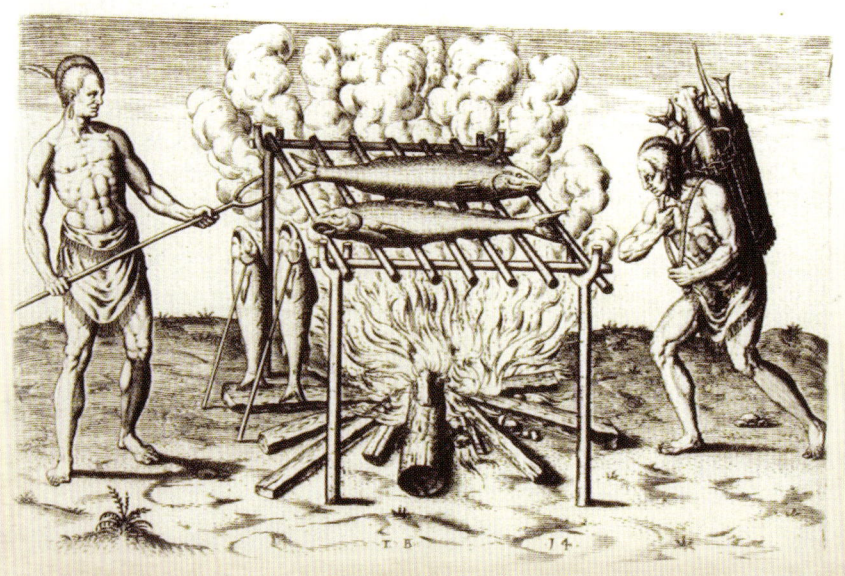

Chapter One

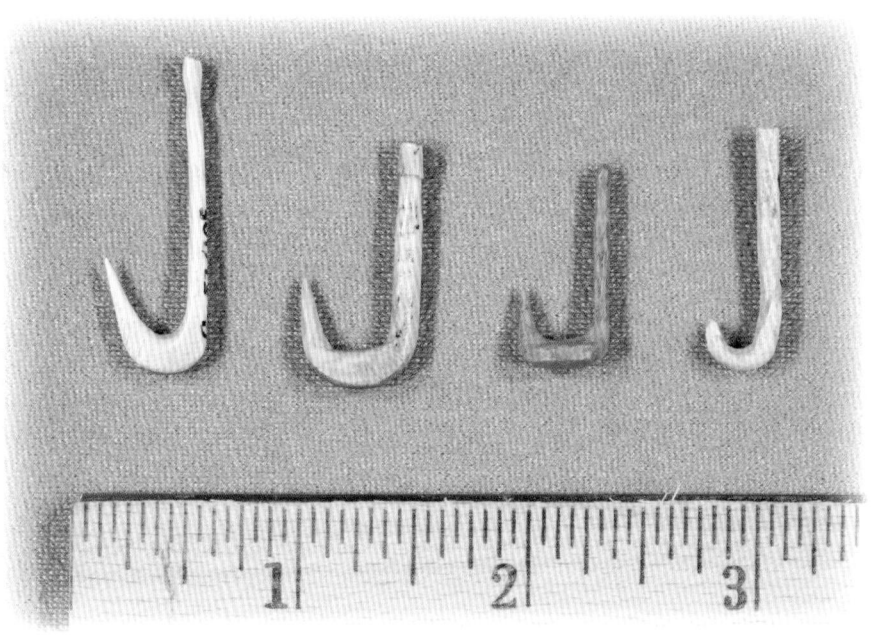

Native American fishing hooks carved from bone.

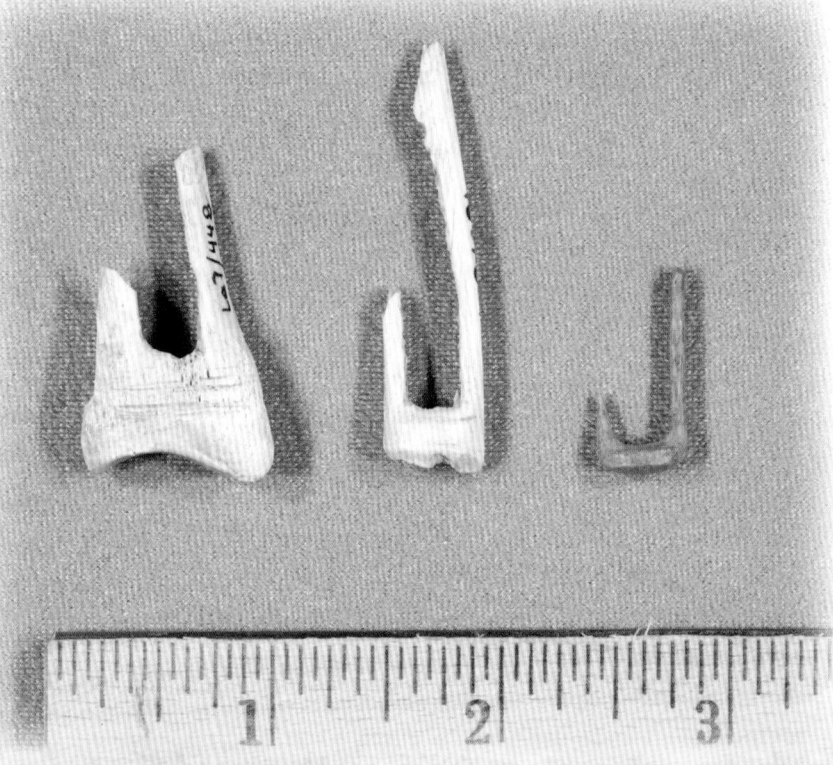

Photographs by Art Michaels, PFBC, in cooperation with The State Museum of Pennsylvania.

The Common "wealth" of Natural Resources 5

which they attached string and primitive hooks carved from stone and other like materials. In terms of the evolution of fishing poles, by the 1800s, metal was used. And, in 1845, Samuel Phillipe, a Pennsylvania-based violin maker, constructed the first split cane rod by dividing cane into three or four small strips and gluing them together. Today, a similar practice is used with as many as six split canes. In the twentieth century, fiberglass rods were introduced. By the end of the century, graphite rods were common.

Skeletons of American Shad from Native American settlements along stream banks reveal that they weighed as much as twelve pounds, while trout sometimes weighed as much as six. They fished in both freshwater and saltwater. Their lives were simple and little was wasted, and their very existence was tied to the land and water. By modern definitions, their cultures might be seen as primitive, yet the plainness of daily existence had a beauty all its own.

White Europeans arrived in North America in the 1600s. Life changed forever on the continent as a result. When Penn claimed his land in 1681—land granted by King Charles II of England in settlement of a debt owed to Penn's father who was an officer in the King's Navy—he granted settlers land rights that resulted in long-term alteration of the landscape. Penn permitted land to be cleared for farming, but he mandated that one acre of trees remain for every five acres that were cleared. Of course, such as mandate was practically unenforceable. In reality, Penn, nor anyone else in authority, had control over natural resources. Quite the opposite, in fact, the natural environment was understood to be something to be controlled for man's benefit. Exploitation became the norm.

Clear-cutting of timber was common. Forests surrounding Philadelphia provided wood for heat and materials for home construction and shipbuilding. Fish and game were taken without consideration for conservation, a concept that was probably unknown at the time. Resources were used as long as they were available. By the late 1600s, Penn permitted hunting, and bounties were offered for wolves and deer. Pigeons, doves, and other fowl were harvested by the thousands. While there is no evidence that Penn's Charter mentioned the taking of fish, he informed the Duke of York in 1683 that rivers had plenty of excellent waterfowl and fish, including sturgeon, shad, herring, and trout.

ARCHAEOLOGICAL SPECIMENS OF CORDAGE.

s - twist

z - twist

Typical two-strand cordage from the Susquehannock levels of the Sheep Rock Shelter.

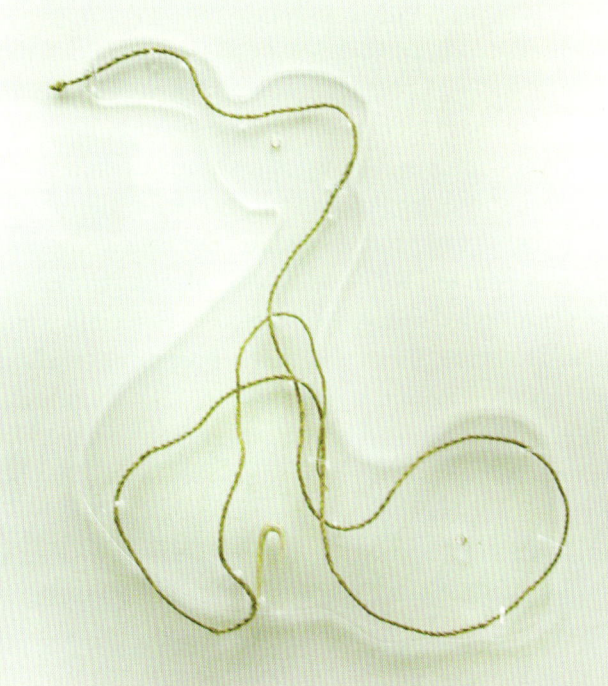

Fish line

Native American fishing artifacts photographed by Art Michaels, PFBC, in cooperation with The State Museum of Pennsylvania.

The Common"wealth" of Natural Resources

Pennsylvania's major towns (later cities) grew up along waterways which were important for transporting people and goods. Philadelphia became the Commonwealth's most populous settlement and a major population center on the East Coast. Other large inland settlements grew from small trapper's trading posts, such as Harrisburg and Shamokin. Fishing was a way of life for many colonists, both as a means of subsistence as well as for economic gain. Places like Head House Market in Philadelphia were common locales for trade. Fish were among foodstuffs offered for sale, sometimes at handsome profits.

In the 1700s, concerns over depleted fish populations, especially the American Shad, became evident. According to one historian, "At the Susquehanna River and its tributaries, 'wars' broke out as those who depended on the abundant shad fought against those who overfished by stretching seines across waterways, and against the millers whose dams prevented the return of fish in the Spring."[3] Fisherman often found that their nets were cut or removed completely by competitors. In some cases, movement of fish was impeded by small dams. Arguments over who held the fishing rights on certain sections of waterways were common, and the taking of fish in large numbers happened frequently.

To mitigate these circumstances, Pennsylvania's Colonial Assembly enacted a statute in 1724 requiring the removal of dams and other barriers that prevented fish from moving upstream in the Schuylkill River. No one knew precisely how many dams existed on the Schuylkill or any river for that matter. Apparently, however, there were enough to cause continued concern. The 1724 law had little or no impact. In 1730, a similar law was enacted that not only reinforced the earlier statute but required the unimpeded movement of fish—especially shad—up and down streams. However, there was no enforcement of either law.

The Assembly followed the principles of the Magna Carta that public rights are inalienable. Assemblymen viewed Pennsylvania's navigable waters as being owned by the public and, therefore, freely accessible to all. The Assembly defined rivers as public highways that could not be controlled by any one interest. British Common Law was also followed, in that the statutes of 1724 and 1730 recognized that the rules of society had to evolve and change as the wants and needs of societies changed. As Governor Martin Brumbaugh (1915–1919) said two centuries later:

"The common law, which is the basis of our laws, is merely crystallized common sense, evolved from the necessity and demand of the people for protection of property and personal rights. The fish of the state are the property of the Commonwealth and are for the use and benefit of the whole people, not only as a very important food supply, but as a means of sport and recreation . . . and economy. The importance of laws protecting fish from wasteful methods of fishing are not new, as we found them to have been enacted in England as far back as the twelfth century."[4]

"American Shad" by Tom Duran Jr.

BROOK TROUT FISHING.

Fishing Clubs Emerge

At about the same time that the Colonial Assembly began regulating the Commonwealth's waters, the first fishing club in the colony was established on the Delaware River. Its name was unusual and changed several times. Originally, the organization was called "The Colony in Schuylkill," then the "Schuylkill Fishing Company of the State in Schuylkill." By mid-decade, its members renamed it "The State in Schuylkill."

Besides what its name suggested, the club had little to do with the Schuylkill River. Rather, its members shared common interests in the outdoors, hunting, fishing, and removal of impediments to the free movement of fish, mainly on the Delaware River. They held meetings in the spring and autumn of each year and had governing rules that were established and enforced by a board that included the Governor and members of the Colonial Assembly. They also held annual outings that were supplied with plenty of food, alcohol, and tobacco.

In 1747, another organization was formed north of Philadelphia and known as the Society of Fort St. David's. Similar to The State in Schuylkill, this organization's members shared common interests in fishing, hunting, and the outdoors. Its members were mainly Welsh, who built a structure for their gatherings that included a small museum. The fort flew His Majesty's flag until 1776. Notables such as Thomas Wharton, head of Supreme Executive Council of Pennsylvania, were members.

During the American Revolution, the Society merged with The State in Schuylkill to form one club. While there is no record that the organization supplied fish for Revolutionary War soldiers, it is a good supposition that it did so as it was a common practice in other colonies. For example, New York anglers regularly provided their catches of salmon and other species to the troops. Obviously, sustenance was essential for those who fought for the Patriot cause. Fishes from Pennsylvania's waters must certainly have been part of that sustenance.

At about the same time that the Constitution of the United States was drafted in Philadelphia, George Washington was invited to a club dinner meeting. While he did not attend, he did send a letter of expressing gratitude for the Revolutionary War service of numerous members of the organization. The State in Schuylkill did gain some notoriety in 1825 when they entertained General Lafayette on his return trip to the new nation. Members greeted him in fisherman's attire, dined on bass, shad, and beef, and presented Lafayette with an honorary membership.

From the adoption of the Constitution in 1789 through the nineteenth century, numerous industries emerged in Pennsylvania, including lumbering, flour and grain milling, shipbuilding, iron making, farming, mining, manufacturing, and fishing. Easy access to the Atlantic Ocean through the Delaware River at Philadelphia meant that products could be shipped to other states and to Europe. Immigrants, primarily from the British Isles, came to Pennsylvania and were comprised of farmers, laborers, craftsmen, miners, fishermen, iron workers, and merchants, among others. Some laborers were indentured servants. And, prior to enactment of Pennsylvania's abolition statute in 1780, the laboring class was supplied by the African slave trade.

While Philadelphia remained the largest city in the Commonwealth, Lancaster grew to become the largest inland town. As both were situated on or near major rivers, fish were easily accessible. This meant that some residents relied on fishing as a means of sustenance. As the Colonial Assembly recognized decades earlier, fishing was an important form of commerce. Shad were particularly appealing.

Before long, commercial fishing began taking its toll on shad and other fish, Pennsylvanians were beginning to see dramatic depletion of shad by the mid-nineteenth century. In the early nineteenth century, the run-of-shad in the Susquehanna River was reported to be the best in the nation. Tens of thousands were caught annually, some weighing in excess of eight pounds. However, this would not last long, as peak fishing for shad in the Keystone State is said to have occurred in the 1830s. Overfishing, and the use of fish weirs and baskets—which greatly reduced the amount of fish which could escape capture in order to reproduce—soon meant that fish in the Commonwealth's waters fell victim to what many saw as inevitable progress.

New Jersey enacted a law in 1808 that prohibited vessels from anchoring on the Delaware River for the specific purpose of shad fishing. Pennsylvania did likewise. A statute was also enacted to create a board of port wardens to issue licenses for wharf construction on the Delaware and Schuylkill rivers. One intent of lawmakers was to get a better handle on who was building wharfs and precisely what they were being used for—shad fishing in particular. Again, however, enforcing these laws was an entirely different matter. Pennsylvania did not have the necessary constabulary or police forces to do as such, and overfishing wasn't the only problem to be dealt with.

When the Columbia Dam was built on the Susquehanna River by the Tide Water Canal Company in the late 1830s, a fish passageway was promised by the company's officers. However, it was never built.

Circa 1900, shad harvesting at Susquehanna flats, Maryland.

A fish ladder installed next to a dam to allow passage by migratory fish species.

photo-Art Michaels, PFBC

And, in short order, the shad population upstream was far fewer than downstream of the dam. Additional construction of dams began cutting off shad migratory runs to the upper portion of the river. It was only in years of high water or when ice breached the dams that shad were able to migrate to upstream spawning areas. The final blow to the Susquehanna's shad population came with the construction of four large hydroelectric dams (York Haven, Safe Harbor, and Holtwood in Pennsylvania, and Conowingo in Maryland), from 1904 through 1932. Similarly, the construction of the North Island Dam on the Juniata River resulted in poorer shad catches upstream.

The same problems occurred on the Delaware River. By mid-nineteenth century, fishermen in Milford, Pike County, were catching fewer and fewer shad than they had in prior years. Those that were caught were of a very small size. Prior to the Civil War, 40 shad filled a pork barrel. By the end of the war, 100 shad or more were needed to top-off a barrel. By this time, most shad weighed three or four pounds.

The problems caused by dams were not only recognized in Pennsylvania, but they had become a national concern. According to *The Roosevelt Wild Life Bulletin* (a publication of the Wild Life Forest Experimentation Station of The New York College of Forestry at Syracuse University), "excessive and untimely fishing were not the only factors concerned in the depletion of fish in lakes and streams. (Another) of the most potent factors was the erection of dams in the streams with no provision for the ascent of fish. Fish which went downstream could not get back."[5]

The depletion of shad, excessive and wasteful fishing, and dams posed threats to Pennsylvania's waters and fishery resources. As Chapter Two further explains, so did the growing problem of industrial pollution. The Commonwealth's public policymakers had no choice but to respond.

The Common"wealth" of Natural Resources

Chapter Two: The Board of Fishery Commissioners is Born

"I found my party at camp; they had butchered the buffaloe and brought in a half dozen very fine trout. My fare very sumptuous this evening: buffaloe's humps . . . and fine parched trout."
—*Meriwether Lewis, June 14, 1805*[1]

When Meriwether Lewis and William Clark set out on their famed journey (1804–1806) to map a route to the Pacific Ocean, they journaled extensively about the abundance of wildlife, rich soil, astonishing Rocky Mountain peaks, and pristine lakes and waters and the aquatic life therein. Fish were plentiful, trout among them as Lewis journaled in June 1805. In Philadelphia, Lewis trained extensively with Benjamin Rush, the American physician, prior to the expedition which was sponsored, in part, by the esteemed American Philosophical Society, headquartered in that city.

Of course, in what was to become the American West, the white man had not yet encroached prior to Lewis and Clark. Their journey is famously called The Corps of Discovery. Yet, what they discovered was nothing of which the American Indian wasn't already aware. Native Americans lived there for thousands of years, and the land, wildlife, and fish were their mainstays that were to be respected and protected, as had been the case in the east prior, to European colonization. By the time of the Lewis and Clark Expedition, man-made threats to the natural environment were becoming apparent in the east. In time, such threats would emerge in the American West as well.

Water Pollution

Pennsylvania's woodlands were worth tens of millions of dollars in the nineteenth century. Forests were ripe for exploitation. Timber was needed for Pennsylvania's growing urban areas and various industries

Oil wells next to Benninghoff Run, Venango County. Photograph by John J. McLaurin.

such as railroads and coal mines. Railroad engines burned wood (they later used coal) and hundreds of miles of rail tracks were placed on large pieces of hewn logs. The increasing number of anthracite and bituminous coal mines required timber to secure mine tunnels from cave-ins. Coal miners referred to this as roof or ceiling "propping" where hundreds of logs were placed from the floor to the ceiling of a mine to prevent collapses.

Lumber workers in the early 1900s in northcentral Pennsylvania's vast woodlands. Photograph by William T. Clarke.

The Board of Fishery Commissioners is Born **15**

Lumber companies such as Ryan and Thompson Inc., owned thousands of acres in Union County and removed trees in large quantities from mountainsides, in some cases as much as 100,000 feet of lumber a day. Fortunes were made by individuals such as Teddy Collins and the brothers Martin and Thomas Quinn, who built homes along "millionaire's row" in Williamsport, which was referred to as Pennsylvania's lumber capital. Lumberjacks, log-skidders, sawmill hands, and river rafters were usually comprised of the Scotch-Irish, as well as Irish immigrants who fled famine in their homeland. Workers lived in primitive camps in and near logging sites. Deforestation became a very serious problem in the nineteenth century. According to the Pennsylvania Department of Agriculture, forests in Columbia, Crawford, Clearfield, and Dauphin counties were among the many being destroyed to meet the demands of the nation's growing industrial economy. And, many parts of Erie County had been entirely clear-cut. Such areas "were heavily wooded. But now the wood has disappeared."[2]

Moreover, the Department of Agriculture report noted that the "welfare of the Commonwealth demands that the present wholesale destruction of our forests shall cease and that there be inaugurated a policy of encouragement of the growth of timber on lands now idle and fit for nothing but timber culture." The report further noted that clear-cutting was "suicidal," because the wanton actions of the forestry industry negatively impacted water quality, wildlife, and fish. Without trees, soils and sawdust from logging operations washed into Pennsylvania's streams and rivers. The report also hinted that the clear-cutters knew as such but chose to ignore the environmental impacts of their work. To them, profit was more important than the environment.[3]

Another common stream pollutant was discharges from tanneries. The Bald Eagle Creek in Clinton County and the Pine Creek—in what would later be called Pennsylvania's Grand Canyon—were heavily polluted with tannins found in astringent chemical compounds drawn from the bark and leaves of plants and trees. Tanneries were described as "unpleasant and malodorous" where "backbreaking labor and low pay" were common. Among tannery workers in the latter half of the nineteenth century were Irish and Italian immigrants. Italian immigrant Vincent Grasso approached tannery work with a "philosophic resignation: better a tannery job than no job at all." Grasso was somewhat unusual though. Realizing that tannery work was hard and

Coal miners from near Hazelton in the early 1900s.

dangerous, he studied English and was appointed postmaster of English Center in 1901. Fishing was his hobby and, apparently, he was quite good at it.[4]

And, the burgeoning coal mining industry created yet another problem: stream pollution from "culm" or coal dirt that ran into waterways. The western world's largest deposit of anthracite coal is located in a 500 square mile area of northeastern Pennsylvania. Central and southwestern Pennsylvania lay claim to large deposits of bituminous coal. The demands of a growing industrial society required both types of coal for railroads, factories, and home heating. Tens of millions of tons of Pennsylvania coal were mined and consumed in the latter part of the nineteenth and early twentieth centuries. And, tens of thousands of jobs were created in the mining industry, mostly filled by immigrants from the British Isles and, later, eastern and southern Europe.

However, the coal mining industry was minimally regulated. Weak laws made it illegal for coal companies to dump waste into waterways, yet, there was no enforcement. Reports of fish kills were common in the anthracite region where culm from mining operations wantonly polluted waterways. Coal operators carelessly cast waste along the stream banks or directly into streams. Citizens informed their legislators of situations in which streams once abundant in fish were depopulated from culm from anthracite and bituminous mines and by acids from tanneries. As Pennsylvania and the United States industrialized, it seemed that the environment was of secondary concern.

To Stock and Supply All Streams

In 1866, a convention was held in Harrisburg to address several environmental and conservation concerns that arose because of industrialization. Water pollution headed the list, as did declining spring shad runs and the depletion of other fishes. The convention resulted in the Act of March 30, 1866 (Public Law 336) signed by Governor Andrew G. Curtin (1861–1867) and resulted in James Worrall (born 1812, died 1885) as the Commonwealth's first Commissioner of Fisheries. Chief among his tasks was to propagate shad. Worrall made it clear "why our food fish supply was diminished:

> "First, the dams which obstruct nearly all large streams. Second, the lack of adequate fish-ways. Third, the non-observance of the close of spawning season. Fourth, the many illegal and deadly devices employed at all the seasons for the capturing and killing of fish. Fifth, the pollution of streams by the deposition of material poisonous to the fish."[5]

Worrall's duties were to ensure "the hatching and propagation of useful tribes of food fishes and to stock and supply all the streams, lakes, and fresh waters of the Commonwealth with the same, by distributing the impregnated spawn or the fry of the said tribes of fishes to all parts of the state, under proper regulations and for the dissemination of any varieties of fish in the waters of the State."[6]

The 1866 law was superseded by the Act of April 28, 1873 (Public Law 887), that officially established the Board of Fishery Commissioners and required the governor to appoint three individuals to serve as Commissioners for a period of three years with the option for their renomination when their terms expired. The 1873 statute defined their duties as establishing hatchery houses and stocking and supplying streams with fish. The Fishery Commissioners were granted a $10,000 budget that year. Another law enacted in 1879 increased the number of Fishery Commissioners from three to six.

The Commissioners were also authorized to appoint fish wardens, sometimes referred to as water bailiffs, and provided compensation of about $100 per year to each of them. However, it is not clear if the Commissioners had sufficient financial means to employ or pay more than a few wardens. In archival documentation, there are passing references to fish

LAWS

OF THE

GENERAL ASSEMBLY

OF THE

STATE OF PENNSYLVANIA,

PASSED AT THE

SESSION OF 1866,

In the Ninetieth Year of Independence.

WITH AN APPENDIX.

By Authority.

HARRISBURG:
SINGERLY & MYERS, STATE PRINTERS.
1866.

wardens keeping a small portion of the fines that were imposed, but it is also not clear whether this practice actually occurred.

As cited below, Pennsylvania was one of the earliest states in the United States to establish a fisheries agency.

- **New Hampshire establishment: June 30, 1865**
- **Pennsylvania establishment: March 30, 1866**
- **Connecticut establishment: May 3, 1866**
- **Massachusetts establishment: May 15, 1866**
- **Vermont establishment: November 19, 1866**

By the mid-1880s, the Pennsylvania's Fisheries Commissioners noted that, "nearly every one of them (states) is now engaged in the commendable work of fostering the great fishery interests of the country."[7]

With regard to American Shad, the *Fishery Commissioner's Report for 1879–80* noted that "it is very much regretted that the streams have become depopulated with this valuable fish."[8] The biggest obstacles in the Susquehanna River were dams that prevented their movement upstream as well as "pirates and outlaws from Columbia to the Maryland line" who had depleted the fish. To enhance shad passage on the Susquehanna, in 1867, the first fishway was constructed at the Columbia Dam. In 1873, 2.7 million young shad were hatched and planted in the Susquehanna River, and more than 2,000 bass were taken from the Delaware River and stocked in other waters of the Commonwealth. Such efforts had the assistance of citizens such as Thad Norris, who, a few years earlier, purchased more than 450 bass at Harpers Ferry, West Virginia, and released them into the Delaware River near Easton. Other citizens did likewise. These efforts appeared to help, at least in the short term.

However, Commissioner Worrall frequently voiced concern that there was minimal staff or financial resources for law enforcement, fish propagation, or programs to educate the public. And, not only were there overfishing and dam impediments, but he opined that the problems caused by water pollution went unabated.

For example, Worrall was well aware that there were large fish kills in the Youghiogheny, Conemaugh, and Allegheny rivers resulting from industrial pollutants. In the eastern part of the Pennsylvania, fish kills were also reported on the Susquehanna River, especially where it flowed through the anthracite coal mining counties. And, similar pollution problems were reported on Casselman River and Stony Creek in Somerset County, which were laced with coal waste; Blooming Grove Creek in Pike County, where tannery discharges were rampant; the Monongahela River near Pittsburgh, where petroleum-based solvents and liquids flowed into it from steel mills, and; Bald Eagle Creek in Clinton County, where sawdust from logging operations clogged the stream.

According to Worrall, "the deposition of deleterious liquids and substances of various natures in our stream from mining and manufacturing establishments . . . may well be found to be a nuisance, causing more inconvenience and loss to the general public than what can be shown to be a gain to those who follow such avocations." Moreover, "the subject commands the attention of the public . . . and an adjustment to our laws. We particularly refer to the introduction of refuse matter from tanneries, oil refineries, dyeing establishments, limestone kilns and oil."[9]

There were also natural enemies of fish, mainly zoological. According to the Roosevelt study, bacterial fungous and plasmodial and parasitic diseases destroyed them (and) "non-parasitic and parasitic worms, crustaceans, and some insects are fatal."[10] However, the most significant threat to fish was man:

> "Man has been the most destructive enemy of fish in general. He has tampered with nature's machinery and thrown it out of balance. The results have not always been correctly attributed to him but, rather, laid at the door of some of the alleged natural enemies."[11]

To better regulate the taking of fish, the Commissioners implemented new rules. One such rule required that a fisherman "will please state the name or person to receive fish," as well as where the fish were caught. They also mandated that "no man shall go to sleep while transporting fish and leave them alone while in the cans, as it will be sure death to the fish (as) six 12-gallon cans filled with fish are all that one man can manage or take care of." It remains unclear, however, how such laws were enforced.[12]

And, the General Assembly enacted more restrictions, such as a prohibition against the use of seines for taking fish within 200 yards of any device erected for the passage of fish. Statutes were also in place that protected shad by making it illegal to fish for them on the Susquehanna and Delaware rivers from June to August (subject to a penalty of $5 per offense), prohibited fishing on Sunday, and mandated that fish were to be caught only with a hook and line (subject to a $100 penalty). Another statute prohibited the use of poisonous bait, nitroglycerin, and explosive—such as dynamite—that killed large numbers of fish.

From 1870 to 1880, the governor and General Assembly appropriated a total of about $188,000 for protection and propagation of fish and for expenses incurred by the Commissioners. For example, in 1874, $3,000 was appropriated for artificial propagation of shad in the Delaware River and, in 1875, $5,000 was appropriated for various species of food fishes to be stocked in all streams in the Commonwealth. Added to this amount was $2,000 to purchase land in Corry, in northwestern Pennsylvania, plus an additional $3,000 to be used for construction of a hatchery at that location.

continued on page 26

Images from Pennsylvania Report of State Fish Commissioners of Fisheries 1900.

Western State Fish Hatchery, Corry, Pennsylvania; old hatchery and office.

Western State Fish Hatchery, Corry, Pennsylvania; old hatchery building and deer.

22   *Chapter Two*

Images from Pennsylvania Report of State Fish Commissioners of Fisheries 1900.

Western State Fish Hatchery, Corry, Pennsylvania; new hatchery.

Western State Fish Hatchery, Corry, Pennsylvania; interior of new hatchery building.

Images from Pennsylvania Report of State Fish Commissioners of Fisheries 1900.

Western State Fish Hatchery, Corry, Pennsylvania; trout ponds and hatchery grounds.

Western State Fish Hatchery, Corry, Pennsylvania; trout ponds and hatchery building.

Eastern State Fish Hatchery, Allentown, Pennsylvania; hatchery grounds and building.

24   *Chapter Two*

Images from Pennsylvania Report of State Fish Commissioners of Fisheries 1900.

THE SMALL-MOUTHED BLACK BASS.

Western State Fish Hatchery, Corry, Pennsylvania; black bass pond.

In 1883, the Commissioners constructed what was called the "Eastern Station," built along the Little Lehigh River on land leased from Mr. Rueben Troxel. In 1885, the General Assembly allocated $5,000 for the Commissioners to build a Whitefish hatchery at Erie that began operating by the end of that year. In addition, $25,000 was appropriated for operating and capital expenditures, including $10,000 for salaries, $9,000 for construction and maintenance of fishways, and $1,000 for improvements to the Corry Hatchery. The Commissioners defended that such amounts were necessary for their work, especially when compared to neighboring New York, where $35,000 had been appropriated in the same year. When it went into operation, the Whitefish hatchery at Erie yielded an impressive 14.6 million eggs that were hatched and placed in Lake Erie. Most of the eggs were obtained from the U.S. Commission on Fish and Fisheries.

The U.S. Commission on Fish and Fisheries

As with Pennsylvania's General Assembly, the U.S. Congress demonstrated its concerns regarding the need to protect and propagate threatened fish species—especially shad—when it created the U.S. Commission on Fish and Fisheries in 1871. Congress specifically charged Spencer Fullerton Baird, the agency's first director, with studying and recommending solutions to reverse the decline of food fish. Soon thereafter, sea salmon were introduced in the Delaware and lower Susquehanna rivers with the assistance of a $5 million federal appropriation, a quite sizable sum at the time. And, some 2.7 million young shad were hatched and planted in the Susquehanna River.

The federal agency also propagated shad on the Susquehanna River at Havre de Grace, Maryland, by constructing the man-made Battery Island on which 25,000 eggs were hatched and deposited just upstream from where the river enters the Chesapeake Bay. Constructing an artificial island proved to be quite an undertaking: More than 200 men and 15 teams of horses were put to work over several months. In short order, more than 63,000 shad were taken from the Susquehanna, many sold at markets in Baltimore and Philadelphia.

According to the U.S. Commission, by the early 1880s, its staff had developed a state-of-the-art method to transfer shad eggs over long distances. Eggs were sent from the eastern United States as far west as Sacramento, California, in moist trays with the voluntary assistance of various railroads, although some occasionally charged for the transport. Hatched fish were also relocated on rail, simply because it was the only expedient mode of transportation.

Congress and President Chester A. Arthur (1881–1885) also appropriated funds for the U.S. Commission to participate in the London International Fisheries Exhibition of 1883. Exhibits consisted of fish that were preserved by professional taxidermists, various types of boats, tackle, lithographs, and printed educational materials. These items and artifacts were gathered from the collections of both the Commission and several states, including Pennsylvania. The Pennsylvania Railroad voluntarily transferred the materials to a ship in New York Harbor that sailed for England in the spring of 1883. The exhibition was held in South Kensington, London, England, and was tagged as the largest special event in the world up to that point in history. Held between May and October 1883, it reportedly attracted more than 2.7 million people or an average of 18,500 per day. Thirty-one countries and colonies of the British Empire participated and, while many won awards, the United States topped the list with 151 gold, silver, and bronze medals. Fish and artifacts related to angling were not the only items on exhibit. Visitors were treated to a special exhibit that introduced them to an entirely new technology that most had never seen or heard of: electricity.

Innovations, Activities, and Efforts at the end of the Nineteenth Century

Back home, the Pennsylvania Fishery Commissioners managed a number of important tasks. For example, in addition to renovating fish hatching ponds at the Corry Hatchery, aesthetic improvements were undertaken, as well as carving a carriage drive, installing graveled walkways, and building two fountains, and constructing a summer house, new offices, and sleeping quarters for the superintendent, Mr. William Buller. Staff at the Corry Hatchery received and hatched 10,000 Brown Trout eggs from Germany in 1886. It wasn't the Board's only "first" when it came to hatching and planting. In 1888, the first recorded planting of Rainbow Trout occurred in the Susquehanna River.

The Commissioners reported that "the streams of this State are believed to be still capable of producing fish enough to feed the nearly five million of our people" provided that they were "not obstructed by dams, polluted . . . and ravaged by unreasoning fisherman who take

THE BROWN TROUT.

From Pennsylvania Report of State Fish Commissioners of Fisheries 1900.

Images from Pennsylvania Report of State Fish Commissioners of Fisheries 1903.

Fishway in Susquehanna River Dam at Clark's Ferry, Pennsylvania (shown during construction).

everything, big or little, in their traps or nets (and) wastefully destroying what they cannot sell." The Commissioners stressed the importance of fishways, especially for shad: "Shad still seek to ascend our streams. In 1885, high waters enabled them to go over the Columbia Dam, which resulted in 139 being caught in the Juniata River just north of its confluence with the Susquehanna River at Clark's Ferry."[13]

The Commissioners were particularly verbose when it came to discussing "the wanton work of fish destruction—which would not be tolerated even in any heathen country and which is a disgrace to our entire civilization." They argued that countries such as China and Japan protect shad because fish were central to their diet. How could it be, then, that a civilized people in a state like Pennsylvania would not give its fish regulatory agency sufficient resources to enforce laws that were already on the books? How could it be that so-called civilized Americans could behave in ways that showed disregard for natural resources? On a more positive note, the Commissioners reported that Pennsylvania had at least kept pace with England when it outlawed fish baskets. Even

Queen Victoria recognized that fish baskets were nothing more than death traps for fish, the Commissioners said. Thus, she and Parliament made them illegal.[14]

An increasingly common occurrence that was noted near the end of the nineteenth century was simple wastefulness. Anglers were apparently catching shad merely for sport rather than for food, sometimes resulting in the fish being discarded and left to rot along stream banks. Ordinary citizens were the usual offenders. Wardens were authorized to make arrests but the problem was occurring with such frequency that it was impossible to even begin to keep pace with violations.

Another growing concern was the depletion of Whitefish in Lake Erie. "The greatest destroyer of Whitefish was the pound net." According to the Commissioners, a pound net is placed by a fisherman as he "sets his first stake very near to the land and from that stretches a line or wing to the distance of a mile offshore. At the other end of the line is placed a heart-shaped net with a funnel leading into a large round net called the pot or pound into which tons of fish are driven daily. The net is strong enough to hold the largest (fish) and the mesh is small enough to prevent the escape of fish too small to be of any commercial value, yet all are destroyed." Those who engaged in such practices were sometimes referred to as "pirates." The Commissioners also reported that "the very small fish are taken in such quantities as to be hauled away and converted into fertilizers. A stringent and unquestionable law for the suppression of pound net fishing within Pennsylvania over Lake Erie should be adopted."[15]

By the late nineteenth century, wardens were granted increasing authority to enforce existing laws and destroy sizable means of catching fish such as oversized nets. And, wardens could secure their appointment with the assistance of the Commonwealth's citizens. Ten or more citizens of any county could write to the Fishery Commissioners requesting the appointment of specific individuals as warden. The Commissioners usually appointed the nominees who were paid an annual salary of about $100.

In the late 1880s, $5,000 annually was appropriated for the salaries and expenses of fish wardens. Although it is unclear exactly how many were employed, the total salary and expenses paid to Warden Peter Williamson in one year totaled $298. Warden J. P. Creveling was paid $250 in salary plus $13.80 for expenses. Ten years later, however, the

THE WHITEFISH.

From Pennsylvania Report of State Fish Commissioners of Fisheries 1900.

The Board of Fishery Commissioners is Born

General Assembly and Governor did not appropriate any funds for wardens, because, in their view, the few wardens who were on the payroll weren't very effective at carrying out their official responsibilities. This problem wouldn't be addressed until the early twentieth century. Volunteers and members of the Fish Protective Association took on the task of policing waterways, as did police and constables who were also granted general authority to enforce fish laws.

Enforcement was dangerous work. Warden Moses Van Gordon was assigned the task of destroying fish baskets in the Delaware River. While he had some success, on one occasion a fisherman drew a rifle and fired at Van Gordon, causing him to run for cover. He was unhurt and the shooter was never caught. Indeed, there were problems, but there was good news as well.

When it came to fishing and the Commonwealth's economy, Erie contributed mightily. By 1886, the town was firmly established as the

A morning's catch on Lake Erie.

Image from Pennsylvania Report of State Fish Commissioners of Fisheries 1909-1910.

Images from Pennsylvania Report of State Fish Commissioners of Fisheries 1903.

Batteries and hatching lake fish at Erie State Fish Hatchery.

Erie State Fish Hatchery

The Board of Fishery Commissioners is Born

Jar or battery system for hatching fish.
Image from Pennsylvania Report of State Fish Commissioners of Fisheries 1903.

Commonwealth's fishing capital. Many residents relied on fishing for their livelihoods and for food. Of its 27,000 residents, men employed in the fish industry totaled 350, while 41 boats were used on Lake Erie along with 19 tugs, 22 sailboats, and 58 small skiffs. The total number of Whitefish caught in Lake Erie in 1886 was 61,500. Other fish species included: 160,000 herring; 320,000 pike; 10,000 trout; 10,000 sturgeon; and various other species totaling 180,000 fish. The dollar value caught and sold that year was estimated at $175,200. When it came to Whitefish, the price paid to fishermen by wholesalers was $5.00 per 100 fish. The fish were then sold at $6.50 per 100 fish at retail in 1886.

To enhance its hatching and propagation program, the Commissioners entered into an agreement for transferring fish and fish eggs that reflected the practice of the U.S. Commission on Fish and Fisheries. The Pennsylvania Railroad agreed to allocate space in freight and passenger cars for 10-gallon cans of eggs to be shipped anywhere in the state. Initially the service was provided free-of-charge. In short order, however, the railroad began charging 20 cents per mile. The typical shipment consisted of 10 to 12 cans, which were accompanied by a warden. One warden reported that water from the cans sometimes spilled onto the floor of passenger cars, apparently making for quite a mess and a foul odor.

In 1892, Jackson and Sharp of Wilmington, Delaware, constructed and delivered the Commission's rail car named "Susquehanna," which was designed to transport fish throughout the Commonwealth. The rail car was delivered and put into service on June 5. And, in 1893, the Commissioners established a shad propagation station at Bristol, Bucks County, Pennsylvania, on the Delaware River.

"Susquehanna" rail car used for transporting and stocking fish.

Sturgeon fishing camp in the early 1900s.

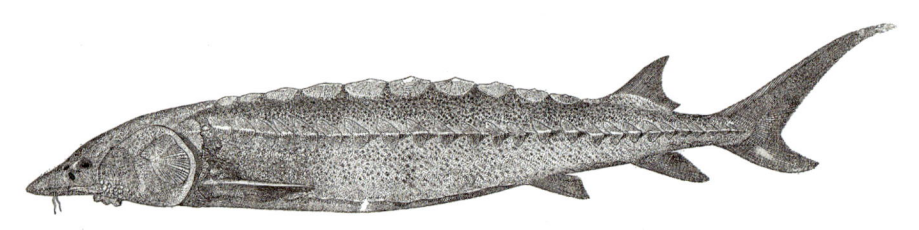

THE SHORT-NOSED STURGEON.

Images from Pennsylvania Report of State Fish Commissioners of Fisheries 1903.

    That same year, the Commissioners developed an exhibit of Pennsylvania fish species, which was put on display at the 1893 Columbian Exposition (World's Fair) in Chicago. Though no exact count was kept, the Commonwealth's $8,000 exhibit attracted thousands of visitors and the Commissioners were pleased that "Pennsylvania would keep her place . . . among progressive fish cultural efforts." The exhibit was 1,701 square feet and situated near one of the major entranceways. It included models of fish hatcheries at Corry and Erie and the Eastern Hatchery, along with 20 aquaria. A few items

36   *Chapter Two*

Interior of Fish Commission display showing aquaria at the 1893 Columbian Exposition.

were gathered from angling associations that also played key roles in propagating certain fish, such as salmon and Brook Trout. Among these organizations were the Blooming Grove Park Fish Association and the Pennsylvania Fish Protective Association.[16]

With the assistance of the U.S. Commission on Fish and Fisheries, raising and stocking various species in the nineteenth century reached its peak in 1898–99 and consisted of more than 100 million fish comprising 26 different species. This number included 37 million shad that were hatched at Havre de Grace, Maryland, by the federal government and planted in the Delaware and Susquehanna rivers. By the end of the nineteenth century, shad brought in impressive prices at market with a total annual value of between $600,000 and $700,000.

Salmon were plentiful in the Delaware River with an average weight range of 12 to 15 pounds. Some were reported to be 25 pounds or more. Philadelphia's restaurants regularly featured Atlantic Salmon on their menu. Some of the more elite restaurants charged $2 to $4 for a full course meal. And, the Board of Fishery Commissioners had success at introducing walleyed pike into the Monongahela River at Pittsburgh.

Total propagation dropped-off to about 165 million in the waning years of the nineteenth century, mainly because the Commissioners lacked sufficient funds to do more. In fact, in 1899, the Commission had an operating deficit of $13,000 and "not a dollar was expended for anything save the most urgent needs."[17] As a result, both the Erie and Bristol stations were closed, as adequate funding for effective operation

THE ATLANTIC SALMON.

From Pennsylvania Report of State Fish Commissioners of Fisheries 1900.

Hatchery workers in 1897.

of the agency would not be restored until the early twentieth century, when the State Treasurer reported balances on hand of $4,634 in 1900 and $431 in 1902.

As the nineteenth century drew to a close, the Commissioners increasingly collaborated with and encouraged the work of angler associations to propagate various species. Quite simply, the Commissioners needed their assistance. For example, salmon and Brook Trout were raised and released by the Blooming Grove Park Fish Association, the Pennsylvania Fish Protective Association, the Fish Protective Association of Eastern Pennsylvania, the Pohoqualine Fish Association in Monroe County, and the Norristown Fish and Game Protective Association. Collaboration with railroads was expanded as well. Besides the aforementioned Pennsylvania Railroad; the Lehigh Valley, Philadelphia, and Reading; Allegheny Valley; and Delaware, Lackawanna, and Western railroads transported fry and gave fish wardens a complimentary seat on trains. The railroads also hauled the Commission's "Susquehanna" rail car to various locales in the Pennsylvania.

From 1866 to 1900, it was apparent that Pennsylvania's Fishery Commissioners were merely getting a handle on problems such as fish depletion, water pollution, and unscrupulous activities by anglers. Moreover, they were defining and clarifying their role as an agency of state government. There was measurable progress in species propagation and hatchery acquisition and construction. And, there were setbacks to be sure. Inadequate funding and insufficient human resources topped this list. It was clear that much work remained to be done as a new century dawned.

Chapter Three:
The Progressive Era

"There Comes an Awakening."
–Pennsylvania Governor Martin Brumbaugh, 1915

"As the angler seats himself by the banks of the streams or wades out into the current, there comes an awakening," said Governor Martin Brumbaugh (1915–1919) in describing the benefits of being in the outdoors and the pleasure to be found in fishing. Brumbaugh said that the ordinary angler was transformed from the daily grind of factory work to the gratification that the natural world provided. The governor encouraged more Pennsylvanians to fish. He also suggested that state government adopt a more proactive role to ensure clean water and to protect Pennsylvania's environment.

Brumbaugh's commentary fitted perfectly with this time period in American history. Later in the twentieth century, historians would refer to the period of 1900 to the early 1920s as the "Progressive Era." This was a time when government and public policy began to have a more significant role in ameliorating the excesses of industrial capitalism, including its negative impact on the natural environment. It was a time of awakening in Pennsylvania and across the nation.

For example, child labor laws were put into effect. The U.S. Department of Labor and the Pennsylvania Department of Labor and Industry were created to investigate problems in industries and monitor and enforce new laws aimed at reducing industrial hazards. Coal mining laws were enacted to reduce the alarming number of deaths and injuries in the nation's coal mines. Banking and insurance laws were created to protect consumers. And, programs aimed at protecting wilderness areas and expanding the nation's national park system were established. These are just a few examples, and there are many more.

Progress in the Progressive Era

When it came to conserving, propagating, protecting, and exhibiting Pennsylvania's aquatic resources, there was indeed, "An Awakening," in

continued on page 44

Early 1900s photos of the Wayne Hatchery (Pleasant Mount State Fish Hatchery).

Images from Pennsylvania Report of State Fish Commissioners of Fisheries 1905.

Wayne Hatchery (Pleasant Mount State Fish Hatchery); hatching house and hatchery grounds.

Wayne Hatchery (Pleasant Mount State Fish Hatchery); hatching house.

Chapter Three

Images from Pennsylvania Report of State Fish Commissioners of Fisheries 1903.

Bellefonte State Fish Hatchery; hatchery exterior (built in 1904).

Bellefonte State Fish Hatchery; interior showing hatching troughs.

The Progressive Era

the form of new and more progressive policies and initiatives that would last well into the twentieth century and beyond.

In 1901, the General Assembly passed a bill classifying fish into two species categories: game and food. Fishery Commissioners stepped-up their law enforcement activities when a 1901 statute granted them authority to hire 12 fish wardens at a salary of $50 per month. When it came to hatcheries, in 1903, the deed for the Wayne Hatchery, Wayne County (now called Pleasant Mount State Fish Hatchery), was officially transferred to the Commissioners, and the Bellefonte State Fish Hatchery, Centre County, opened on October 9 with the assistance of local citizens who raised $3,500 to acquire additional hatchery land and to secure railroad sidings. Three years later, the Spruce Creek Hatchery, Huntingdon County, opened, and smelt were successfully hatched at the Torresdale Hatchery, near Philadelphia, Bucks County, and planted in Bigelow Lake, Wayne County.

A major administrative change occurred on April 2, 1903, when Governor Samuel Pennypacker (1903–1907) signed legislation creating a Department of Fisheries. The new law established a Commissioner of Fisheries, much like an Executive Director, and it mandated that four citizens be appointed to the Fisheries Commission which was,

Bellefonte State Fish Hatchery building
Image from Pennsylvania Report of State Fish Commissioners of Fisheries 1905.

Torresdale State Fish Hatchery: Hatching house and supply tanks.
Image from Pennsylvania Report of State Fish Commissioners of Fisheries 1909-1910.

interchangeably, referred to as the Board of Fishery Commissioners. The board appointed Mr. W. E. Meehan as Commissioner of Fisheries and president.

Meehan made his management style and views known early, "I have endeavored to place all branches of the work of the Department of Fisheries on a firm business-like foundation and to conduct it on business principles. I have been greatly hampered in performing my work thoroughly and to the best advantage by the meagerness of the appropriation to the Department of Fisheries." The agency was allocated a total of $50,000 in 1903–1904. Meehan continued, "the Board feels that the Department does not possess adequate means for the protection of the fishes of Pennsylvania. The appropriation is so small that it is impossible . . . to make both ends meet."[1] This wasn't a new problem.

Despite its meager appropriations, in 1904, the Commissioners agreed to a suggestion by Meehan that a few department staffers participate in the St. Louis World's Fair to exhibit items similar to those that it had at the 1893 Chicago World's Fair. Pennsylvania's exhibit was more than 1,000 square feet and included models of several of the Pennsylvania's fish hatcheries along with a dozen aquaria and a

The Progressive Era 45

pamphlet that described the work accomplished by the department. As with the 1893 Columbian Exposition, a few exhibit items were gathered from fishing associations.

That same year nearly 100,000 frogs were distributed throughout the Commonwealth and 10.2 million Chain Pickerel were propagated. This was a "first" as pickerel had never before been propagated in the United States. The agency also began raising Yellow Perch. And, in 1905, citizens of Crawford County provided a gift to the Commonwealth that officially established the Crawford Hatchery, located about a mile from Conneaut Lake.

PICKEREL.

From Pennsylvania Report of State Fish Commissioners of Fisheries 1900.

THE YELLOW PERCH.

The Commission's exhibit at the 1904 St. Louis World's Fair. Poster for fair shown at right.

The Commissioners became more aggressive when it came to problems posed by dams. For example, The Trenton Water Power Company constructed a dam at Scudders Falls on the Delaware River in the late 1890s. A group of fishermen and raftsmen later filed suit in Bucks County claiming that the company violated Pennsylvania law that mandated that dams could only be constructed with permission from the state government. Moreover, they argued that the company's actions had impeded shad migration and, as a public waterway, the Delaware River could not be controlled by any one interest. Oddly, the Commissioners could not secure a copy of the transcripts of the court's proceedings, and there were many rumors and general confusion as to outcome of the case or even if a decision had been made at all.

Regardless of the court's actions—or lack thereof—the New Jersey Fish Commission and Pennsylvania's Commissioners collaborated for the first time to address the matter. Meetings were held between Pennsylvania Commissioner Meehan, New Jersey Fish and Game Protector Charles A. Shriner, Assemblyman Oliver P. Blackwell (who had the dual role of serving as legal counsel hired by Delaware River fishermen to protect their interests in the matter), and Mr. Charles A. Hewitt, president of the Trenton Water Power Company. Their discussions resulted in the company removing the dam, placing a net with a five-eighths-inch mesh to prevent young shad from passing down the river past Trenton and constructing a log boom above the net to

The Progressive Era

catch debris. Mr. Hewitt reportedly cooperated because he realized that fishery interests and the sanctity of the river were on par with his company's interests. The Trenton Water Power Company was apparently trying to be a good corporate citizen.

The forces of nature helped when it came to the problem of dams. For instance, the accumulation of ice at the Sunbury dam on the Susquehanna River destroyed the structure. The Pennsylvania Railroad owned the dam, and company management was disinclined to rebuild it as they saw no appreciable return, should they make the investment. The Commissioners reported to Governor Pennypacker that shad would now be able to move upstream unimpeded from Sunbury to a dam at Nanticoke in Luzerne County.

The Commissioners continued to embrace novel ideas. For example, in 1907, $6,000 was secured from the General Assembly for the construction of a boat to be used to patrol Lake Erie. It was appropriately named the *Commodore Perry*. Among problems on the lake was that commercial fishermen, often from out of state, fished without licenses and used illegal nets to capture large amounts of fish. The *Commodore Perry's* purpose was to mitigate such matters. Paasch Brothers of Erie was hired to construct the boat. Upon completion, it weighed-in at 43 gross tons, was 62 feet long, 15.7 feet wide and had a depth of 6.7 feet. Its engine could generate 80 horsepower and had a top speed of 12 miles per hour.

Jeremiah R. Driscoll, Captain of the Commodore Perry.

Governor Edwin S. Stuart (1907–1911) had the pleasure of naming the vessel. As Commodore Oliver Hazard Perry was a naval hero of the War of 1812, Stuart chose his name for the vessel's moniker. It was officially launched at 3:00 p.m. on April 21, 1908. Jeremiah Driscoll was its captain. His family was well known for having a lineage of fishermen on the Great Lakes. He owned several commercial fishing vessels and was highly respected as an expert angler. The crew included James Dailey as engineer and Lawrence Scully who served as fireman.

Commodore Perry, 1908.

Philip Hartman, a department employee, occasionally worked on the boat when extra help was needed. The entire crew hailed from Erie. When the ship seized fish illegally caught in Lake Erie, they were distributed to area hospitals and homes for orphans and the needy.

The *Commodore Perry* also proved critical to saving lives. According to one account:

> "Apart from the usefulness of the *Commodore Perry* in fish protection and cultural work it has made, through its staunchness and the heroism of the officers and crew, (it has) a brilliant record in the cause of humanity. In April (1909), it made two trips in the midst of a raging seas to the rescue of disabled tugs and brought them safely to port together with the crews of 10 men in all. Before the storm had disappeared and while the captains of most craft considered it too dangerous to set forth, Captain Driscoll and the crew steamed out into the lake in search of a third tug that had not returned up. It failed to save the craft sought for but did find and restore to the sorrowing friends two bodies. Later, Captain Driscoll and the crew, by means of the *Commodore Perry*, saved the crew of a boat that had been driven ashore during a summer storm."[2]

Addressing Water Pollution

When it came to water pollution, a new fish protection law forbade industrial establishments from polluting waters with chlorine (used for bleaching at paper, cotton, and wool mills), hydrogen chloride, carbon monoxide, and ammonia-based pollutants, which caused fish to "frantically dash about in the water as if attempting to free itself from some object" and then die from irritated gills. During the next several years, approximately 250 industrial establishments installed water purification systems that reduced pollutants.[3] In addition, a Sanitary Water Act was enacted to mitigate the potential for a typhoid epidemic. The act empowered the Pennsylvania Department of Health the authority to regulate the discharge of pollutants into public water supplies. Municipalities were required to secure a permit from the department before they discharged human waste into streams. However, municipal sewage treatment was usually primitive, if it existed at all, and the Department of Health had insufficient resources to enforce the law.

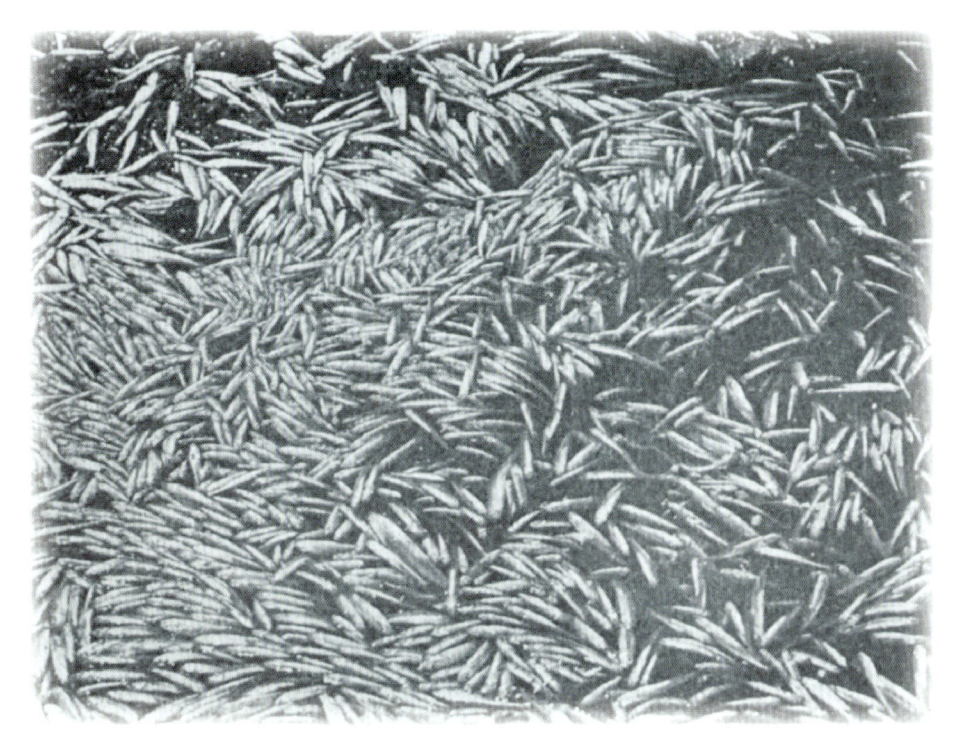

Fish killed by water pollution in Lake Erie.
Image from Pennsylvania Report of State Fish Commissioners of Fisheries 1908.

    The Fish Commissioners reported that pollution of streams had been lessened, but that it continued and "has been caused by that careless habit of wastefulness of the American people (where) immediate profits and a disregard for the right of the people living below on the stream were the causes of every manufacturer allowing his refuse to flow away." They reported that Americans could learn from Germany, where strict laws were in place that regulated pollutants and raw sewage from entering waterways.[4]

    Moreover, the Commissioners and newly appointed Commissioner of Fisheries Nathan Buller (who assumed office on September 1, 1911) reported to Governor John Tener (1911–1915) that . . . "In the matter of pollution, it was decided that the best plan was to take up various sections notifying all the manufactories on a certain stream that pollution must cease at a certain time," and that "the problem of pollution is a very large one, but the Department finds that the majority of manufacturers are anxious to cooperate . . . in bringing about the purification of the streams."[5]

The Progressive Era

Despite new laws and policies aimed at reducing stream pollution and the outspokenness of the Commissioners when it came to this issue, the problem continued. A decision in the case of Commonwealth of Pennsylvania v. Russell (1914) determined that the health and welfare of the public was indeed threatened by man-made pollutants, and the public had a right to clean water. The court concluded that stream pollution was unlawful and the Commonwealth should engage in further actions to mitigate the problem.

The following year, a new law gave Fish Wardens and Deputy Fish Wardens the power to make arrests in a variety of circumstances, including instances of wanton stream pollution. This law amended and reinforced provisions of a 1909 statute that authorized the Commissioners to hire up to 30 wardens and at a salary of $75 per month. Wardens were quite busy. A typical year consisted of more than 300 arrests and convictions or guilty pleas. About 10 percent of the violators served jail time, and aggregate, yearly fine collections ranged from $4,000 to nearly $7,000. The most common violations were for fishing on Sunday and using dynamite and large nets to secure as many fish as possible.

The reality was that neither the Fish Commissioners, the Department of Health, nor any other state agency had adequate financial resources and personnel for enforcing water pollution laws, try though they might. Often, their efforts were outweighed by powerful industrial lobbies that influenced public policymakers more towards their interests than for the good of the Commonwealth.

For example, Pennsylvania historically has 50 elected State Senators seated at the State Capitol Building in Harrisburg. However, there were 52 seats on the floor of the Senate from the late nineteenth to the mid-twentieth century. The two extra seats were assigned to the chief lobbyists for the Pennsylvania Railroad and the Sun Oil Company. This was common knowledge and accepted practice. According to Pennsylvania Governor George M. Leader (1955–1959): "look, there were two extra desks on the floor of the State Senate, one for the Pennsylvania Railroad and one for the Sun Oil Company. Everyone knew it. I knew it when I was a State Senator from York County before becoming governor. And, of course, I knew it when I was Governor. When a bill that would affect certain industries came up for a vote, the Republican Senators would go to the corporate lobbyists and ask for their advice on how to vote! Naturally, the Senators voted the way that the lobbyists told them to vote. It was abhorrent! But that's the way business was done!"[6]

The interests of industry—coal mines, railroads, steel mills, and the like—would outweigh environmental concerns for several more decades in the Keystone State.

Hatching, Educating, and Licensing: The Commission's Work Continues

It was during the Progressive Era that, for the first time, commercial fish hatcheries were required to provide data to the Commissioners. This was important, because these hatcheries were reported to earn $600,000 or more in annual business. There were 10 in all and included Paradise Brook Trout Company in Lancaster County, Crystal Spring Brook Trout Company in McKean County, and R. S. Kemmerer Company in Carbon County. Besides hatching thousands of trout annually, these companies also produced pickerel, bass, carp, and pike.

Commission Hatcheries at Corry, Erie, Bellefonte, Wayne County (Pleasant Mount), Torresdale, Erie, Spruce Creek, and Crawford were quite busy as well. During the latter years of the first decade of twentieth century, the Commission produced nearly 1.2 million pounds of fish per year from its hatcheries. Though this number was impressive, the Wayne Hatchery proved practically useless for trout breeding. Drought conditions caused the spring at the hatchery to give-off scarcely 10 gallons of water per minute.

Educating the public about fish and angling became part of the Commissioners' agenda, as well. Staff implemented an educational program specifically aimed at children so that they could "watch the sunfish build its nest or see the black bass build its nest and see the speckled male trout take on all of his most brilliant colors, red and golden, outshining the resplendent costumes of the dandies of the court of Louis XIV." In short order, Fish Wardens placed educational cabinets in schools throughout the Commonwealth, displaying various species and showing the phases of development of Brook Trout and Whitefish. Remarkably, the cabinets were installed in 79 schools across Pennsylvania.[7]

One of the schools which received a Commission exhibit was in Governor John Tener's hometown of Charleroi in Washington County. Tener, though not particularly outspoken on many issues, was somewhat

Educational cabinet for public schools.
Image from Pennsylvania Report of State Fish Commissioners of Fisheries 1914.

of the more progressive genre of the Republican Party. In one instance, his actions directly impacted the makeup of those appointed as Commissioners, or, nearly so.

Tener wasn't only a politician. Prior to holding elected office, he was a professional baseball player who pitched and played outfield for the Chicago White Stockings and Baltimore Orioles. It is the nature of the sport that players acquire many fans, friends, and a few foes during their careers. Apparently, one of his very close friends was Baseball Hall of Famer Johannes Peter Wagner, otherwise known as Honus Wagner, shortstop for the Pittsburgh Pirates. Wagner was known for his lightning speed that enabled him to be one of greatest base stealers of all time. His 1908 season has been cited by many baseball experts as the single greatest season for any player in baseball history. Wagner held a record 109 RBIs and a consistent batting average of .354.

Honus Wagner, 1902.

Tener thought enough of Wagner to appoint him as a Fish Commissioner in April 1914. However, it isn't entirely clear what relationship Wagner had with angling, the outdoors, or conservation. His tenure was short. When Governor Martin Brumbaugh (1915–1919) took office in January 1915, he "balked" at Wagner's renomination by delaying it in the State Senate. In short order, the new administration terminated Wagner's service. It was probably a good thing for Wagner, as he devoted full-time to playing baseball for the next several years. He set a few more records and, in short order, became a manager and later the coach for the Pirates.

Despite terminating Wagner's service, Governor Brumbaugh supported the work of the department. Perhaps the best example of his support came in a major address he gave before the "Third Pennsylvania Welfare, Efficiency, and Engineering Conference," held in mid-November 1915, in the chamber of the House of Representatives at the State Capitol Building. The purpose of the conference, initiated by Governor Tener, was to educate the public and state agency personnel about the various workings of state government bureaucracy and, especially, state engineering projects and natural resource initiatives.

The Progressive Era

On Tuesday, November 16, Governor Brumbaugh gave an extensive address on the Department of Fisheries to those assembled. He began his address by saying:

> "(My purpose) this afternoon is to explain to you the purposes of the Pennsylvania Department of Fisheries. The Department . . . was organized under the provisions of the Act of April 2, 1903 (and) . . . authorized the appointment of a Commissioner of Fisheries and four other citizens . . . who constitute the Fisheries Commission. The duties of the Department . . . is to provide for the protection and propagation of fish and to promote and encourage the development of the fishery interests of the Commonwealth, and to obtain and publish information respecting the extent and condition of the fisheries of the Commonwealth (and) make rules and regulations . . . for the protection, extension and propagation of fish."

The Governor continued, with both good and bad news:

> "The Department has under its control six hatcheries, which are devoted to the hatching and propagation of fish . . . located in Erie, Centre, Wayne, and Philadelphia counties. The Department, since my incumbency, has devoted much time and labor to the rehabilitation of the hatcheries, to bring them up to the highest point of efficiency so that they will be entirely up-to-date. The next factor is efficiency, because without efficient workmen the best implements are no better than poor ones. It is here that the Department finds it is badly handicapped.
>
> "The work of the fish culturalist is hard and the hours long, and it is only after years of training that a man attains efficiency which is so essential in the propagation of fish. The men are not only overworked, but are unable from the fewness of their number (2 or 3 at each site) to get all out of the hatcheries that (they) . . . would do if properly manned. Lack of appropriations accounts for this condition.
>
> "It has been difficult to obtain men in the employ of the Department owing to the inadequate salaries that the Department is able to pay. The result has been as the men are trained by the Department and become efficient, they are sought for and bought up by offers of a much higher salary then the Department is able to pay. The result is that the Department makes the man and someone else gets the benefit of the training."

The Governor also addressed the inadequacy of the Department's ability to enforce laws:

> "Another duty which devolves upon the Department is the enforcement of the laws governing the protection of fish in our streams. The enforcement of the law comes under the small force of wardens which the Department is able to employ. The law allows the appointment of 30 citizens to act as Fish Wardens, but, unfortunately, the Legislature only appropriated sufficient money employ regularly 10 men.
>
> "As the angler seats himself by the banks of the stream or wades on into the current there comes an awakening and it is hugely jarred into his mind that there is no such thing as perpetual motion, and if he wishes the wheels of the Government to keep turning and turning smoothly, he must at times apply his own shoulder to the wheel to assist the officers entrusted with enforcement of the law."[8]

It was just a few years later, in 1919, that the first Pennsylvania fishing licenses were issued. A license was required only for non-residents at a fee of $5 per year. A 1921 state law required Pennsylvania resident fishing licenses, and, the following year, such a license was made available at $1 per resident. Licenses took the form of buttons of about 1.75" in diameter in 1923, and anglers were required to display them on an outer garment. The buttons were then replaced by the display of paper licenses in 1960. License buttons were introduced again in the mid-1970s. Then, in 1976 they returned to the paper form and featured

An array of past fishing license buttons is shown with the lower right button provided free to the public as a button commemorating the 1923 introduction of the license buttons. They were produced until 1960 and then, again, in 1974 and 1975. Reintroduced in 2014, they presently continue to be sold by PFBC.

The Progressive Era   57

In Honor and Memory of Warden William E. Shoemaker

March 2, 1865 - September 22, 1921

While on routine patrol in Bradford County, Fish Warden William E. Shoemaker became the first Pennsylvania Fish Commission law enforcement officer to lose his life in the line of duty. Warden Shoemaker started his 18-year career in 1903, when acceptance of fish and game laws, and the brave officers who enforced those laws, was virtually non-existent. Life was difficult at best for those early officers, but late in the evening of August 25, 1921, Warden Shoemaker made the ultimate sacrifice. With his son Gregory, a "special" fish warden, Officer Shoemaker was returning to his home in Laceyville, when he spotted a light in Wyalusing Creek as the pair crossed over the bridge at Merryall. After instructing his son to remain with the vehicle, Officer Shoemaker approached two men spearing fish. One of the men had a permit, the other did not. Officer Shoemaker informed the violator he was under arrest. After the warden collected the evidence, he and the two men headed up the embankment single file. Near the top, the man following Officer Shoemaker, who was not under arrest, grabbed the .38 caliber revolver from the warden's holster. At point-blank range, he pointed the revolver at Officer Shoemaker and pulled the trigger. The bullet entered the back of his neck, instantly paralyzing the warden from the neck down. On September 22, 1921, Officer Shoemaker lost the month-long struggle for his life. He was laid to rest in the Lacey Street Cemetery in Laceyville.

The man who shot and killed Warden Shoemaker received a sentence of nine years and a fine of $100. On the same day, in the same courtroom, a man who stole an automobile was sentenced to nine years and a fine of $500.

On May 13, 1999, Officer Shoemaker was inducted into the National Law Enforcement Officers Memorial in Washington, DC.

Memorial plaque located at the PFBC Harrisburg Headquaters. *photo-Spring Gearhart, PFBC*

Chapter Three

the Liberty Bell in honor of the nation's bicentennial. From that date, forward, fishing licenses regularly featured artwork of Pennsylvania fish—either the Brook Trout as the state fish or other predominant game fish species. By the early 1920s, the Commission became fully self-supporting with a total income of $207,425.53 reported for 1922, which was the first year's income from licenses sold to all citizens 21 years of age and older. Resident fishing license cost was increased to $1.50 in 1928.

Throughout the agency's history, Fish Wardens and, later, Waterways Conservation Officers, faced inevitable danger. Sadly, this became apparent on August 25, 1921. Bradford County Warden William E. Shoemaker attempted to apprehend two fishing law violators. They shot Shoemaker. He died on September 22 from the gunshot wound. Shoemaker had been an 18-year veteran of the agency. Earlier, he worked as a warden for the Pennsylvania Game Commission, where he received no salary but was allowed to keep one-half of the amount of fines he imposed. He came to work for the Fishery Commissioners in 1904, when he was offered a full-time, salaried job. He and Warden Raymond L. Schroll Jr. remain the only two Commission law enforcement officers to be killed in the line of duty (Schroll is discussed later in this book). Both were inducted into the National Law Enforcement Officers Memorial in Washington, D.C., on May 13, 1999.

New legislation, in 1925, officially established (or re-established) the Board of Fish Commissioners, supplanting the Fishery Commissioners moniker of 1866. While the Board's basic statutory provisions didn't change much, its work continued to expand with the times. For example, creel limits were established for the first time in 1925, which limited the taking of trout to 25 per day, 10 for bass and Walleyes, 15 for pickerel, and 3 for Muskellunge. And, the Commission continued to build new hatcheries. In 1925, a site was purchased in Bedford County (one mile northwest of the town of Reynoldsdale, New Paris) and was called the Reynoldsdale Hatchery. Three years later, the Tionesta Hatchery went into business. Moreover, in 1928, Lake Wallenpaupack (located in the Pocono Mountains) was opened to the public for fishing (it was created two years earlier by Pennsylvania Power and Light Company for hydroelectric power generation and for flood control), a new Bureau of Research was created by the Commissioners, and the Commission stocked a newly created lake at the Conowingo Dam.

The Progressive Era

On a somewhat similar note, the Board of Fish Commissioners implemented a new and innovative program to distribute fish from its hatcheries into the waterways of the Commonwealth. In 1927, a fleet of new trucks were purchased and distributed to the various hatcheries. Modern technology—at least when it came to vehicles—had been embraced.

Commission staff began to conduct substantive research and rely on science more so than they had in the past. For example, C. R. Buller, Deputy Commissioner of Fisheries at Wayne Fish Hatchery, Pleasant Mount in Wayne County, issued a novel study in 1927 entitled *The Aquatic Life Maintained at the Wayne Fish Hatchery for Educational Purposes*.[9] Buller took seriously the task of "educating fishermen to be real conservationists and sportsmen, particularly the youthful angler." In order to do so, the Wayne Hatchery engaged in a number of educational endeavors. These included "portraying in motion pictures the life history and artificial propagation of various species, distributing pamphlets and bulletins on the conservation of fish life, talks and lectures by men qualified in the work, sending specimens of fish and fish eggs to our institutions of learning for research work, and by maintaining aquariums in the major hatcheries where many forms of aquatic life can be seen and studied at close range."[10]

As Buller pointed out, in one example, the Wayne Hatchery had several display tanks that were open to the public. They could view various methods used to artificially incubate fish eggs. In addition, staff and volunteer guides conducted public education programs. And, school classes were brought into the hatchery to learn about the work of the agency, especially fish propagation. Educating the public was essential according to Buller: "when the anglers, both present and future, learn somethings of the life history of the fish for which they are angling then, and only then, can they be called real conservationists and fishermen."[11]

Buller was a busy man. In 1928, he issued another study entitled, *Methods Employed in Producing the Bullfrog* (Rana Catesbiana) *Tadpoles at the Pennsylvania State Hatcheries*.[12] In addition to describing the appearance and distinctive markings of Bullfrogs, Pickerel Frogs, Green Frogs, and explaining how they can be differentiated between male and female, Buller provided detailed accounts of the ways in which the state fish hatcheries were attempting to rear the species. The hatcheries included Wayne (Pleasant Mount) and Union City. "Our tadpoles are produced

Bullfrog

in connection with the rearing of certain species of warmwater fish ... and is carried on in ponds ranging in area from one-half to 100 acres."[13]

Propagating frogs was not without its difficulties, however. In the mid-1920s "a series of unsuccessful attempts were made to artificially propagate and rear the frog." Among the problems were that "frogs could not be induced to take artificial food" and "frogs of all sizes had to be securely penned to keep them from migrating to more desirable quarters," though, in several cases, keeping them penned was unsuccessful. Finally, "because of their cannibalistic tendencies ... the adult had to be removed from the areas containing the tadpoles," which proved to be a tedious task for which there was insufficient staff. Thus, Buller reported, the agency downscaled these efforts.[14]

By the end of the 1920s, angling remained largely a man's game. Catching fish was both a form of recreation and a means of securing food. Most fishermen were ordinary, work-a-day citizens who were usually employed in factories, coal mines, railroads, and other industrial establishments. Most had families. There were also commercial fishermen, especially on Lake Erie.

What lay on the nation's horizon was largely unforeseen as the 1920s drew to a close. Few could have anticipated that the country's economy—and its entire social and cultural fabric—was about to be shaken-up as never before.

The Progressive Era

Commissioner Oliver M. Deibler congratulates David Shuey for landing the largest trout of the day, 1934.

Chapter Four: The Great Depression

"This progress, I feel, is forerunner to even greater advances in Pennsylvania."
—*Commissioner Oliver M. Deibler*[1]

    The Great Depression began with the stock market crash in October 1929. Its economic and social impacts were devastating and widespread. Millions were unemployed, factories were shuttered, coal mines closed, Wall Street limped along, insurance companies became insolvent, and banks locked-out customers. For the first time in U.S. history, citizens felt the impact of widespread scarcity: scarcity of food, money, and work.

    Pennsylvania wasn't immune. As a highly industrialized state, several industries fell on very hard times. The extraction of coal from the Commonwealth's anthracite and bituminous mines slowed, and steel and textile mills laid-off workers. Many industrialized areas of the Commonwealth saw double-digit unemployment rates, as well as massive underemployment. The only industry that did increase was clothing manufacturing. More and more garment factory owners relocated from New York City to Pennsylvania in towns such as Shamokin, Wilkes-Barre, and Allentown. They did as such, because labor was far less costly due to excess labor (mainly women), and because they could avoid labor unions that had organized workers in New York.

    One Pennsylvania woman who, by coincidence, was born in October 1929, recalled that her father lost his job in an anthracite coal mine. There were nine children to feed, and food was scarce. "My father worked in the mines. Naturally, he lost his job when the Depression hit. He had a lot of free time and a family to feed so he took to fishing in the Susquehanna River and in other streams to catch fish for our family to eat. As a young girl, I remember him coming home with a bucket of fish. My mother would clean and cook the fish. It tasted so good. Sometimes it was all we had to eat. He fished all the time, because we had to eat and couldn't afford meat or anything like that."[2]

    As with the Progressive Era, the federal and state governments stepped-up their involvement in the private economy to ameliorate the many problems caused by the Great Depression. For example, banks, investment houses, and insurance companies were more closely regulated. Public works projects were created to employ some of the tens of millions of men that lost their jobs. The Civilian Conservation Corps was launched, and its workers were assigned to many tasks, such as building roads in national parks and planting trees, especially in deforested locales; unemployed artists, teachers, and writers—women among them—were hired with federal funds to undertake a variety of projects that tapped their expertise. Entire communities were built, such as Norvelt in western Pennsylvania, to house the homeless and unemployed. Norvelt derived its name from Eleanor Roosevelt: "Nor" for the last consonant in her first name and "velt" for the last consonant in her surname. As people had more free time, angling became an increasingly important form of recreation. Pennsylvania's waters continued to be among the best in the nation; anglers had no doubt about that.

By the early 1930s, Pine Creek in Pennsylvania's so-called "Grand Canyon" offered some of the best fishing in the Commonwealth. Fish Warden Horace Boyden of Wellsboro reported that Pine Creek held real promise for bass fishermen who often stayed overnight at a public camp in Ansonia, Tioga County, built by the Department of Forests and Waters with the help of the Civilian Conservation Corps. Boyden witnessed numerous sizable bass caught from the creek, along with the occasional Brown Trout. He also reported a few violations, such as anglers who fished without a license.

In the southwest corner of Pennsylvania, the Allegheny River had some of the best bass fishing to be offered in years. Careful stocking of the river near Pittsburgh, along with enforcement of new anti-pollution laws, had begun to pay-off. Fish Warden J. Albert Johnson reported that anglers caught dozens of healthy bass and were often surprised by the quality of the fish, even though he said that the water quality wasn't always ideal.

Moreover, when the Safe Harbor Water Power Company created the Safe Harbor Dam in 1931 for hydroelectric power, it created Lake Clarke, which provided excellent angling opportunities. In 1935, the first three-day license was issued for $1. It is worth noting that the Commission did not increase any license fees during the Depression years. A 1937 state law made Sunday fishing legal, and the Commission produced its own Brown Trout and Rainbow Trout eggs for the first time in 1938.

DO NOT BLOCK FRIEND FARMER'S LANE

W.P.A. poster from the 1930s, emphasizing landowner courtesy.

1933 view of Lake Clarke, Susquehanna River.

The Great Depression

In another significant accomplishment, the Commissioners opened Fisherman's Paradise along Spring Creek in Centre County. Located not far from the Benner Spring Research Facility in what is known as Spring Creek Canyon, the locale was the first specially regulated stream in the nation. Fishing was (and is) limited to using fly-fishing gear only and a catch and release mandate. In 1934, nearly 3,000 anglers fished the Paradise section of Spring Creek. Today, Fisherman's Paradise remains a favorite spot for anglers from across the Commonwealth.

Fish were an increasingly important food source during the Great Depression. Many anglers fished not for pleasure but as a means of survival. This might help to explain why the Board of Fish Commissioners reduced creel limits on several occasions in the Depression years. For example, in 1933, the creel limit for trout was reduced to 20 from 25. In 1937, the creel limit was again reduced, this time to 15. And, in 1938, it was reduced to 10. It may well be that the Board was engaging in distributive equity among the 400,000 licensed anglers. Lower creel limits meant that more people could fill a creel. Thus, more people had access to an important food source during an era of scarcity.

Additional public policies were put in place to deal with the continuing problem of water pollution. In 1937, the Clean Streams Law was the most sweeping legislation yet to mitigate water pollution problems. It gave municipalities the authority to issue bonds for the construction or upgrading of sewage treatment facilities, brought most industrial wastes under legal control for the first time, and enabled the Sanitary Water Board the authority to issue penalties. The law would be amended several times in years to come.

For Better Fishing— Kill the Watersnake

Another Commission policy was to control the watersnake population. Commissioner French encouraged Pennsylvanians to "Kill the Watersnake!"

"With the abnormally low water prevailing in many sections of the Commonwealth, there has been brought to our attention more than ever before, the serious damage the watersnake is doing to our streams. Trout waters have been the most seriously affected, and might I suggest that a special effort be made for the removal of this natural foe to good fishing?

"An appropriate bronze medal, inscribed "Junior Conservationist," is awarded those under 19-years of age for killing ten (10) or more watersnakes.

"By doing your part, you will be very definitely improving the fish habitat which will mean for better fishing next year."[3]

Pennsylvania Angler is Launched

In a major accomplishment, the Commissioners launched *Pennsylvania Angler* in December 1931. The cost was 50 cents for a one-year subscription. At the time, the Commissioners were:

O. M. Deibler, *Chairman, Greensburg*   John Hamberger, *Erie*
T. H. Harter, *Bellefonte*   M. A. Riley, *Ellwood City*
Dan R. Schnabel, *Johnstown*   Leslie W. Seyler, *McConnellsburg*
H. R. Stackhouse, *Secretary to the Board*

Early issues of *Pennsylvania Angler* contained little in the way of data, statistics, and other factual information or reports of Commission activities, policies, or laws. However, this would change in short order. Initially, *Pennsylvania Angler* was more proficient in poetic verse such as the following:

Season's End

"When the curtain fell on the 1931 fishing season in Pennsylvania, another season was at hand—the season of reveries. For the ardent angler, memories of days astream—in the spring when pussy willows blossom along the trout streams, of dusk on a summer evening when bass wallow in the minnow shallows, and of frosty October mornings—are close to the heart.

"Perhaps to these reveries may be attributed the checking over of trout tackle in January and the collecting of new flies when ice mantles many of the streams. In all probability, that giant Brook Trout still lurks under the high log below the eddy, and in the weed-fringed flat a mammoth Smallmouth Bass that smashed tackle last year still holds sway.

Front cover of the December 1931 issue of Pennsylvania Angler *magazine.*

Editor's note: As this time period in the Commission's history marks the beginning of *Pennsylvania Angler* magazine, we begin to include many images extracted from past issues in the book. Our original selection included as many as 1,500 images, which were then culled down to those included in the book and identified by the month and year datelines for when they appeared in the magazine. As most prior documentation for these images is non-existent, we use this dateline identification as a consistent reference for when the image was first presented to the public. In addition, these datelines provide the opportunity for readers to know more about the images and possible extended context with articles appearing in the magazine. To view and reference our digital archive of magazine issues since 1931, visit: **www.fishandboat.com/PaAnglerLegacyIssues.htm.**

The datelines provided are on two progressive timelines: One chronologically shows the Commission's activities, and the other chronologically depicts Pennsylvania anglers and boaters through the decades. With respect to these extracted images, provided for context with the former magazine articles, whether it was a result of printing methods of the day or a poor original photograph, image quality as it appears in this book may have been sacrificed in order to provide the desired depiction of the historical topic. Color-coded gradient screens have been added to the pages from this point forward to assist in grouping each subsequent decade's span of time.

Chapter Four

"Whether memory holds a shadow of mottled green and red and the chant of swift waters, or the scream of a reel as the monarch bass takes line, the season of reveries brings contentment of the finest to those who answer the call of rod and reel."[4]

Pennsylvania Angler often reported on the achievements of fishermen (and women). In "Giant Trout is Landed at Wallenpaupack," it was noted that, "One of those rod busters responsible for the spinning of fish yarns was conquered on Lake Wallenpaupack in October. And, as the season for Brown Trout was closed, this 38-inch specimen still roves the inlets of that mecca for anglers of the state." Warden John A. Schadt of Lake Ariel was on hand when two fishermen had hooked into it several times, but in each instance, it had snapped their lines before it had been brought into the boat. Of course, it was released back into the lake and "perhaps next spring will furnish the basis for more than one 'fish story.'"[5]

Warden Schadt also told of seeing other large "brownies" in one of the inlets while patrolling Wallenpaupack with Warden Brink: "A number of Brown Trout, ranging in size from 18 to 26 inches were caught on the lake this fall as they moved toward the headwaters to spawn," and he noted that "I have measured a number of pickerel this year— 26-, 28-, and 30-inches long."[6]

Lake Wallenpaupack, Pennsylvania's third largest lake, remained a well-liked locale for anglers. Yet, some conservationists apparently lamented the damming of the Wallenpaupack Creek to create the lake in 1926 by Pennsylvania Power and Light Company. It created the 52-mile shoreline lake for hydroelectric and flood control purposes. The following poem which appeared in *Pennsylvania Angler* expresses such lament:

The Great Depression

The Wallenpaupack
Slow Wallenpaupack, swift Wallenpaupack,
Tell us the talks of the days that are o'er
When the darn Delawares, awed by your whimsies,
Gave you the name you will wear no more.

Then came the time, when brown men and white men
Vied for the vale, where you placidly dream;
Block house and power vanquished the arrows.
Never again will the birch canoes gleam.

Soon the keen axes entered your shadows;
Down your slow current the great trunks you bore,
Catching in anguish some to your bosom—
Still they lie thick in the sands of your floor.

Now men would tame you, put you in harness,
Over the Poconos lead you away,
With your great power chase back the darkness,
Turn your bright spirit to work, not to play.

Service is noble, but beauty is glorious!
Grieving we'll cherish your joyness still,
Know the glad leap and the song of your waters
Seeing the dry bed you shaped to your will.

We'll miss your beauty! How we have loved it!
Weave once again the mystical spell
Of tall hemlocks sprayed with jewels of winter.
Then Wallenpaupack, old Paupack, farewell!
–*Nora Del Smith Gumble*[7]

 The 1931 inaugural issue of *Pennsylvania Angler* also reported on exciting catches of pickerel with artificial bait. For example, Warden E. W. Davis of Scranton reported an unusual catch with an artificial grasshopper. "While fishing in Fords Lake, Mr. C. M. Shriner hooked and landed a 22-incher using the artificial hopper. Pickerel are typically voracious feeders on other fish, particularly minnows, and when they strike at a grasshopper, artificial or otherwise, it's quite unusual."

Female anglers were featured as well with such angling success exemplified in the following story:

Feminine Anglers Land Big Bass

"When fishing at Twin Lakes, two feminine disciples of Izaak Walton, Mrs. John A. Rishel and Miss Maude Hostetter, of Harrisburg, landed six Smallmouth Bass, some over two pounds, in an hour's fishing in August. Frank V. Stutsman, of Twin Lakes, in a recent letter to Frank Brink, warden, at Milford, tells of this instance coupled with numerous other fine catches during the past season. Mr. Stutsman said that perch running to two pounds in weight were caught in abundance. A group of Reading fishermen, Messrs. Sherman, Weidner, Pflurn, Frazier, and Garman, landed 80 perch in one day and topped their catch with a pail full of Bullhead Catfish, some of them 15 inches in length."[8]

Children became part of the storyline as noted in an article entitled "Kids Score Again." According to Warden C. Joel Young of Fullerton, a big Brown Trout was sighted early in the morning of the opening day of trout season. The fish swam under a bridge near the hatchery on the Little Lehigh River. "Fly fishermen and bait fishermen whipped the pool without a rise. The 20-inch trout gave every lure a cold and glassy stare until, nonchalantly carrying an old rod and line and a can of fishin' bait,

August 1934

October 1938

April 1934

The Great Depression

a 12-year-old approached the scene of action. Swinging the trusty rod into action, he dropped the garden hackle in front of the big trout." The brownie must have liked the "particular brand of fishing bait. It struck with a rush and the proud youngster toted it home with him after a hard struggle."[9]

Young also reported that "although the lakes are stocked with both large and Smallmouth Bass, fewer largemouths were caught that year. Almost without exception, these fish weighed four pounds or more. Mr. Blickius, of Carbondale, caught a Largemouth Bass weighing five pounds and fifteen ounces." Young concluded that, "in August, the Smallmouth Bass went on a striking rampage. Billy Kriesock, of Carbondale, caught the limit before breakfast and a number of other unusually good catches were reported. Several nice catches of pickerel were made, a five pounder taken by H. B. Gardiner and son."[10]

Pennsylvania anglers were inventive as well. Consider Walter Mingle of Selinsgrove, for example:

> "Walter Mingle. . . recently demonstrated his newly invented fishing rod, on which he has just received a patent from the United States Government, before the annual reorganization meeting of the Snyder County Sportsmen's Association.
>
> "Mingle . . . has equipped an ordinary rod with an electric light for night fishing. Batteries are located in the handle and the bulb for illumination at the tip of the rod. The light is small enough to be within the laws governing night fishing but large enough to show when the angler has a bite.

December 1933   *November 1934*

72   *Chapter Four*

"The local sportsmen were much interested in the new invention and enthused following the demonstration."[11]

By 1933, Commissioner Oliver M. Deibler was quite verbose in his reports that appeared routinely in *Pennsylvania Angler*, especially, when it came to reporting on agency stream acquisitions and fish propagation matters. For example, his report entitled "Fish Commission Scored Advances in Past Year," he stated the following . . .

"Accomplishments during 1932 may be grouped under the following heads:
- increased facilities for fish output,
- virtual completion of the stream survey,
- increased Brown Trout stocking, and
- increased fishing waters.

"In line with increased facilities for fish output, purchase of the Huntsdale site in Cumberland County for establishment of a trout farm will serve a dual purpose. It will greatly increase stocking facilities of the Fish Commission in the central counties, and will cut costs of transportation of fish from hatcheries in other sections of the state to streams in these counties. Establishment of the Huntsdale nursery and purchase this month of a tract of land on Spring Creek in Centre County are, I feel, noteworthy steps in our drive for better fishing.

continued on page 82

February 1934

September 1936

The Great Depression

Pennsylvania anglers and boaters in the 1930s

March 1936

September 1934

July 1935

June 1935

74 Chapter Four

June 1939

June 1934

June 1934

June 1938

The Great Depression 75

January 1934

76   Chapter Four

HONORABLE GEORGE H. EARLE
Governor of Pennsylvania

A Message to Pennsylvania Sportsmen From Governor Earle

FELLOW SPORTSMEN:

I am grateful to the Editor of your ANGLER for this opportunity to send a message to you.

Pennsylvania has achieved an enviable position as a leader in game conservation, largely through the efforts of the organized sportsmen in holding true to two great principles. The first, that the Game Commission should be constituted and its affairs administered on a non-political basis. Trouble has followed as a result of relaxation of this rule.

The second and equally important, is the preservation of the Game and Fish funds. Hunting and fishing license fees are in no sense a tax. They are rather voluntary contributions by the Sportsmen of the State to the cause of conservation. It would be a breach of trust to divert them.

The first of these principles I propose to restore to activity, and the second to uphold. In this I ask your loyal support, so we may keep Pennsylvania in front as the best game State of the Union.

Message to sportsmen from Governor George Earle.
February 1935

February 1934

PERSONALITIES AT SPRING CREEK

Sketches by George Gray

DAN R. SCHNABEL
MEMBER
BOARD OF FISH COMMISSIONERS

E. W. NICHOLSON
MEMBER
BOARD OF FISH COMMISSIONERS

ART NEU
FORMER NATIONAL FLYCASTING CHAMPION

T. F. O'HARA
CONSTRUCTION ENGINEER
BOARD OF FISH COMMISSIONERS

O. M. DEIBLER
COMMISSIONER OF FISHERIES

ADOLF MULLER
PRESIDENT BOARD OF
GAME COMMISSIONERS

DEWEY SORENSON
SUPT., BELLEFONTE HATCHERY

C. R. BULLER
DEPUTY COMMISSIONER
OF FISHERIES

E. W. DAVIS
WARDEN IN CHARGE
SPRING CREEK

June 1934

78   *Chapter Four*

July 1934 **Pennsylvania Angler** *editorial cartoon*

Commission activities in the 1930s

January 1937– fish stocking

November 1933– hatchery battery

March 1934– hatchery staff

January 1938– conservation presentation in schools

March 1938– W.P.A. stream habitat improvement project

November 1935— Commission exhibit at Philadelphia show

June 1935— fly-tying class

April 1939— truck fish stocking

The Great Depression   81

"The tract on Spring Creek known a "Forked Springs" was purchased from Joseph Bertram and comprises 90 acres of land including a trout dam and the famous springs. We hope to make this site a model in stream improvement.

"Trout fry in excess of the number that may be successfully raised at the Bellefonte hatchery will be transferred to the "Forked Springs" trout farm. The "Forked Springs" farm affords facilities for development equal to our present Bellefonte hatchery. Trout above legal size will be stocked from this fish farm to many streams in central counties, in this way greatly increasing the output.

"We expect to stock Spring Creek heavily from time to time and are receiving cooperation from the prison board through Dr. Claudey, superintendent of Rockview Penitentiary, in improving the stream and giving us additional mileage on prison property. Between two and three miles of Spring Creek will be improved by dams, retards, winter holes, transplanted vegetation, and an increased supply of natural food. This model stream will be open to fishermen, and governed by certain rules to be announced later.

"Facilities for rearing fish for distribution were also increased during the past year at five other hatcheries. A four-acre brood pond for retaining bass and other warmwater species has been constructed at Pleasant Mount Hatchery, Wayne County. Plans now call for construction of 26 additional ponds at Pleasant Mount, Construction work completed at other hatcheries this year follows:

June 1936— Spring Creek project

May 1934— Administration building at Spring Creek. This became the H. R. Stackhouse School of Fishery Conservation and Watercraft Safety School (see page 348).

"At Bellefonte, increased trout production (has occurred) through a system of water aeration, changing of a number of pond intakes, and the addition of four new ponds. At Corry, new ponds (have been) constructed and land purchased. At Reynoldsdale, the completion of 16 additional trout rearing ponds (has been completed) and at Tionesta warmwater ponds produced their first crop of warmwater fishes.

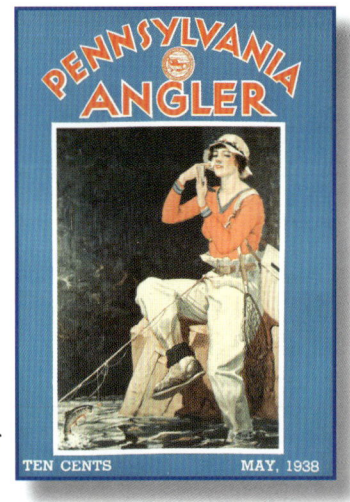

"To provide more varied sport for fishermen we have distributed millions of fish such as black bass, pike perch, Bluegill, sunfish, catfish, suckers, pickerel, Lake Trout, and minnows to Pennsylvania's streams and lakes. Suitable waters have been well stocked with frogs.

"A stream survey, now virtually complete, was of great assistance. It served as an index to waters suitable for stocking, and eliminated guess work in distribution of species.

"The Brown Trout is here to stay and is a favorite game fish. In the survey, waters adaptable to Brown Trout have been carefully checked, and distribution of these fish, all above the legal size of six inches, was increased this year.

"Through the efforts of the Board many additional waters were made available to the public, including 25 miles of excellent trout streams, located in Susquehanna, Clinton, and Wayne counties.

continued on page 86

March 1939— fish stocking

March 1939— stocking truck

The Great Depression 83

January 1934— Reynoldsdale State Fish Hatchery

February 1934— Bellefonte State Fish Hatchery

April 1934— Corry State Fish Hatchery

84   Chapter Four

October 1933— Pleasant Mount State Fish Hatchery

August 1934— Torresdale State Fish Hatchery

April 1935— Huntsdale State Fish Hatchery trout rearing ponds

Completion of the Safe Harbor Dam on the Susquehanna provided ten and one-half square miles of fishing water, while the dam of the Evitts Creek Water Company, located above Lake Gordon, Bedford County, makes available approximately two and one-half square miles. Work on the great Pymatuning Dam, which, when completed, will have a shoreline of 70 miles, was pushed steadily ahead.

"This progress, I feel, is forerunner to even greater advances in Pennsylvania."[12]

Around the same time, Mr. M. M. Kauffman, chair of the agency's by-laws committee, made educating political candidates on conservation and species protection a top priority. He wrote the following: "As soon as a name is announced in a newspaper or newspapers by any and all candidates for United States Senator or Congressman; for Governor of Pennsylvania; State Senator or Assemblyman or candidates for any other legislative, executive or law enforcement office, the (agency) Secretary shall publish the following in (various newspapers): 'Mr. (or Mrs.) you have announced your name for the office of _____. If elected to the office will you at all times vote for and use your influence and best endeavor to pass laws and aid in enforcing present laws to stop pollution of the Lakes, Rivers, Brooks and Springs of the State and particularly the Clarion River and its tributaries?'"

The northcentral and northwest regions of Pennsylvania were targeted for the publication of this question. Water pollution in the region's streams and tributaries was the rationale. The question was posted in the *Clarion Republican* and the *Clarion Democrat,* as well as the *Oil City Derrick* and *Sun-Telegraph* and also newspapers in Brookville,

September 1936— Presque Isle Sportsmen Club (700 plus members)

Tionesta, Ridgway, DuBois, and Kittanning. Copies of the question were also mailed to each candidate.[13] It isn't clear how successful Kauffman's effort was, but it undoubtedly caught the attention of some candidates for public office.

In addition, the Commissioners were increasingly involved in collaborative conservation efforts in the 1930s. For example, the Pittsburgh Sportsmen's Luncheon Club was established in 1938. Its primary aim was to educate Pittsburghers about the alarming pollution problem on its rivers—a problem that was probably already apparent to many residents. *The Pittsburgh Press* employed Johnny Mock as its outdoor recreation writer. Besides writing for the newspaper, Mock saw another outlet to get the word out by forming the club. Regular luncheons featured speakers on conservation and environmental issues, citizen outreach programs were initiated, members met with legislators to discuss their views on these issues, and the club collaborated with like-minded organizations such as Trout Unlimited, the Pennsylvania Audubon Society, and, of course, the Pennsylvania Board of Fish Commissioners.

The Commissioner's also collaborated with junior conservationist programs which were established in many parts of the Commonwealth. According to Commissioner French:

> "Our hats are off to the Junior Conservationists of Pennsylvania. More than ever before, organized sportsmen and individuals have taken these lads under their wing, and we now have hundreds of Junior organizations in Pennsylvania.
>
> "We older sportsmen certainly owe a vote of thanks to these boys for their efforts in furthering the conservation program in Pennsylvania. It has been my good fortune to be intimately associated with some of these groups. The Board, in cooperation with various sportsmen's groups . . . have set aside a large number of ponds or lakes to be fished exclusively by youngsters under the age of 16.
>
> "One of the things we particularly like about the program is the fact that it gives many thousands of under-privileged children who never saw a fishing pole, a chance to enjoy this most healthful recreation."[14]

One such program was at State College High School where a Junior Conservationist Club was created in 1937. Among the goals of the club were to educate youth on hunting and fishing topics such as hunting and angling safety, identifying various types of wildlife, and fly tying. Youth even assisted in trout stocking, as reported in *Pennsylvania Angler* "with the coming of the trout season, our spring program has been launched. Many streams have been stocked, all with Junior Conservationist aid." "Stoddardt, C. W. Jr. "Junior Conservation."[15] Though the vast majority of the club's 160 members were boys, about a dozen girls were among them.

Boating Regulations and Other Laws

Act 121 of 1931 provided the Commissioners the responsibility of administering boating laws in Pennsylvania. Licenses were required for all motorboats operated on inland waterways. The fee was $1 per cylinder for internal combustion engines and $2 per electric motor. Boats were to be tagged with two metal license plates, similar to those found on automobiles. The plates were required to be placed on both sides of the boat at the bow (front of boat). Fines for non-compliance ranged from $25 to $100, hefty sums during the Great Depression. In lieu of paying the fine, violators had to serve 30 days in jail. License fees and fines were allocated to the Commission.

Motorboating for pleasure had become popular in the pre-World War II era. It was mainly limited to well-healed Americans who weren't greatly impacted by the Great Depression. As a result of the growth in recreational boating, President Franklin D. Roosevelt signed the federal Motorboat Act of 1940 which gave the U.S. Coast Guard regulatory authority to ensure safe boating practices. The law mandated that boats carry lifesaving and flotation devices, horns, lights, and fire extinguishers. The Coast Guard could issue fines or make arrests for non-compliance. In 1947, Pennsylvania's boating statute was re-written to be in conformity with the federal law.

Though many state and federal measures were undertaken to end the Great Depression, it was not until the United States entered World War II in December 1941, when Japanese air forces bombed Pearl Harbor in Hawaii, that the economic doldrums dissipated. Hundreds of thousands of young men went off to war in Europe and the Pacific and, on the home front, tens of thousands of men and women worked in factories that supplied munitions, uniforms, food, and other essentials to the troops.

As men went off to war, fishing slowed in some areas of the Commonwealth, but not on Lake Erie where the commercial Blue Pike catch rose by four-hundred percent from 1941 to 1942. And, the work of the Board of Fish Commissioners continued. Regulations in

1941 prohibited trolling from a motorboat, and, in a landmark 1942 regulation, the agency prohibited the operation of a motorboat while intoxicated. In 1944, the Commission purchased Trexler Fish Hatchery in Allentown. As the troops began to return home, Act 145 of 1943 granted them free fishing licenses. A few years later, Act 81 of 1947, granted free licenses to disabled veterans.

July 1, 1937-Patrol boat launch during opening of Pymatuning Reservoir.

Interestingly, the manufacturing of fishing equipment employed some disabled American veterans. Ernie Hille came to the United States from Germany just prior to Adolph Hitler's rise to power and established a small fishing tackle manufacturing business in Williamsport. "When the United States Government hit upon fly tying as a vocation to be taught to wounded veterans in government hospitals, Ernie Hille and his wife, Hilda, bid on the business of supplying fly-tying materials. They won the contract." Hille and his wife provided 400 fly-tying kits, each weighing 83 pounds, and contained enough material to keep 10 men busy tying flies for a period of over 2,400 hours. The disabled veterans were delighted to have the work, for which they were paid a stipend, and their products enabled the Hille duo to expand their business throughout the United States, Canada, and several other countries.[16]

When both the Great Depression and World War II had come to an end, the United States experienced a sustained period of unprecedented economic expansion. Jobs were plentiful, labor unions became more powerful than ever, suburbanization took hold as exemplified by the construction of Levittown in southeastern Pennsylvania, and, before long, many homes would have televisions, electric appliances, and numerous other modern conveniences. The typical American household consisted of a working father, a stay-at-home mother, two to four children, and sometimes, even a dog or cat.

It was a new era and Pennsylvania's fisheries agency was an active part of it.

continued on page 108

Fred Everett: *Artist Profile*

Homage, in the context of the Commission's history, must be provided to Fred Everett as one of the national pioneers of fish and game magazine illustration. In the timely tradition of J. C. Leyendecker and Norman Rockwell of the famed *Saturday Evening Post* cover renditions, Everett was busy conveying capsulized short stories and fishing and hunting depictions in his own, painterly artistic style. Born on September 13, 1892, in Castle Creek, New York, Fred Everett was the son of Edwin and Elizabeth Everett. He worked as a printer's apprentice in 1910 and graduated from Binghamton High School in 1912. Everett attended Colgate University, where he graduated with a Bachelor of Science Degree in 1916.

Everett's pen and ink story illustrations appeared in magazines such as *Wild West Weekly, Western Stories,* and *Clues Detective Magazine.* He also painted covers for magazines such as *Ace-High, Complete Stories, Cowboy Stories, Frontier Stories, Mystery Magazine, Rangeland Stories,* and *West.* In addition, Everett illustrated nationwide, subscription magazines included *St. Nicholas, Outdoor Life,* and *The Elks.* Later, he wrote and illustrated three books—*Wild Ducks* (1946), *Fun With Trout* (1952), and *Fun With Game Birds* (1954).

In 1937, he began illustrating covers for *Pennsylvania Angler* magazine and produced more than 100 pieces of art for the magazine during the 1930s and 1940s with at least 70 of those artworks gracing the covers. It is believed that he was the only out-of-state member of the Fly Fishers' Club of Harrisburg in the late 1940s and early 1950s.

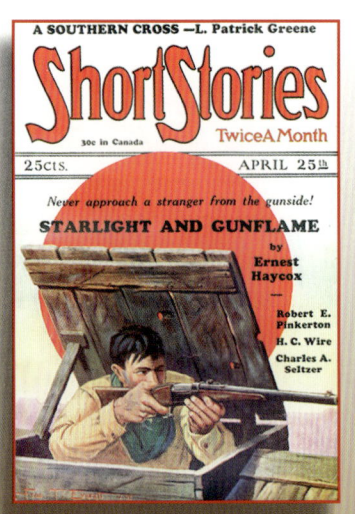

Everett became Senior Editor of Publications in the New York State Conservation Department in 1945, and he retired from that position in 1953. After retirement, he moved to Chatham, New York. There, he produced portraits of local dignitaries and paintings of wildlife. Everett died on September 20, 1957.

March 1937 **Pennsylvania Angler** *cover by artist Fred Everett*

The Great Depression 91

January 1938 **Pennsylvania Angler** *cover by artist Fred Everett*

92 *Chapter Four*

February 1938 **Pennsylvania Angler** *cover by artist Fred Everett*

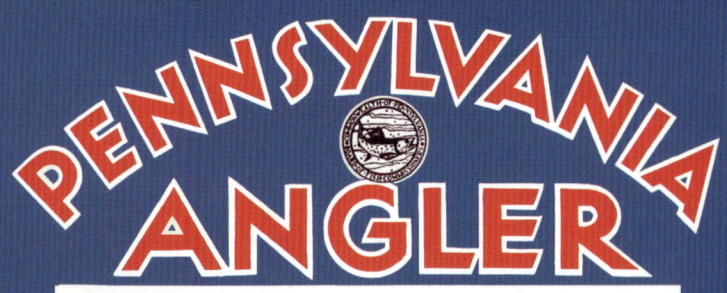

The Great Depression

March 1938 **Pennsylvania Angler** *cover by artist Fred Everett*

94   *Chapter Four*

April 1938 **Pennsylvania Angler** *cover by artist Fred Everett*

November 1938 **Pennsylvania Angler** *cover by artist Fred Everett*

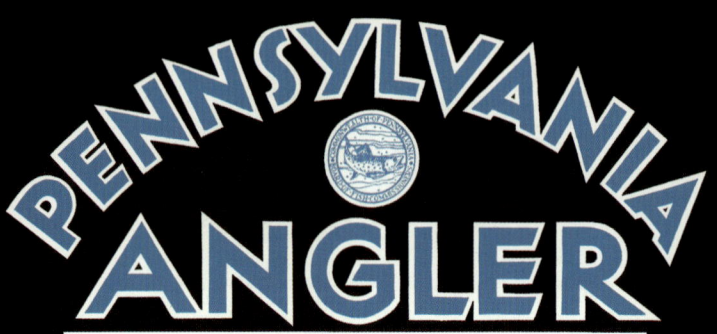

96 *Chapter Four*

January 1939 **Pennsylvania Angler** *cover by artist Fred Everett*

The Great Depression 97

July 1940 **Pennsylvania Angler** *cover by artist Fred Everett*

98 *Chapter Four*

September 1940 **Pennsylvania Angler** *cover by artist Fred Everett*

The Great Depression

October 1940 **Pennsylvania Angler** *cover by artist Fred Everett*

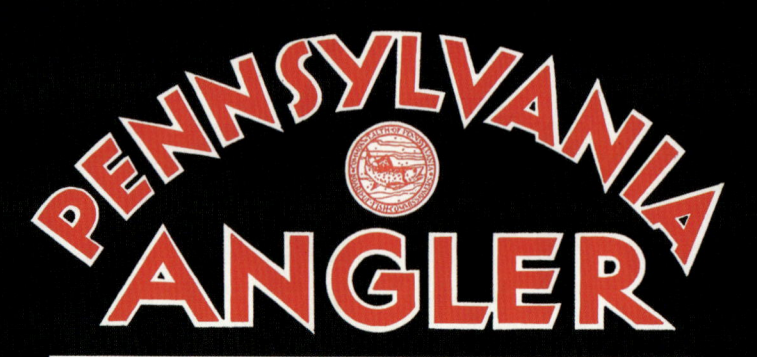

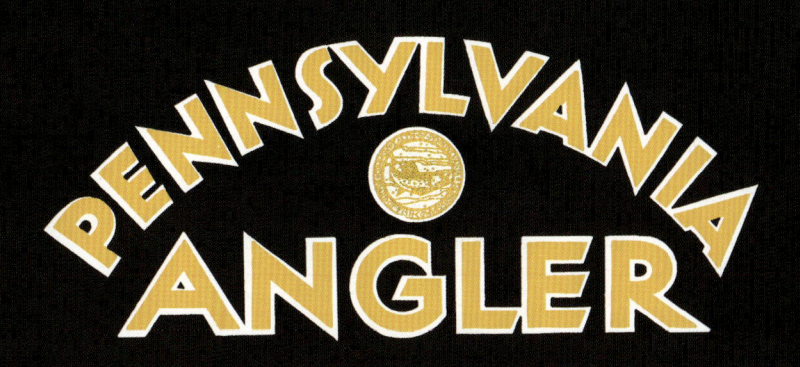

February 1941 **Pennsylvania Angler** *cover by artist Fred Everett*

May 1941 **Pennsylvania Angler** *cover by artist Fred Everett*

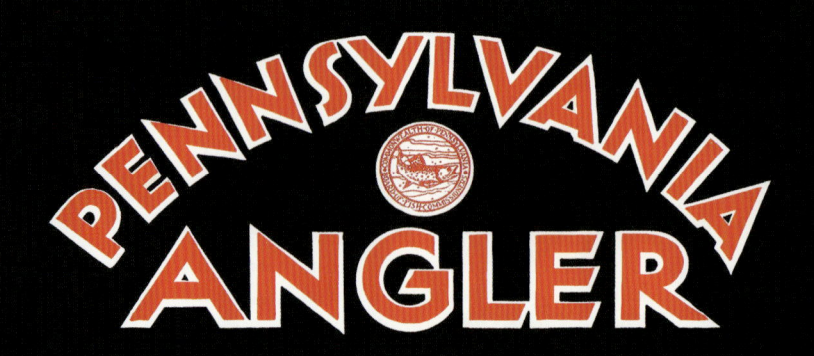

102   *Chapter Four*

June 1941 **Pennsylvania Angler** *cover by artist Fred Everett*

The Great Depression 103

August 1941 **Pennsylvania Angler** *cover by artist Fred Everett*

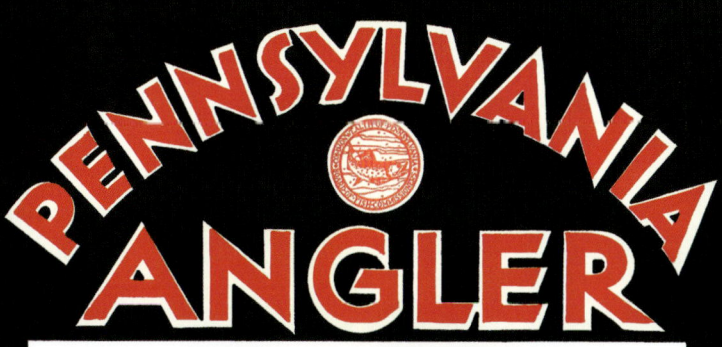

December 1942 **Pennsylvania Angler** *cover by artist Fred Everett*

The Great Depression **105**

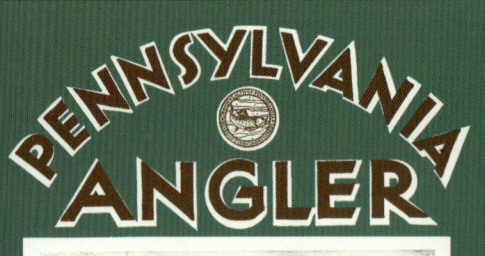

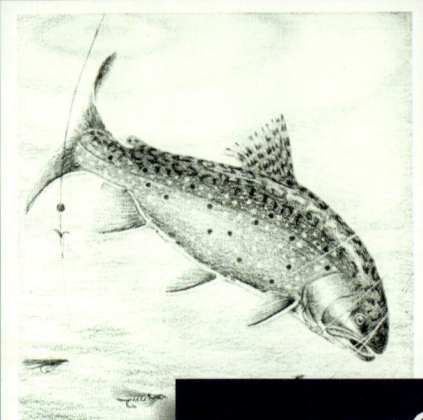

April 1943
*Pennsylvania Angler
cover by
artist Fred Everett*

*June 1943
Pennsylvania Angler
cover by
artist Fred Everett*

106 *Chapter Four*

January 1940 **Pennsylvania Angler** *cover by artist Ned Smith*

One of Ned Smith's first professional assignments in magazine illustration and authorship was for the cover painting of the January 1940 Pennsylvania Angler and a companion article in that issue.

The Great Depression

Chapter Five: From the Post-War Era to Earth Day

"I wanted a State Park within 25 miles of every Pennsylvanian. The parks had to have water. Water gives you fishing, boating, and swimming."
—Governor George M. Leader (1955–1959)

During the immediate post-war era, the profile of the average angler began to change. On one hand, fishing remained largely a man's sport, as did boating. In the 1940s and 1950s, of course, World War II and Korean War veterans were among the ranks of anglers. Many worked in factories and other industrial establishments that produced goods en-masse for the growing consumer marketplace. Saturdays and Sundays were the days on which they typically fished, although, from spring to fall, they could do so after putting-in the typical eight-to-five work shift. The number of resident fishing licenses issued grew steadily from 554,000 in 1946 to more than 700,000 in 1956. The cost of an annual resident license was $2.50. Act 330 of 1957 raised resident fishing

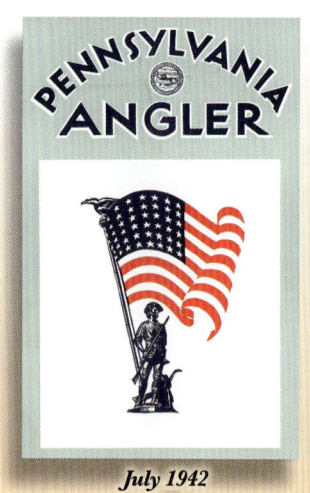

July 1942

July 1945– tackle donation to servicemen

108 Chapter Five

licenses to $3.25, causing a drop-off in the number of resident licenses to 585,000 by 1960. Yet, angling still remained relatively affordable in an era when a gallon of gas was 31 cents, and a gallon of milk cost $1, while the average annual salary was $5,500, and the minimum wage $1 per hour (1957 dollars).

Besides the average male angler, women were increasingly starting to fish: "They say that marriage is a partnership but most fellows don't feel that this axiom applies when it comes to their hunting and fishing. If they take the little woman along at all, they usually do so grudgingly," author Keith Schuyler pointed out in an article entitled "Why Not Take Her Along?" that appeared in a late-1949 issue of *Pennsylvania Angler*. Schuyler hinted that it could very well help a marriage if the couple enjoyed the outdoors and bagging a deer or filled-out a stringer together. Besides, he said, "the only additional expense (could be) for freckle cream (as) the wind brings out her spots that worry her much more than snakes or wet feet!" While there were no precise statistics yet kept, more and more women were becoming anglers.[2]

Another particular audience that was addressed by the *Pennsylvania Angler* was retirees. For example, a February 1958 article entitled "So You've Retired," said:

> "So you're retired. The magic birthday has been reached and crossed and time is yours to do with what you wish. You are at last unhampered by work schedules, vacation limits and employment responsibilities. This age of leisure, an achievement of the modern

November 1949

July 1949

From Post-War Era to Earth Day

civilizations, can be the most creative and splendid of your life. And, one of the most important assets your retirement can bring you is freedom to take rod, reel and all equipment to a spot dear to your heart and remembrance. Not only is this a dream come true of your dreaming. It is a glimpse of Paradise!"[3]

Yet, another trend was that fishing was increasingly a family activity, perhaps no surprise given the post-World War II "baby boom." For example, researcher Carol Lane, who served as women's travel director for the Shell Oil Company, conducted a 36-state survey to determine the types of vacations that families typically enjoyed. In summarizing the findings of her survey, Lane reported that "taking the family to the lake for a week of fishing was the most popular pastime . . . because it proved to be easy, fun—and, most of all—reasonably economical."[4]

Some women, retirees, and families probably fished in the 100-acre Raccoon Lake at the newly opened Raccoon Creek State Park in Washington County. Governor James Duff (1947–1951) cut the ribbon in October 1949. He also helped to place 400 Largemouth Bass, 2,000 catfish, and 2,000 Bluegills in the park's lake. The park began as a Recreational Demonstration Area operated by the National Park Service in the 1930s. Civilian Conservation Corps workers developed recreational areas, trails, and camps in the 7,600-acre park that remains one of the jewels of Pennsylvania's State Park System.

September 1949

September 1942

A New Name:
The Pennsylvania Fish Commission

Act 180 of 1949 officially changed the name of the Board of Fish Commissioners to the Pennsylvania Fish Commission (PFC). At their first official meeting following the reorganization, the Commissioners had to select an Executive Director. Apparently, it was quite an easy decision. When they gathered in a conference room in the South Office Building at the State Capitol Complex in Harrisburg for their April 25, 1949, meeting, Commissioner Charles A. French called the meeting to order, explained provisions of the new statute, and, when he was finished, he was immediately asked to leave the room by the other Commissioners. Some agency staff seemed surprised by the abrupt request. However, the reason for his removal was auspicious for French. The Commissioners very briefly discussed appointing him as Executive Director and unanimously voted in the affirmative. French was called back into the conference room in short order and asked if he would accept the position. Without hesitation he said "yes." His salary was set at $9,500 per year.

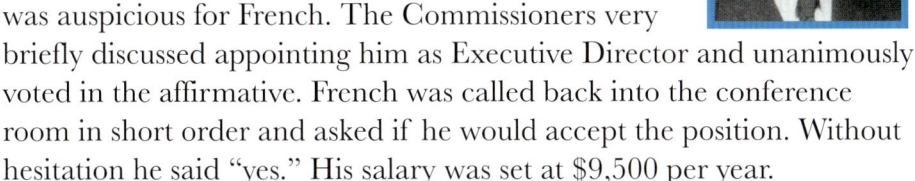

After thanking the Commissioners, French indicated that "the old board of Fish Commissioners had done a magnificent job" and "that as Executive Director of the new Pennsylvania Fish Commission, he would do everything within his power to maintain the high standards under which we are now operating."[5]

Of course, French was no stranger to the agency. Governor George Earle (1935–1939) appointed him as a Commissioner in April 1935.

On Wednesday, December 22, 1948, the Harrisburg office staff of the Pennsylvania Fish Commission held its annual FISH-MAS Party in the Rose Room of the William Penn Hotel, Harrisburg.

French was active in northwestern Pennsylvania's sportsmen's organizations and was well known in the region. He was an avid hunter and angler, particularly well versed when it came to bass fishing. French was no rookie, and the Commissioners recognized that.

While the Fish Commission remained an independent agency and was statutorily funded by licensing fees and other exclusive forms of revenue, such as fines, the Governor's Office did have some say in the agency's operations. The Commission set its own budget, for example. Yet it was subject to review and final approval by the Governor's budget staff. In addition, some Commission office staff, such as stenographers, had to meet job requirements set forth by what was then called the Governor's Personnel Office and the Civil Service Commission. Before long, all Commission staff, salaried and non-salaried, were required to join and make regular contributions to the State Employees' Retirement System. They could also participate in medical insurance programs offered by the Commonwealth. Moreover, fish wardens were required to retire at age 62, while other employees could remain on the job until age 65.

Embracing science was still a fresh idea at the Commission, although some of this work had been done by Mr. Buller in the 1920s. Novel or not, the agency embraced scientific and technical know-how when it implemented its first official statewide fish management program in 1950. Gordon Trembly described it this way: "In recent years we have heard the term 'management' used frequently as applied to our forests, our soils and our game. Much less have we heard it applied to

January 1940

October 1945

112 *Chapter Five*

our fish." Field investigations were required under the new program with the primary aims to collect and analyze data on water quality, fish growth, and "to determine existing relationships between the different environments and the various species . . . in those environments. In each case, an attempt is the made to control or adjust the population . . . in such a way (that) anglers may have a maximum sustained yield." According to Trembly, "expressed simply, fish management aims to provide better fishing."[6]

Concurrently, the Fish Commission received financial assistance from the federal Dingell-Johnson Act that went into effect in 1950, ending a 10-year struggle by conservationists from across the nation. Also called the Federal Aid in Sport Fish Restoration Act, the statute granted federal financial assistance to states for fish restoration, management, and acquisition plans and projects. At its outset, Dingell-Johnson rebated monies to Pennsylvania that were collected from a 10-percent excise tax on tackle. From 1951 to 1963, a total of $1.5 million was granted to the Commonwealth with the average annual amounts ranging from $100,000 to $130,000 in federal monies matched by an additional one-quarter of (of the federal share) of state monies. Virgin Run Lake in Fayette County was the first PFC project to use federal aid from Dingell-Johnson. The 35-acre lake was built from start to finish by the Commission and was dedicated on July 11, 1953. Preceding Dingell-Johnson was the federal Pittman-Robertson Act (1937) that similarly supported state wildlife conservation. *continued on page 118*

June 1948

January 1949

From Post-War Era to Earth Day

Commission activities in the 1940s

October 1941– refrigerated stocking truck

November 1940

April 1947– stocking fleet

April 1947 *April 1942– tank truck*

114 *Chapter Five*

March 1947– Fish Wardens at training school

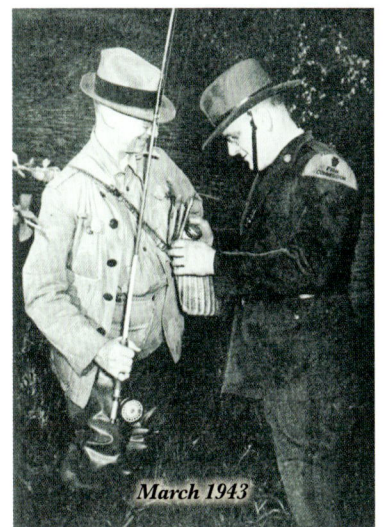

March 1943

November 1940

May 1949– fish culturists

From Post-War Era to Earth Day

Pennsylvania anglers 1940s

October 1944– Susquehanna River at Harrisburg

January 1942– license button collector

March 1941

June 1947– fly-tying classes

116 Chapter Five

October 1944

February 1945

November 1946

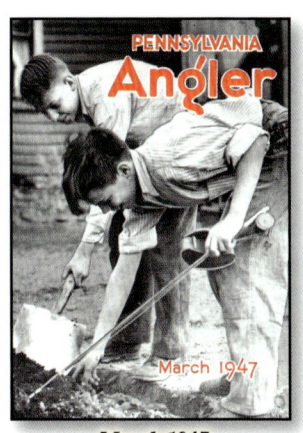

March 1947

August 1947

IMPORTANT TO FISHERMEN!

NO FISHING OF ANY KIND FROM MARCH 15TH UNTIL APRIL 15TH SIGNED PENNSYLVANIA LAW!

SPECIAL NOTICE!

"By Special Amendment of the Fish Laws passed by 1949 Legislature--All Fishing is Prohibited in Any Waters from March 14 to April 15, 1950, Except in Rivers, Lakes or Ponds Not Stocked with Trout."

PENNSYLVANIA FISH COMMISSION

January 1950

From Post-War Era to Earth Day

Ground-breaking ceremonies on May 2, 1952, for Benner Spring Research Station. Executive Director of the Pennsylvania Fish Commission, C. A. French, in foreground with shovel, turns first shovelful of sod.

On the heels of Dingell-Johnson came the good news that Fisherman's Paradise set a record attendance in 1950 at 34,796 and that the Commission acquired the Benner Spring Research Station property in Centre County. The Benner Spring Research Station began full operation in 1957. Equally important were the following:

- Act 65 of 1949 prohibited fishing in trout streams that were stocked by the Commission one month prior to the famed opening day of trout season.
- In 1951, fish were placed in the Schuylkill River for the first time in a decade. This followed a massive clean-up effort and acid mine drainage mitigation project undertaken by the Pennsylvania Department of Forests and Waters.
- Act 68 of 1951 directed the Commission to study the migratory habits of fish—particularly shad—for the first time.
- The legal size of pickerel was raised to 15 inches from 12 inches in 1951.
- In 1952, the creel limit for trout was reduced to eight from ten.
- Pymatuning Reservoir was first stocked with Muskellunge in 1953.
- Ground was broken for Lake Somerset in 1955.
- In 1956, taking carp with a long bow and arrow was legalized.

Change and new ways of doing things—such as embracing science and putting federal dollars to good use—became the norm at the Pennsylvania Fish Commission. Change, too, was on the political horizon in Harrisburg.

continued on page 126

June 1953– Early boating safety poster within the pages of **Pennsylvania Angler.**

Temporary hatch house during the construction of the Benner Spring Research Station in 1953.

Fisherman's Paradise in the 1950s

From 1934 through 1961, only fly fishing with barbless hooks was permitted at Fisherman's Paradise. Wading was prohibited. During this time, visitation grew to more than 50,000, annually, at this location on Spring Creek in Centre County. This gallery of photos presented over this and the next five pages provides a glimpse of the participation and experience of fishing at "Paradise" during the 1950s.

120 Chapter Five

From Post-War Era to Earth Day 121

Fisherman's Paradise in the 1950s

Located next to the Commission's Stackhouse School and the Bellefonte State Fish Hatchery, large crowds at Fisherman's Paradise required the construction of a booth for check-in, as seen in the above photograph.

Chapter Five

From Post-War Era to Earth Day 123

While the above photograph provides the appearance of a male-dominated fishing spot, Fisherman's Paradise became heralded as a family-fishing destination. A 1956 article about the project in The Fisherman, *a national sporting magazine, read much like a travel brochure: "The area surrounding the fishing project is somewhat of a park in itself . . . Picnic tables are spotted around the grounds.*

Fisherman's Paradise in the 1950s

Paths wind beneath shady trees among walled-up spring holes which hold specimen trout for visitors to see." The article continued to extol the virtues and amenities of fishing at the location, noting, that in keeping with the era's sense of equality "a separate stream is maintained for women and teen-age girls."

From Post-War Era to Earth Day

A New Governor and Executive Director

At the remarkably young age of 36 years old, George M. Leader of York County was elected Governor of the Commonwealth in November 1954, defeating the incumbent Republican Lieutenant Governor Lloyd Wood by 280,000 votes. Leader had served as a State Senator and Chairman of the York County Democratic Party and was quite well known in political circles, though he was given little chance to secure the governorship for two reasons: First, he was far too young some said, and, second, Leader was a liberal Democrat in a solidly Republican state where GOP stalwarts had consistently been elected to the Commonwealth's highest office since the Civil War with just two exceptions. Agrarian and labor support bolstered his campaign, which focused on rooting-out political patronage in state government, implementing economic development policies to help distressed areas of the Commonwealth, such as its anthracite coal region, and focusing efforts on environmental protection and conservation.

Leader promised that he would hire qualified professionals at all levels of state government and root out political patronage. Of nearly 50,000 jobs in state government, Leader expanded civil service rules and regulations to 13,000 of those positions. This meant, simply, that people had to be qualified to do the jobs for which they were hired. Applicants had to pass civil service exams, clear background screenings, and hold the proper credentials for the job.

When it came to environmental and conservation issues, chief among Leader's many goals was that, "I wanted a State Park within

Governor George M. Leader shown, in 1958, signing the proclamation for National Wildlife Week.

126 *Chapter Five*

25 miles of every Pennsylvanian. The parks had to have water. Water gives you fishing, boating and swimming." To help him accomplish this goal, Leader hired Maurice K. Goddard, a forestry professor at Penn State University, to head the Department of Forests and Waters. There were 44 Pennsylvania state parks in 1955. Both Goddard and Leader worked with the General Assembly to enact the Oil and Gas Lease Fund Act, which earmarked royalties from oil and gas taken from state-owned land to be spent on conservation development and land acquisition. One hundred seventy-five potential park sites were evaluated by the end of the 1950s based on criteria such as water, location, topography, subsurface conditions, availability, and scenic and historical significance. Acquisition of some of the new state parks soon began and continued for the remainder of the twentieth century and well into the twenty-first century.[7]

In fact, when Governor Leader passed away in 2013, at the age of 95 years, his vision had largely been achieved. Pennsylvania had 120 state parks, including some of the finest state parks in the nation. In time, recreational fishing and boating opportunities were greatly expanded within the Commonwealth's growing state park system. Some park lakes were stocked by PFC staff. Boat mooring and launch sites were built, and, naturally, all angler and boaters could enjoy the opportunities made available to them. In 2015, three Pennsylvania state parks were ranked among the top ten family friendly places to boat and fish in the United States, according to the Recreational Boating and Fishing Foundation. The parks were Keystone State Park, Westmoreland

Maurice K. Goddard in 1960.

December 1950

From Post-War Era to Earth Day   127

County; Presque Isle State Park, Erie County; and Lackawanna State Park, Lackawanna County.[8]

As with his selection of Maurice Goddard, Leader stuck to his rule of hiring qualified professionals for cabinet, sub-cabinet, and commission appointments. When Fish Commission Executive Director French retired in mid-1955, Leader appointed William Voigt Jr. on September 12, 1955, to head the agency. The appointment came as a surprise—as did many of Leader's appointments—since Voigt wasn't well known in and around Harrisburg or in Pennsylvania for that matter. He did have an eclectic background to say the least.

Voigt was a businessman who managed a large Georgia pecan farm and was among the largest producers of jellied and jarred pecans for retail markets in the United States. What was attractive to Leader, however, was that Voigt was also a crusader for conservation and had served as President of the Izaak Walton League of America. He was passionate about clean streams, wildlife management, and protection of endangered species. Himself a fisherman, Voigt "talks fish and fisherman in the language of a bank fisherman, a fly rod man, an expert with the spinning gear." Voigt, said that "my business is to conserve" whether it came to pecans or the environment. James Finnegan, Governor Leader's Secretary of the Commonwealth, gave the oath-of-office to Voigt in September 1955.[9] Yet, to the surprise of some, Voigt's tenure with the agency wasn't all that remarkable. And, it was relatively short. One critique was that he

August 1958—fish culturists

May 1958

Chapter Five

was more of a part-time Executive Director, rather than someone who was fully dedicated to the job.

He pushed-through a resident fishing license increase from $2.50 to $3.25 in 1957. One dollar of the cost of license was specially earmarked for property acquisition and development. Such a policy was consistent with the Leader Administration's push to expand public ownership of land and waters, including forests, wetlands, and stream encroachments. Voigt also convinced the Commissioners that, based on staff recommendations, trout season should be extended to October 31 in selected lakes. He also oversaw the establishment of the first Fish-for-Fun area along the Left Branch of the Young Women's Creek in Clinton County in 1958. This event attracted female anglers, amateurs, and pros alike.

Anglers are always excited about opening day of trout season. It is probably the one day of the year when thousands of them simultaneously line stream banks across Pennsylvania to catch these prized fish. Voigt and the Commissioners supported passage of Act 673 of 1959 which established the opening day of trout season as the first Saturday after April 11. Casting could begin at 5 a.m. A later policy mandated that opening day was to be on the Saturday closest to April 15 and was to begin at 8 a.m., rather than 3 hours prior. Numerous landowners whose properties were adjacent to streams complained to the Commission that the 5 a.m. start time prompted anglers to camp overnight on their land. Setting the time at 8 a.m. mitigated the problem of overnight camping. The selection of Saturdays was for practical reasons. Most anglers were working people whose workweeks were defined by the usual Monday through Friday schedule.

continued on page 134

Harold "Whitey" Solomon, popular Erie County Fish Warden keeps his audience on the edge of their seats as he talks about fish and fishing. These youngsters are a few of the approximately 600 who attended day-camping sessions during the summer of 1958.

Pennsylvania anglers and boaters in the 1950s

April 1953

October 1952

April 1954

June 1954

130 Chapter Five

April 1951

September 1951– boating on the Susquehanna River

August 1951

July 1954

July 1957

June 1953

From Post-War Era to Earth Day **131**

Pennsylvania anglers and boaters in the 1950s

April 1951

October 1958

April 1955

April 1953

132 *Chapter Five*

May 1951– Miss Fisherman's Paradise 1950

From Post-War Era to Earth Day

There was one item of sad news during Voigt's tenure. In April 1958, Fish Warden Raymond L. Schroll Jr. died in an accident in the swollen Susquehanna River at Williamsport. He and Paul A. Ranck, a game protector, were checking waterfowl nestings and fishermen law compliance when their motorboat suddenly encountered a heavy, swift current and capsized, throwing them into the raging river. Ranck clung to the overturned boat, while Schroll, an expert swimmer, tried to make it to shore. Witnesses said that he had almost reached the shore when he realized that his partner needed help. He turned and started swimming back to the capsized boat to assist Ranck. However, he made it just a short distance when he disappeared in the turbulent water. Ranck was rescued by members of the Williamsport Fire Engine Company No. 2 when he caught hold of a life-line lowered from a railroad bridge.

Search parties looked for Schroll's body for several weeks. On Monday afternoon, April 28, 24 days after the accident, the body was sighted floating under a bridge some 30 miles downstream from the site of the accident. Schroll was from Glenville, York County, and was appointed as a Fish Warden on June 23, 1952. He was assigned to Lycoming County. During World War II, he served with the U.S. Navy aboard the aircraft carrier *U.S.S. Midway*. Schroll left behind his wife Jean and two children, Linda Jean and Jeffery Allen.

When Executive Director Voigt decided to return to his pecan business on a full-time basis, the Commissioners appointed a leader who was well-suited to manage the agency's affairs. Albert M. Day assumed the job on July 18, 1960.

The Pennsylvania Fish Commission under the Leadership of Albert Day

Day was a veteran of more than 40 years of service in fish and game work. Most of his career was with the U.S. Fish and Wildlife Service, where he served as that agency's director for many years. Prior to coming to Pennsylvania, Day was head of the Oregon Fish Commission, where he had led major efforts to clean-up that state's streams.

In 1960, Day oversaw the full implementation of the Federal Boating Act of 1958, which affected boats on all navigable waters in

134 *Chapter Five*

In Honor and Memory of Warden Raymond L. Schroll Jr.

September 11, 1927 - April 28, 1958

On April 4, 1958, Lycoming County District Fish Warden Raymond Schroll and Paul Ranck, a Game Commission officer, were patrolling the Susquehanna River below Williamsport. It had been a wet spring and the river was unusually high and swift. The two officers were returning from checking the duck hatch from Muncy to Williamsport. They attempted to navigate the "chute" in Williamsport, but the swift water was too much for the small craft to handle. The boat capsized, throwing both Officer Schroll and Officer Ranck into the river. Officer Schroll was an excellent swimmer and quickly made it safely to shore. As he exited the water, he turned and saw Officer Ranck clinging to the overturned boat. Without hesitating, Officer Schroll dived back into the water in an attempt to assist his friend. Witnesses say he was gaining on Officer Ranck when Officer Schroll just disappeared under the raging water. Officer Ranck clung to the boat for over a mile, before he was rescued by a volunteer fireman who threw a rope from a bridge over the river. Recovery teams searched unsuccessfully for Officer Schroll in the following few weeks. His body was recovered April 28, 1958, in Lewisburg, PA, over 30 miles downstream.

Witnesses say Officer Schroll had saved his own life and was out of danger. He didn't have to return to the water, but he saw a fellow officer in trouble and instinctively responded.

Officer Raymond Schroll is a genuine hero, who unselfishly laid down his life for a friend.

Officer Schroll began his career with the Pennsylvania Fish Commission on June 23, 1952. He was well-respected and admired by his fellow officers and the sportsmen of Lycoming County. All who knew him were not surprised by his act of putting his life on the line in an effort to assist a friend in need.

On May 15, 2000, Officer Raymond L. Schroll was inducted into the National Law Enforcement Officers Memorial in Washington, DC.

Memorial plaque located at the PFBC Harrisburg Headquaters. *photo-Spring Gearhart, PFBC*

From Post-War Era to Earth Day

Pennsylvania. The law resulted in dual jurisdiction (federal and state) over boat operators who used motors that delivered more than 10 horsepower. For these boats, dual licenses were required, and both state and federal regulations were applicable. The Boat Safety Act of 1971 further prescribed licensing requirements and, for the first time, mandated that unpowered boats carry personal flotation devices. The National Association of Engine and Boat Manufacturers produced several films in 1958 on recreational boating, one that included discussion of the provisions of the 1958 federal law. The association provided the 16-millimeter film free of charge to sportsmen, boater, and angler associations.

In the 1960s, the Fish Commission collaborated with other state agencies to address continuing water pollution problems. Working with the Sanitary Water Board, Commission staff conducted studies of stream pollution. Both the Sanitary Water Board and PFC investigated an acid mine discharge in October 1961 that ranked as the worst fish kill on the Susquehanna River up to that time.

During the summer and fall of 1961, the Glen Alden Mining Corporation, a subsidiary of Blue Coal Corporation, dumped excessive amounts of acid mine waste into the river in the Wyoming Valley. When large fish kills were reported, staff from PFC and the Sanitary Water Board investigated and traced the source to the company's south Wilkes-Barre mining operations, where two continuously operating mine pumps discharged acid-laced water. Damage was reported on a 50-mile stretch of the river from Wilkes-Barre to Sunbury. Thousands of

May 1960

April 1961– hatchery fish grader

136 *Chapter Five*

fish were killed, and the river turned an orange-rust color. Glen Alden, the last large anthracite coal operator in the nation, was mandated by the Commonwealth to pay over $58,000 in fines and had to cover all clean-up costs. Besides being a polluter, the company had a reputation for poor labor relations and unsafe mining practices. Its principal owner was James Durkin of nearby Dallas, Pennsylvania. A silent partner in Blue Coal was James R. "Jimmy" Hoffa, famed former President of the International Brotherhood of Teamsters, though his ownership of Blue Coal would not become known until after his disappearance in 1975.

Despite such bad news, the agency had other tasks to attend to as well. In 1962, a federal-state cooperative trout stocking program went into effect. That year Fisherman's Paradise opened on April 14 on a "fish-for-fun" basis. And, 1963 marked the last year that non-resident trout stamps were required. When it came to boating, Act 400 of 1963 approved a numbering system for boats and set boat registration fees at $4 per year for motorboats less than 16 feet in length, while the owners of larger motorboats had to pay $6 per year. Moreover, in 1964, resident fishing licenses increased to $5.

During Day's tenure, the agency remained on firm financial footing. For example, during the Fiscal Year from July 1, 1964, to June 30, 1965, the Commission sold nearly 500,000 resident fishing licenses at $3.25 per license. Licensing fees, fines, and miscellaneous sources of income brought revenues of more than $2.8 million. When added to budget surplus carryovers from previous years, the Commission had more than $4.4 million on hand by mid-decade. During the same period, expenses totaled nearly $2.3 million, leaving a hefty reserve.

The twenty-fifth anniversary of the signing of the Pittman-Robertson Act was commemorated at a dinner in Washington, D. C, in 1962. Albert M. Day (center), Executive Director, Pennsylvania Fish Commission, was given a scroll in recognition and appreciation of his efforts in wildlife restoration in America by Frank P. Briggs, Assistant Secretary for Fish and Wildlife, U.S. Department of the Interior. At left is C. R. Gutermuth, Vice President, Wildlife Management Institute.

A reserve was prudent. Earlier that year, PFC's comptroller had forewarned that, "there is mounting pressure of increased costs for the Commission's operations . . . without accompanying increased revenues." Thus, "tight control and close supervision of finances" were absolutely necessary. Part of the reason for increased costs was a five-percent, across-the-board pay raise for Commonwealth employees that took effect July 1, 1965, resulting in additional costs to the Commission of $75,000.[10]

When it came to expenditures, 37 percent or $850,000 (out of total expenditures of $2.3 million cited previously) of the Commission's budget was for fish propagation and distribution, and the numbers were impressive. During Fiscal Year 1964–1965, the Commission hatched and planted over 3.5 million trout alone, which was augmented by U.S. Fish and Wildlife Service's Hatchery Division depositing another 600,000, bringing the grand total of trout to 4.1 million trout. Propagation of warmwater species was equally as impressive. The Commission hatched and planted 14 million Walleyes, 600,000 Northern Pike, 454,000 Muskellunge, and 105,000 Largemouth Bass, during the same period.

Law enforcement expended $400,000 during the same period. Besides imposing fines and making arrests, Fish Wardens spent a good deal of time educating the public by conducting regional fishing schools, which taught the basics on how and where to fish as well as the essentials of laws and regulations. And, they conducted watercraft safety programs across Pennsylvania where most of the participants were reported to be first-time boaters.

August 1963– PFC exhibit staffed by Fish Wardens.

October 1966

Engineering expenditures ranked third for a total of $323,000. The agency's engineering work was enhanced by the Commonwealth's Project 70 Land Acquisition and Borrowing Act of 1964. This law enabled the Commonwealth to issue bonds totaling $70 million for acquisition of public lands for parks, reservoirs, and other conservation, recreation, and historic preservation purposes. As a result, a good deal of the Engineering Division's time at mid-decade was focused on conducting feasibility studies for acquisition projects. PFC engineers also worked on developing trout raceways, hatchery renovations, and maintenance of more than 90 public access areas.

PFC Fisheries Management Research and Land and Water Management programs spent $158,000 and $124,000, respectively. Research focused on fish diseases, habitat impediments, evaluation of the impact of herbicides such as DDT (discussed later), and analysis of physical and chemical conditions necessary for hatching shad. Land and Water Management program staff worked closely with the Real Estate Division to acquire and maintain properties, among other activities. Finally, conservation education and public relations were allocated $100,000 to publish and distribute *Pennsylvania Angler* and other educational material, develop and deliver slide presentations to youth and adult audiences, and to create live and mounted fish exhibits at county fairs and sportsmen's shows. Commission staff also produced live radio and television appearances to address conservation, angling, and boating issues.

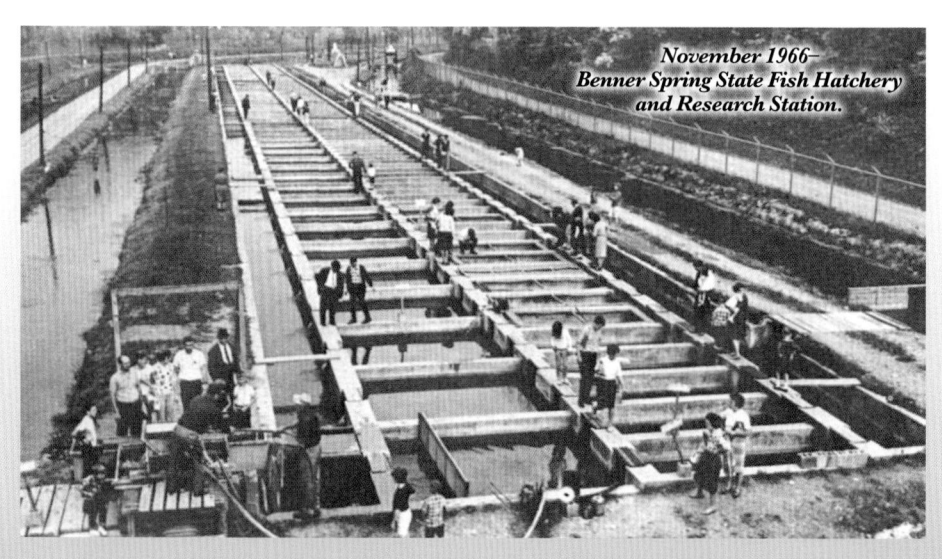

*November 1966–
Benner Spring State Fish Hatchery
and Research Station.*

Another very important milestone was marked in 1964. The agency officially opened the H. R. Stackhouse Fishery Conservation and Watercraft Safety School on November 9 *(see page 348)*. The locale was (and remains) the agency's training facility at Fisherman's Paradise near Bellefonte in Centre County. The Commission used (and uses) "Stackhouse" to hold seminars on topics such as law enforcement, propagation, and watercraft safety. A three-month regimen of instruction was required for each newly hired warden. Twelve men graduated from the first training program and were assigned to fill warden vacancies. The Pennsylvania Game Commission (PGC) and the U.S. Coast Guard (USCG) occasionally took advantage of Stackhouse to train its personnel as well.

A Study of the Commission by the Wildlife Management Institute

Even though PFC appeared to be functioning smoothly during Day's tenure, the General Assembly's Joint State Government Commission called on the Washington, D.C.-based Wildlife Management Institute to conduct an analysis and review of the agency. This included its organizational structure, management practices, enforcement program, regulations and policies, and its overall operating efficiency and effectiveness. The same type of study was conducted of PGC.

Many of the Institute's recommendations were not very surprising. For example, it was recommended that dedicated funding be continued and that only individuals who meet clear qualifications and employment standards be hired, so as to prevent the influence of partisan politics.

January 1967

April 1967– PFC exhibit

Chapter Five

The H. R. Stackhouse School of Fishery Conservation and Watercraft Safety opened in 1964 at the administration building along Fisherman's Paradise near Bellefonte. Here, in 1968, John Buck, Region II Warden Supervisor, provides some law enforcement training to the cadet class.

The Institute also recommended that employees be granted regular, merit-based pay increases and be adequately trained to carry-out their duties. The Executive Director (sometimes referred to as "the Chief Fish Warden") was to have full administrative and supervisory responsibilities over all Commission employees and should continue to serve on the boards of various collaborative organizations such as the Sanitary Water Board and the Atlantic States Marine Fisheries Commission. It was also recommended that PFC retain all enforcement authority involving fish and boat laws, including establishment of seasons and creel limits, as well as prosecuting law violators.

Some recommendations raised eyebrows, particularly when it came to issues relating to Fish Wardens. For example, the Institute found that the salaries for PFC Fish Wardens were about average with other states at $5,000 annually. However, the study indicated that base pay should begin at $5,000 and be subject to regular merit increases if "the Commission is to hire and keep good men." Quite simply, wardens weren't paid enough. And, it was apparent that they were to be "men." While it was important that all wardens possessed a least a high school education, the Institute also recommended that PFC adopt stricter educational standards by requiring a college education but admitted that recruiting such personnel would be difficult "at the present time," because the number of candidates who could meet this requirement was very small and would grow slowly.

Other recommendations were vague or generalized, such as "it is recommended that existing pollution laws be reassessed, strengthened, and rigidly enforced"[11]; that "a modernization plan be initiated at all hatcheries,"[12] and that staff be enlarged to meet the growing needs of the agency. Day and agency staff agreed with these ideas, but careful thought had to be given to the details and funding necessary to accomplish each one.

Among its practical and well-received recommendations, some referenced PFC education and outreach programs. For example, the study recognized that "the increasing public demand for education has placed a heavy load upon the limited force of this division."[13] To reach larger audiences, the Institute recommended that audiovisual aids be used, especially slide presentations, and live and mounted exhibits continue to travel to fairs, expositions, and other locales where they could be seen by as many people as possible. The agency was all-too-quick to implement these recommendations.[14]

Though the report didn't address this matter, there was an equally pressing and practical issue: Fish Wardens were in desperate need of new uniforms. The Commission and staff agreed that "our present uniforms are not sufficiently distinctive and do not reflect the modern trend in Conservation dress." Therefore, at its March 1965 meeting, the Commissioners approved a motion for an updated warden uniform and spelled out its details: "The style (is to) be similar to that displayed by the U.S. Fish and Wildlife Service, the U.S. Army green-gray color" and would carry the Commission insignia and a name plate. Commission President Raymond Williams cast the only nay vote. He preferred "a chocolate-brown color."[15]

The Commission under the Leadership of Robert J. Bielo

A few major administrative changes occurred in 1965 when Albert Day decided to retire. The Commissioners appointed Robert J. Bielo as Executive Director on January 11. Bielo had been employed by the Commission since 1950, had served as a Regional Fisheries Manager for six years, and as a District Fish Warden for five years. He had also worked for the Hatchery Division in northwestern Pennsylvania. Bielo earned a Bachelor of Science degree in biology from Elizabethtown College and a Master of Science degree in marine sciences at the University of Delaware, a graduate school highly regarding for the quality of its marine science program. Bielo, an avid angler, was paid $13,000 per year. He resided in East Petersburg, Lancaster County.

At the same time, the Commissioners appointed Gordon Trembley as Assistant Executive Director. Like Bielo, Trembly had been with the agency for quite a few years. He was appointed as Chief Aquatic Biologist in 1946. Prior to that he served as a Professor of Zoology at Pennsylvania State University. His salary was set at $11,500 per year. Trembly's promotion precipitated another personnel change. Keen Buss, who had been employed by PFC since 1951 as a Research Biologist, was named as Chief Aquatic Biologist.

It was during this era that Rachel Carson (1907–1964), a marine biologist, conservationist, and native Pennsylvanian, published her landmark work, *Silent Spring*. According to Al Gore Jr., who served as Vice-President of the United States from 1993 to 2001, "Major

From Post-War Era to Earth Day

chemical companies tried to suppress *Silent Spring*, and when excerpts appeared in *The New Yorker*, a chorus of voices immediately accused Carson of being hysterical and extremist."[16] However, the outcry from the public and environmentalists far outweighed private interests following the publication of her book in 1962. Her writings documented the destructive impact of chemicals such as benzine hexachloride and dichlorodiphenyltrichloroethane (DDT) on the environment. Human cancers and birth defects, as well as bird, wildlife, and fish kills were among the many caustic impacts of such chemicals, Carson argued.

According to Carson, "Some (chemicals) are deliberately applied to bodies of water to destroy . . . unwanted fishes."[17] She continued, "A sample of drinking water from an orchard area in Pennsylvania, when tested on fish in a laboratory, contained enough insecticide to kill all of the test fish in only four hours."[18] She also pointed out that the U.S. Fish and Wildlife Service had evidence that fish stored ingested insecticides in their tissues and that the harm to humans from consuming fish, while not yet fully documented in 1962, could not have been healthy.

Echoing the arguments of Supreme Court Justice William O. Douglas, who documented the negative impacts of applied chemicals

continued on page 147

Governor Scranton is shown in 1966 at the signing of the "July is Clean Streams Month" proclamation as members of the Sanitary Water Board and guests look on. They are (left to right): Robert L. Reitinger, Pa. Society of Professional Engineers; Leonard Goodsell, Great Lakes Commission; William T. Evans, Pa. Section, American Water Works Association; Mrs. Lawrence Haner, League of Women Voters of Pa.; Walter Cain, Pa. State Chamber of Commerce; H. Bruce Gerber, Water Pollution Control Association of Pa.; Jack C. Sheffler, DuBois, Sanitary Water Board member; Arnold L. Edmonds, Pa. State Chamber of Commerce; John K. Tabor, State Secretary of Commerce; George Adams; Robert J. Bielo, Executive Director, Pa. Fish Commission; Harvey Adams, Pa. Division, Izaak Walton League of America Inc.; Rep. William F. Renwick, Chairman, House Game and Conservation Committee; Oscar A. Becker, Izaak Walton League of America Inc.; and (seated) Dr. C. L. Wilbar Jr., State Secretary of Health and Board Chairman.

To herald PFC's century mark in 1966, Pennsylvania Angler magazine commemorated the agency's history in a special January 1966 edition. A wealth of historical accounts, information, and photographs provided readers with a consolidated presentation of the Commission's 100 years.

Below, from September 1966 Pennsylvania Angler, *PFC's Delano Graff is shown instructing students. Like so many employees, Graff remained with the agency for many years, eventually becoming Bureau of Fisheries Director.*

September 1966

From Post-War Era to Earth Day **145**

September 1967

Governor Raymond P. Shafer is shown in 1967 dedicating the "Palomino Streamer" fly to commemorate the "Golden Age of Conservation" in Pennsylvania. At the Governor's right is Pennsylvania Fish Commissioner Clarence Dietz, Bedford. On the Governor's left is nationally known sportsman Samuel Slaymaker, Gap, Pennsylvania, who designed the streamer, and Robert J. Bielo, Executive Director of the Commission. The ceremony was part of the signing of the proclamation for "Let's Go Fishing in Pennsylvania Week." The streamer has palomino-colored wings with a brilliant gold tinsel covered body–a pattern designed to tempt all species of gamefish in Pennsylvania's waters.

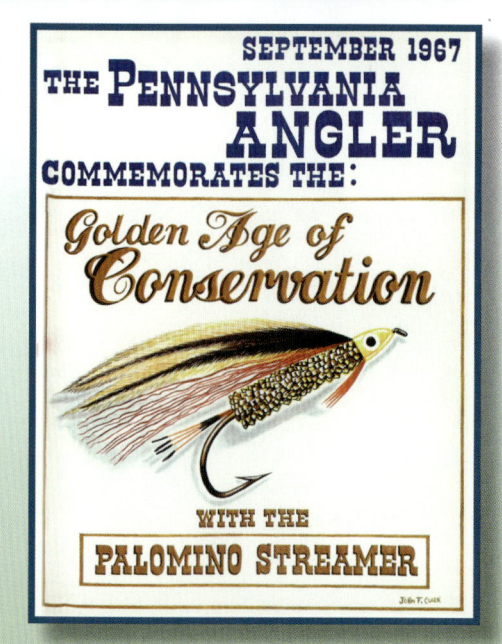

SEPTEMBER 1967
THE PENNSYLVANIA ANGLER
COMMEMORATES THE:
Golden Age of Conservation
WITH THE PALOMINO STREAMER

Chapter Five

on wildlife in his book, *My Wilderness*, Carson noted that when chemicals had been applied to sage lands in the Bridger National Forest in Wyoming, runoff into streams had not only blinded and killed innumerable trout, the chemicals had also impacted their growth.[19] Trout were seldom more than six inches in length, whereas, prior to chemical applications, trout sometimes grew to five pounds.

Though despised and even covertly threatened by chemical companies, Carson did not withdraw her strong viewpoints and the science that backed her up. In fact, Carson's work influenced the U.S. Environmental Protection Agency (EPA, which was created in 1970 by an executive order issued by President Richard M. Nixon) to phase-out the use of DDT and other chemicals deemed harmful to the environment. And, her work resulted in the EPA's strict enforcement of 1972 amendments to the 1910 Federal Insecticide Act. The amendments required federal registration of hazardous chemicals and mandated full disclosure of environmental and biological impacts. Known by its full title, the Federal Environmental Pesticide Control Act, the statute made it clear that protection of the environment and human health were top priorities.

Carson's work may well have had another impact when it came to Pennsylvania: expanding state ownership of land and waters where the use of hazardous chemicals was prohibited. From the mid-1960s to the early 1970s, the Fish Commission expanded its acquisition programs pursuant to Project 70, as did several other state agencies. For example, PFC reported to the Governor's Office of Administration and the State

In 1968, District Officers Norm Ely (left) of Erie County and Joe Kopena (right) of Forest and Clarion counties demonstrate electroshocking gear at Linesville State Fish Hatchery.

From Post-War Era to Earth Day

Planning Board that acquisition of Piney Creek Springs in Blair County and Ingram Springs in Bucks County was in its plans. Total cost of land acquisition for the two sites was estimated at $255,000. Meanwhile, the Governor and State Planning Board approved of the Commission's acquisition of Harmon Creek in Washington County, at a cost of $58,000, and Big Spring in Cumberland County, at a cost of $40,500. By the end of the 1960s, the agency spent over $3 million, in aggregate, for Project 70 initiatives. From 1965 to 1972, the cumulative dollar amount allocated to PFC was $4.9 million.

By the end of the decade, the Commission also accomplished a great deal pursuant to another major state government initiative: Project 500, which was a voter-approved bond issue that created the State Land and Water Conservation and Reclamation Fund used for the development of public recreation areas and protection of environmental, cultural, and historical resources of the Commonwealth. Among the main provisions of Project 500 ($500 million total) were:

- $100 million for municipalities to construct sewage treatment plants;
- $200 million to the Department of Mines and Mineral Industries for abate acid mine drainage and to prevent pollution from culm banks;
- $75 million to the Department of Community Affairs to provide grants to local municipalities to create parks and retain open space areas; and
- $125 million allocated among the Pennsylvania Historical and Museum Commission to acquire and preserve historic sites, the Department of Forests and Waters for preservation and better management of state forests, and the Fish Commission for acquisition of lakes, streams, and the construction of boat launches.

The cumulative total amount of funding allocated to the Fish Commission from 1965 to 1972 was $11 million.

Pursuant to this initiative, PFC acquired or expanded 10 sites for a total expenditure of $3.8 million in 1969, alone. These included three lake projects, one hatchery, and several water access areas.

Projects 70 and 500 were timely in many respects. An obvious outcome was that the Commission expanded angling and boating opportunities for Pennsylvania's residents. And, the impact was measurable. Executive Director Bielo reported that resident fishing license sales grew by an unprecedented 12 percent for both 1968 and 1969, bringing in more than $3 million in 1969, alone. Boat registration fees grew by 10 percent during this same time period, yielding nearly $500,000 during Fiscal Year 1968–1969. Bielo also reported that the Oswayo State Fish Hatchery went into service in 1968, and that he was very proud that Pennsylvania remained a premier fishing and boating locale. He also noted that water pollution was being addressed, hatchery operations improved, and habitat and biology was better understood. Yet, he remained unsatisfied. Bielo wasn't happy that "much of our present day policy . . . has been carried forward from the 1940s and 1950s."[20]

More had to be done, he said, to bring the Commission up-to-date, and his agenda included improved and expanded education programs with direct outreach to schools, enhanced review of PennDOT highway construction projects with special consideration given to stream and environmental impacts, modernizing hatching facilities, and increased collaboration with conservation groups on such initiatives as cleaning-up

September 1968

At left, District Officer Paul Swanson of Centre County explains the use of a spin-cast outfit to a group of young visitors to the Commission's Open House at the Linesville State Fish Hatchery in 1968. Swanson would go on to serving the Commission for many years and becoming Northcentral Region Law Enforcement Manager.

From Post-War Era to Earth Day **149**

In 1969, Pennsylvania Angler Junior Citation Winners Dwight Romberger, Ronald Yurcic, and Frederick Williams are presented with their citations by Special Waterways Patrolman (now termed as Deputy Waterways Conservation Officers (DWCOs)) Stanley Long of Lehigh County. Romberger won his Citation for a 21-inch shad taken in the Delaware River; Yurcic caught an 18-inch Brown Trout from the Little Lehigh; and Williams landed a 21-inch Brown Trout from Lake Wallenpaupack.

And, here's DWCO Stanley Long in 1997, 28 years later, after serving 50 years as a deputy and part of PFBC's "Thin Green Line." His legacy continues with the Commission's "Stanely Long Outstanding Volunteer Service Award."

acid mine drainage and water pollution. These things would come in time—some sooner and others later.

Lake Erie

Another issue on which many experts and citizens alike agreed was that Lake Erie was "dead." For centuries, Pennsylvania's 48-mile Lake Erie coastline was pristine. Native Americans and New World settlers regularly fished its waters for Whitefish, pike, perch, herring, and other species. However, by the twentieth century, pollution was a very real concern, not only to the leisure fisherman but to commercial operations, as well. Fishing on Lake Erie was big business, as it had been for more than a century. In the immediate post-World War II era, as much as 4.4

million pounds of fish earned nearly $700,000 to more than $1 million annually for commercial fisheries. While the value of fish at-market grew largely as a result of ordinary inflation, the number and quality of catches declined in the 1960s. There was widespread knowledge of the lake's deteriorating condition. Little was done, however, to address the problem. Apparently the Commission wanted to abate some of the problems, but it didn't have the resources to do so on its own.

The Great Lakes Water Quality Board was established, resulting in the Canada-United States Great Lakes Quality Agreements. The PFC was a party to the agreements that addressed the discharge of raw sewage into the lake. Pursuant to the agreements, sewage treatment facilities were constructed along streams that fed into the Great Lakes by Ohio, Michigan, and several Canadian locales. Moreover, New York, Indiana, Michigan, Minnesota, and Akron, Ohio, as well as Canada, implemented statutes limiting the levels of phosphorous in household laundry detergent. And, PFC allocated funds to study pollution in the lake and the long term effects of mitigation measures. It would take another decade for any measurable progress to be made in cleaning up the lake. By the early 1980s, the damage done in earlier decades was being reversed, thanks to the concerted efforts of several American states and Canadian provinces.

October 1969– The **Perca**

The Emergence of the Modern Environmental Movement

The so-called "environmental movement" emerged in the United States in the 1960s. This crusade resulted in unprecedented conservation and environmental public policies at the federal, state, and local levels. People like Rachel Carson greatly influenced the movement.

The 1955 Federal Air Pollution Control Act funded research on air quality, especially when it came to industrial pollutants. As a result of these studies—which demonstrated both growing air pollution problems and the harmful impact on humans—a Clean Air Act was passed in 1963. It was the first major federal law specifically aimed at controlling air pollution and was among the most comprehensive air quality laws in the world. The law established federal oversight and regulatory programs within the U.S. Public Health Service designed to research, monitor, and control air pollution.

This was followed by the Air Quality Act of 1967, which enabled the federal government to increase its activities to investigate and enforce anti-air pollution measures. The 1967 act also authorized expanded studies of air pollutant emissions from many sources, such as automobiles, and established ambient air monitoring and control techniques. The Clean Air Act was enacted in 1970, and there were major amendments to the law in 1977 and 1990. The Clean Air Act and amendments spelled-out additional regulatory provisions and mandated industry to mitigate air pollution in a variety of ways, including employing the latest technologies to reduce the toxicity of industrial emissions.

In addition, the Wilderness Act established criteria defining wilderness areas and protected 9.1 million acres of public land. This statute was the result of a long effort to protect wilderness dating back to the early twentieth century. The Wilderness Act was signed into law by President Lyndon B. Johnson on September 3, 1964. Congress approved additional landmark legislation, including the Wild and Scenic Rivers Act of 1968, which protected unspoiled stretches of waterways in the United States. Other significant federal environmental and resource protection laws were enacted by Congress and the administrations of Presidents John F. Kennedy, Lyndon B. Johnson, and Richard M. Nixon.

When it came to conservation and environmental protection at the state and national levels, what was on the horizon was to be unequaled.

continued on page 156

Pennsylvania anglers and boaters in the 1960s

February 1961

January 1962

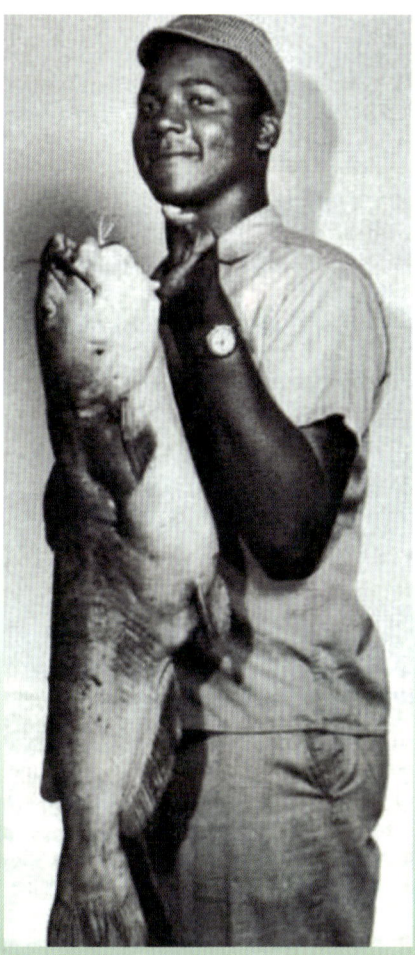

September 1969

From Post-War Era to Earth Day **153**

March 1961

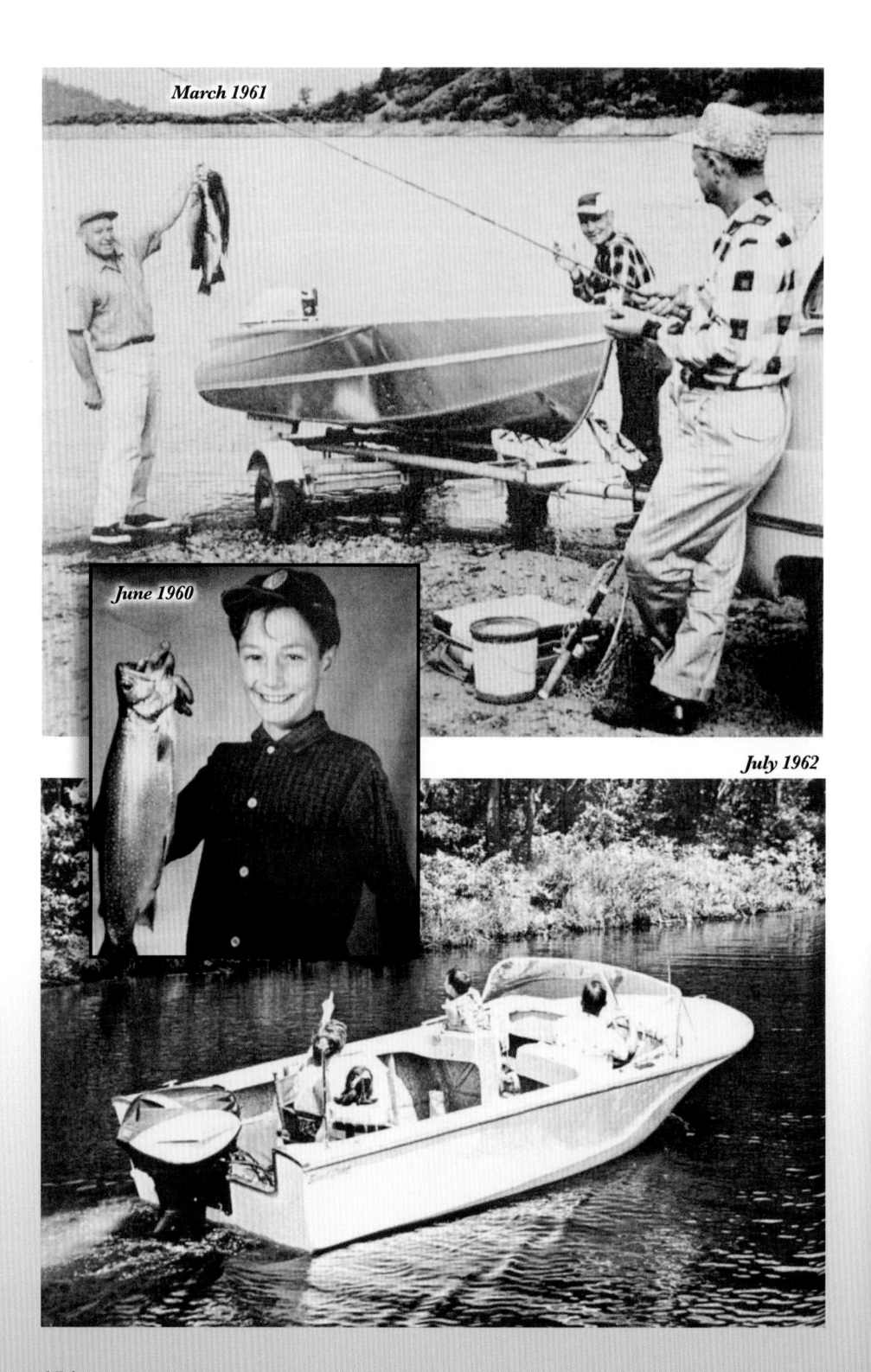

June 1960

July 1962

March 1968

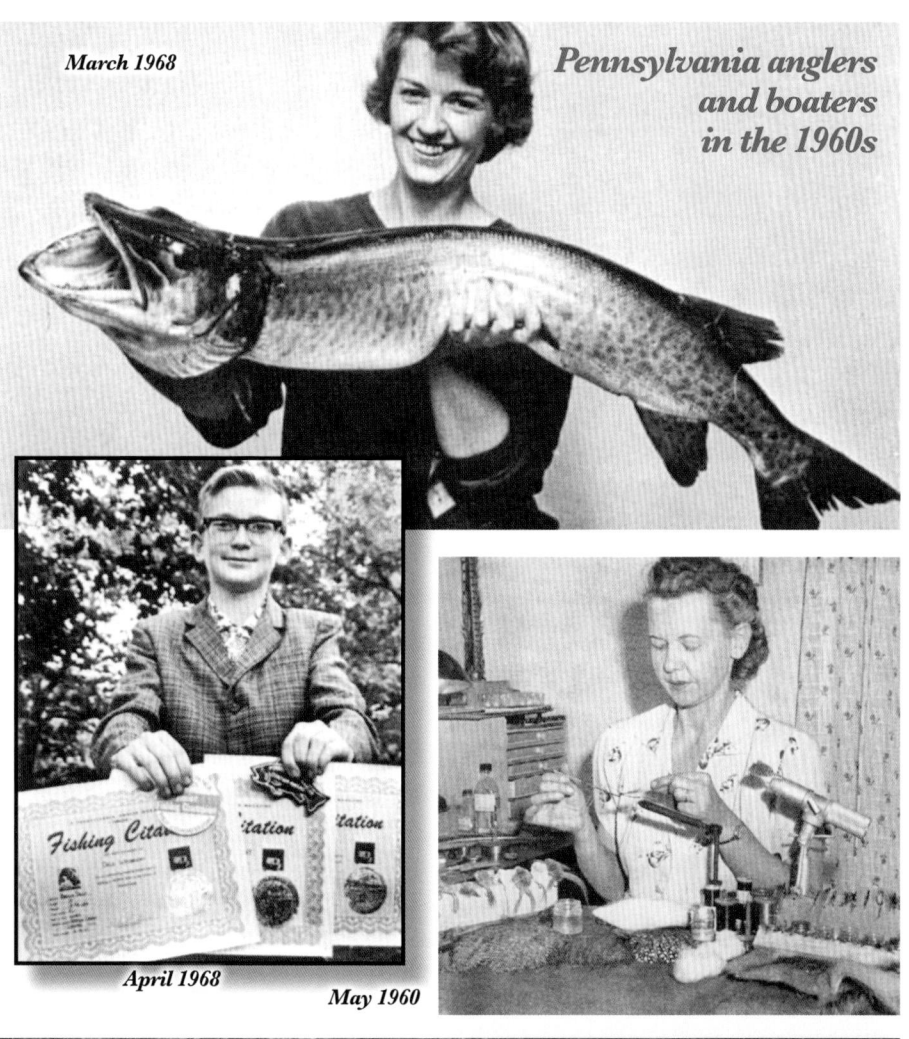

Pennsylvania anglers and boaters in the 1960s

April 1968

May 1960

July 1960

From Post-War Era to Earth Day **155**

Chapter Six: Earth Day to the End of the Twentieth Century

"Do Your Duty and Fear No One."
–Ralph W. Abele, Executive Director Pennsylvania Fish Commission, 1972–1987

Perhaps the most significant landmark event in the history of conservation in Pennsylvania emerged with the adoption of a new amendment to the state constitution on May 18, 1971, specifically, Article 1, Section 27, titled "Natural Resources and the Public Estate." This provision states that "the people have a right to clean air, pure water, and to the preservation of the natural, scenic, historic and esthetic values of the environment. Pennsylvania's public natural resources are the common property of all the people, including generations yet to come. As trustee of these resources, the Commonwealth shall conserve and maintain them for the benefit of all the people."

These few sentences made it abundantly clear that Pennsylvania's government, our executive, legislative, and judicial branches, have an on-going obligation to conserve, protect, and enhance the Commonwealth's environment for the benefit of the public. There could have been no clearer statement. There is no clearer intent.

"Amendments to the state constitution must be approved by each house of the General Assembly in two successive legislative sessions and then approved by a majority of voters in a public referendum. Article I, Section 27 was agreed to in the 1969–1970 and 1971–1972 sessions of the General Assembly, and approved by the state's voters on May 18, 1971. It was one of five ballot questions for that election. Voters overwhelmingly approved the Environmental Rights Amendment 4 to 1. Adding environmental rights to the Constitution was a "strong bipartisan effort," according to its author, Franklin Kury, who was a state representative at the time. As he confirms, "The leadership of both parties was for it."

COMMONWEALTH OF PENNSYLVANIA

The people have a right to clean air, pure water, and to the preservation of the natural, scenic, historic and esthetic values of the environment. Pennsylvania's public natural resources are the common property of all the people, including generations yet to come. As trustee of these resources, the Commonwealth shall conserve and maintain them for the benefit of all the people.

SECTION 27
ARTICLE 1
PENNSYLVANIA CONSTITUTION

Courtesy of the Pennsylvania Fish and Boat Commission

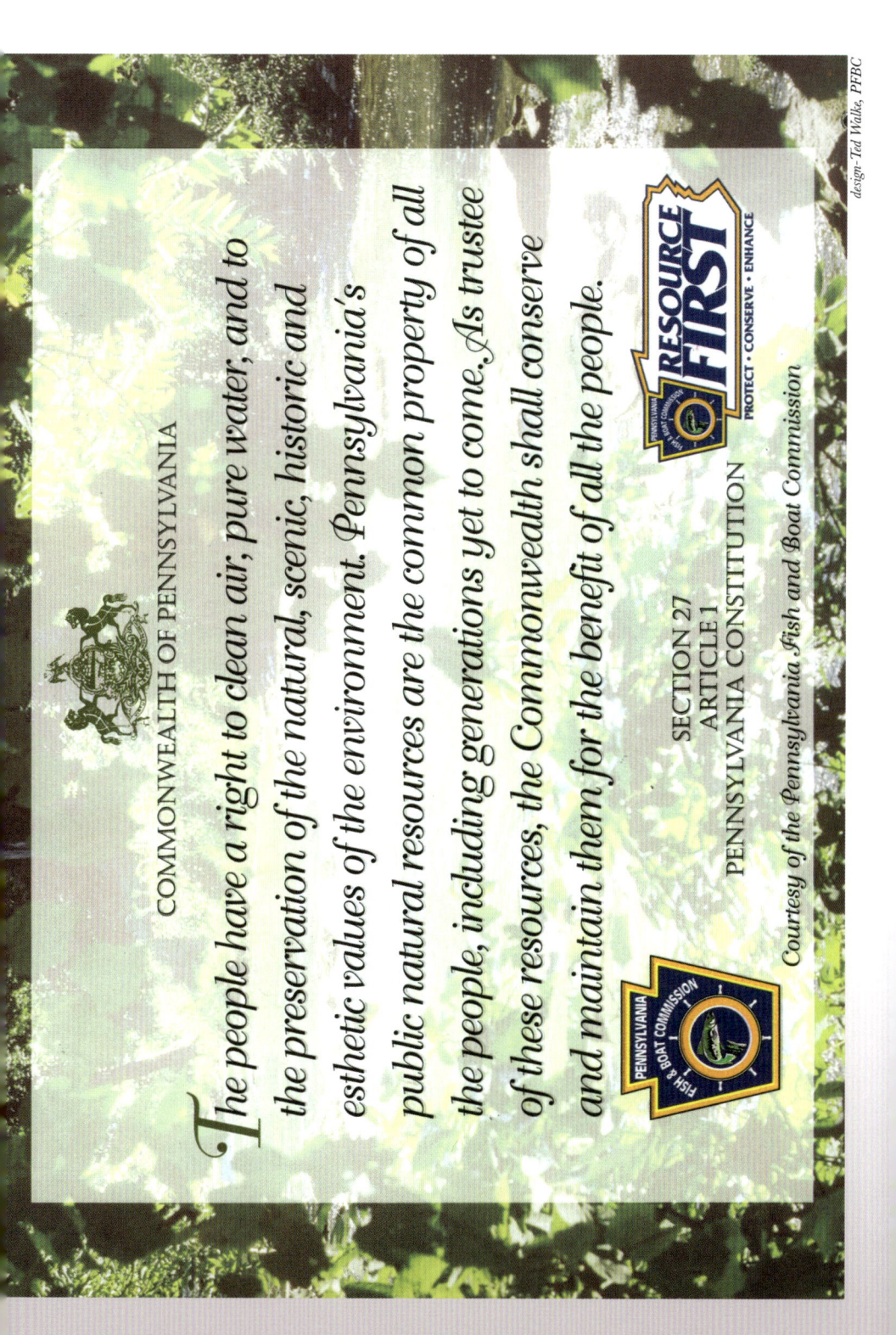

Earth Day to the End of the Twentieth Century

Consistent with Article 1, Section 27, the Commonwealth improved the ways in which it addressed water pollution problems. For example, Governor Raymond P. Shafer (1967–1971) signed a new Clean Streams Law that consisted of sweeping reforms to protect and conserve Pennsylvania's waterways. Specifically, it enhanced the regulatory authority of the Sanitary Water Board and the Department of Forests and Waters by closing loopholes that, for example, allowed industry to dump hazardous waste into waters with impunity. It also required municipal governments to secure permits for discharging waste and gave state agencies additional police powers to levy fines for non-compliance. The money was earmarked for water pollution control projects and measures to help restore polluted waters to an unpolluted condition. Fines up to $10,000 per occurrence can and are levied whether or not the violator discharged waste willfully or by accident.

In addition, Governor Shafer created a Pollution Strike Force that consisted of staff from several state agencies. In signing the bill into law, Governor Shafer commented, "Pennsylvania (now) has the finest law(s) . . . covering water pollution in the nation, but the mere existence of laws on the books is not enough to ensure that all Pennsylvanians (have) their God-given right to live in an unpolluted environment."[1]

Executive Director Bielo was a member of the Pollution Strike Force. And, with the full weight of law and in collaboration with officials from other state agencies, he went after polluters with little mercy. In one instance, the American Viscose Corporation of Meadville became a target of the Pollution Strike Force. In mid-July 1971, extensive fish kills occurred on French Creek. High stream flows made it impossible to narrow-down the exact pollutant that the company was suspected of discharging. Moreover, there was a pattern to the company's actions: American Viscose had earlier paid a $15,000 fine for a similar violation. This time, Bielo reported that "this particular fish kill points up the serious problems we often encounter when the case is on a large stream or when there are other circumstances that mask the true identity of the killing substance."

In this instance, something had been discharged, but "the company does not cooperate by advising of spills or emergency discharges of either toxic or oxygen consuming materials." Though the Pollution Strike Force sought a court-ordered injunction to prohibit any discharges by the company until the matter was fully investigated, a judge refused the request. The Pollution Strike Force didn't relent. It continued to pursue legal action against American Viscose, and the company agreed to pay a hefty fine.[2]

Polluted waterways were sometimes addressed by court rulings. For example, Judge Carl Shelley of the Court of Common Pleas in Dauphin County, handed down an order against a municipality in western Pennsylvania to cease and desist discharging raw sewage into the Monongahela River. The mayor was previously ordered to do so by the Sanitary Water Board but had wantonly ignored the directive. The Board and PFC filed a petition with the court requesting a cease-and-desist order. The court affirmed the petition. Executive Director Bielo referred to the court's decision as a landmark ruling that set a precedent by making it clear that all municipalities had to abide by state law that untreated sewage could not be discharged into waterways.

However, of the three rivers in the Pittsburgh area, the Monongahela River remained the most polluted. Besides raw sewage, unchecked effluent from steel mills and acid mine seepage killed off a great deal of aquatic vegetation. For several decades, anglers simply tagged the "Mon" as "dead." Permitting and enforcement actions by

Governor Milton Shapp and PFC Executive Director Robert J. Bielo in 1971.

the Sanitary Water Board, sealing of bituminous coal mines, shuttered steel mills, and stocking of such species as paddlefish eventually brought life back to the river, in fact to all three rivers in Pittsburgh. The results were impressive. So much so, that, to showcase its cleaned-up rivers, Pittsburgh hosted the largest bass tournament ever held in the state in the spring of 1992. Anglers caught Largemouth Bass, Smallmouth Bass, and Spotted Bass—species unheard of 20 or 30 years earlier.

As his work with the Governor's Pollution Strike Force and his restlessness with the status quo demonstrated, Bielo did not shy away from tough issues and problems. He used his voice and the power of his position to take a stand on a variety of issues. He often used *Pennsylvania Angler* to get his points across.

For example, Bielo discussed the importance of highway construction and maintenance when it came to economic growth and ease of transportation. However, he lamented its impacts on streams when they had to be diverted and when materials used in construction—such as coal tars—found their way into water. New road construction, particularly interstate highways, had resulted "in a long list of trout stream casualties." What was needed was balance, according to the Executive Director. "The policies of road-building agencies to firmly and completely ignore the lasting damage to streams when they get in the way of a road project is not new. It seems that's the way it has always been. However, we believe that this attitude can and will

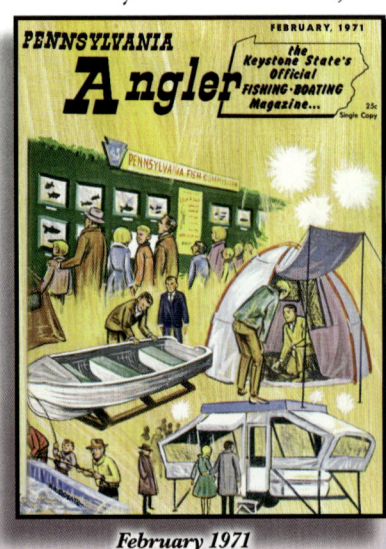

February 1971

September 1972

PFC educator Steve Ulsh (who later became the Bureau of Education & Information Director) is shown in 1972, instructing youth at a conservation camp.

160   Chapter Six

change. There is no reason we cannot have good roads throughout our rural and mountain areas without sacrificing our streams." The federal government had legislated that agencies cooperate in regards to balancing conservation and road construction where federal monies were appropriated, Bielo pointed out. And, the federal government had the authority to withhold funds, if and when fish and wildlife resources are not considered in road construction projects. Why shouldn't Pennsylvania do the same with state funds, he asked? If there were greater collaboration between state and municipal roadway programs and conservation interests, these problems could be mitigated. However, he didn't hold out much hope.[3]

Bielo also used his bully pulpit to take on additional controversial issues. These included the unknown long-term effects of chemicals such as DDT on soil, vegetation, and wildlife; the dangers to air quality that resulted from automobile emissions; and the release of warm water from nuclear power which impacted fish that required cool waters.

The environmental movement was on its march. Its zenith was in the spring of 1970.

Earth Day

April 22, 1970, marked perhaps the most significant turning point in world history with regard to protection of and care for the natural environment. It was the first Earth Day. U.S. Senator Gaylord Nelson

September 1973

PFC electroshocking during a stream survey in 1973.

(D-Wisconsin) and various peace and environmental activists, such as Ira Einhorn, Ralph Nader, and Allen Ginsberg, spearheaded efforts to organize Earth Day programs in the United States. Teach-ins, marches, educational programs, speeches by prominent public figures and activists, and numerous other activities occurred in cities across the country, all with the same goal in mind: raising environmental consciousness. Earth Day became a national event, and, by the 1990s, it had expanded globally. There was more public outcry than ever that policymakers, corporations, governments, and individuals must balance economic progress with natural resource conservation and environmental protection.

In Pennsylvania, Earth Day marches and demonstrations occurred in many locales. One of these locations was the campus of Pennsylvania State University at State College, where thousands of students, professors, activists, and ordinary citizens gathered to hear policymakers, such as Republican U.S. Representative John Saylor of Johnstown speak on the lawn in front of the Old Main Building. He introduced himself as a veteran of many battles on behalf of the environment who had incurred many political scars as a result and urged his listeners to both participate in protests on behalf of the environment and engage in constructive approaches to bring middle-America around to the point where they could also see the dangers facing their way of life if uncontrolled pollution continued.

Immediate changes occurred in Pennsylvania. In 1970–1971, the General Assembly created the Department of Environmental Resources

November 1974

Waterways Patrolman underway in patrol boat.

(DER), and Governor Shafer appointed Maurice Goddard as Secretary. The new agency combined water quality programs housed in the Department of Health, forestry and state park programs lodged in the Departments of Forest and Waters, and regulatory and permitting programs in the Department of Mines and Mineral Industries. The super-agency became Pennsylvania's premier environmental watchdog and developed a tough reputation.

Additionally, the Pennsylvania Game Commission more aggressively applied scientific principles to managing the white-tailed deer herd. And, when it came to the Fish Commission, the agency named 75 streams in Pennsylvania in its "Wilderness Trout Program," continued to propagate millions of fish, and became a partner with DER in protecting and cleaning up lakes and streams. Likewise, the aforementioned Pollution Strike Force continued to take no back seat when it came to going after polluters, big and small.

Pennsylvania also emerged as a national leader in recycling. Conshohocken, located in the southeast corner of the state, was home to the first plastic recycling mill in the country, which opened in 1972. Efforts continued at the community level throughout the decade. Leaping forward, in 1988, the Commonwealth's Municipal Waste Planning Recycling and Waste Reduction Act (Act 101) required larger municipalities to recycle. Act 101 established a $2-per-ton fee on all waste disposed at municipal waste landfills and helped to make Pennsylvania the first state to require recycling plans from each county. The state required each county to manage its own waste to assure a minimum of 10-years' disposal capacity. By the early twenty-first

Shown in 1974, Waterways Patrolman Frank Schilling of Philadelphia County uses his patrol boat to check bank anglers along the Schuylkill River. Schilling went on to become PFBC Southcentral Region Law Enforcement Manager.

century, nearly 94 percent of the state's population recycled plastics, newspapers, cardboard, aluminum, and other waste that would otherwise end-up in landfills.

The Federal Water Pollution Control Act of 1948 was the first major U.S. law to address water pollution. Growing public awareness and concern for controlling water pollution led to sweeping amendments in 1972. As amended in 1972, the law became commonly known as the Clean Water Act. Major changes were subsequently introduced through amendatory legislation, including the Clean Water Act of 1977 and the Water Quality Act of 1987. The objectives of the statute were to identify and regulate sources of water pollution, such as inadequate public wastewater treatment facilities and to provide federal aid to municipalities to improve wastewater treatment. The law also required states and local governments to protect wetlands from residential and industrial encroachments. As with the Air Pollution Act, this law fell under the purview of the U.S. Environmental Protection Agency.

Clearly, progress was being made when it came to conservation and environmental protection at the state and federal levels. Public policy began to significantly balance economics with protecting natural resources. The Pennsylvania Fish Commission was an important part of the protection of these resources.

On a more practical yet very important note, the work of PFC was of life-saving emphasis. Samuel Hall, a Waterways Patrolman assigned to Lancaster County, was given the Governor's Award for Excellence in early 1970. Governor Shafer presented the award to Hall in the Governor's Reception Room in the State Capitol Building. In late 1969, Hall "swam into the lake (Speedwell Forge) twice to rescue a man and his wife who

Shown in 1975, PFC biologist Richard Snyder is shown handling fish during a stream survey. Snyder went on to become PFBC Fisheries Management Division Chief.

164 *Chapter Six*

had overturned their boat while fishing. Hall applied mouth-to-mouth resuscitation" and the pair were rushed to Lancaster Hospital where the man remained semi-conscious for several days while his wife recovered more quickly. Governor Shafer commented that Hall "had shown an outstanding dedication to duty while risking his own life."[4]

Something else of significance happened around 1970, but it wasn't widely known. Future PFC Executive Director Ralph Abele, DER Secretary Maurice Goddard, State Representative John Laudadio of Westmoreland County, trout enthusiast Ken Sink (later national president of Trout Unlimited), and a few others formed a club that they called "The Old Bastards" or the "OBs" for short. The groups met several times a year usually at the Spruce Creek Rod and Gun Club in Huntingdon County. They talked state environmental issues and policy, mapped-out conservation strategies, and, otherwise, discussed business. It is hard to guess just how much environmental policy resulted from these informal get-togethers, but, surely there must have been some. However, these gatherings were not all serious. It was reported that the OBs played cards, drank a bit of whiskey, and fished in a nearby trout stream. If nothing else, it was a chance to blow off the proverbial steam.

Executive Director Bielo departed the agency in early 1972. He credited the dedicated staff of PFC for enforcing laws, enhancing fish production facilities, ensuring safe boating practices, and acquiring and maintaining access areas, lakes, and streams. He also

Graduating in 1974, the Sixth Class of Waterways Patrolmen. From left to right, standing: Deputy Chief of Law Enforcement Edward Manhart, Terry Hannold, Barry Mechling, Kerry Messerle, Robert Kish, and Robert Steiner. Kneeling are: Bud Flyte, Gary Deiger, Harry Redline, and Stanley Plevyak.

thanked Governors, the General Assembly, partner agencies, and the Commissioners for supporting the agency and providing funding (though not always adequate enough in his opinion). Bielo concluded by saying, "I am very grateful to have the opportunity to serve its people and our sportsmen."[5]

"Do your Duty and Fear No One"

Along came Ralph W. Abele, the most revered Executive Director in the agency's history, so much so, that staff seldom called him by his first name. Rather, they respectfully referred to him as "Mr. Abele." Abele had an impressive background. He was no stranger to Harrisburg having served as the head of the General Assembly's Joint House-Senate Conservation Committee. Abele was a leader by nature. He headed a Boy Scout troop in western Pennsylvania for a number of years, served in the U.S. Army during the World War II and was on the school board for the Greenwood School District located where he lived in Millerstown, northwest of Harrisburg. He had a commanding presence and a clear, distinctive voice.

Abele's vision was best summed up in his first article in *Pennsylvania Angler*. "As for dreams, let us resolve them into one: an educated public with a conservation conscious. Twelve million Pennsylvanians—plus! Fishing clinics, boating safety classes—that's just part of it. But if we can get people to try these activities and enjoy them they'll want to protect the resources that make them possible." He concluded, "Impossible dreams? Piece of cake!"[6]

Many of those who knew Ralph Abele held a great deal of respect for him. According to Peter Duncan, who once worked for Abele at the Conservation Committee and later served as Secretary of DER and as Executive Director of the PGC:

> "Ralph could be very tough and uncompromising when he strongly believed in something. He could be both a tyrant and very charming. He took a genuine interest in people and was a mentor to many, including myself. It was not unlike him to send personal notes to people to congratulate them on an accomplishment or to chastise them when he disagreed with them. His management style was one of 'pick the best and the brightest, trust them, let them do their jobs, and back them up.' He had a long-term vision to sustain

Chapter Six

PFC Executive Director Ralph W. Abele and Peter Duncan.

natural resources ranging from forests to waterways. Ralph was a true conservationist in every sense of the word. And, he worked with several organizations that were like-minded and were guided by such vision such as Trout Unlimited and the State Federation of Bass Anglers. Ralph cared more about the perpetuation of the resource(s) than its immediate enjoyment."[7]

Another Abele confidant was former State Representative Harry Bittle of Franklin County, who was elected to the General Assembly in 1968 and served eight terms (he was also Deputy Secretary of DER from in the early-to-mid 1980s). According to Bittle: *(continued on next page)*

November 1972

Earth Day to the End of the Twentieth Century **167**

"Abele was a true conservationist and one of the most environmentally conscious people I ever met. Ralph was a real advocate of the Commission's staff. In one instance, he pushed to give Waterways Patrolmen broad police powers, similar to the Pennsylvania State Police. He wanted absolute protection of natural resources. Though some members of the General Assembly were reticent to go along, Abele succeeded in broadening their powers.

"On one occasion Ralph and I visited Westmoreland and Fayette counties to view surface mining operations. We stood in the mouth of a dragline shovel bucket and were awestruck at its size. We also witnessed the scars on the landscape from surface mining activity. Ralph was especially upset by what he saw and became a strong advocate of DER's powers to enforce surface mining laws, especially reclamation laws.

"On other occasions Ralph and I took canoe trips on the Youghiogheny River in western Pennsylvania to assess water quality and to look at land that was under consideration for purchase by the Western Pennsylvania Conservancy. He wasn't an office person. He was in the field and wanted to be where the natural resources were."[8]

Tom Qualters Sr., the Commission's former Western Pennsylvania Regional Manager, also witnessed Abele in action and his commitment to the agency's enforcement arm, "The Thin Green Line" as Abele referred to it: "Sometimes Ralph would receive a call from a legislator or other public official demanding that an enforcement action against a citizen be withdrawn. He hardly ever conceded to demands from legislators on any issue. In fact, I don't recall one time when Ralph conceded on an enforcement issue. He was a firm believer in enforcement of the law."[9]

According to current PFBC Executive Director John Arway, "Ralph was my mentor. He was a role model. He was a real conservationist. Ralph always supported his staff and sought their advice before making important decisions. He was the type of person who could probably have done anything with his life. Instead, Ralph chose conservation and natural resource protection as his career. I've never met anyone like him, and I am proud to have worked for him."[10]

Abele's children were firsthand witnesses to their father's commitment to conservation. According to Ralph Abele Jr.:

PFC Executive Director Ralph W. Abele shown at his retirement celebration in 1987 with his son Ralph Abele Jr.

"On one occasion, when I was very young, we were driving in the family car when my father witnessed a group of bikers (motorcyclists) discarding empty beer cans along the side of the road. We came to a red light, and my Dad chastised the bikers for littering. With his stern voice, he caught their attention. I don't know if they cleaned up the beer cans. But my Dad's reaction made an impression on me. He just had that commanding presence."[11]

According to Abele's daughter, Jennifer Smith:

"His main interests were in the environment and conservation and, of course, his family. He was very active in the Boy Scouts, earlier in life. I think this made him more aware of the environment and the need to protect it. His job took him away from home a lot. I remember him being both happy and tired when he came home. He was very active in his church in Mount Lebanon (near

April 1973

Earth Day to the End of the Twentieth Century 169

Pittsburgh), and later, in Newport and Millerstown. He was a firm believer in the principles of the Presbyterian Church."[12]

The Commissioners issued a special statement in *Pennsylvania Angler* when Abele was appointed on January 3, 1972:

> "Today, the Commission is enjoying its greatest prosperity . . . in its ever expanding fisheries program which, coupled with an aggressive land and water acquisition and development program, has succeeded in bringing trophy-producing fishing and access to prime boating waters within easy driving of all Pennsylvanians. (This is) in no small way (the result of) the hard work of nearly 400 employees.
>
> "Throughout our history, many dedicated administrators have directed the Commission's progress, and each has left an indelible mark in the Commission's annals.
>
> "To continue this tradition of service, the Pennsylvania Fish Commission has chosen Ralph W. Abele as our new Executive Director. Mr. Abele was concerned about a deteriorating environment many years ago and his achievements as a citizen won him the coveted American Motors Conservation Award in 1969, a tribute shared by only nine other non-professional conservation leaders in a nation of 200 million.
>
> "We welcome and introduce to you, Executive Director Ralph W. Abele."[13]

Abele proved himself as a very capable manager whose style permeated PFC. Given his military background, he firmly believed in a

February 1976

chain-of-command. He delegated and expected full accountability from all PFC staff. Hard work, dedication to public service, collaboration with like-minded organizations, and building productive relationships with legislators, other public sector agencies, private entities, and the Governor's Office led his agenda. He was what some may call, "no nonsense." And, he was never afraid to speak his mind.

Tropical Storm Agnes

Abele took the leadership post a few months prior to Tropical Storm Agnes that devastated many parts of the Commonwealth. Damage totaled $2.3 billion (in 1972 dollars) and was more extensive in Pennsylvania than in any other state. Rainfall totals reached as much as 19 inches, mainly in eastern areas of the state. In Harrisburg, the first floor of the newly constructed Governor's Mansion on Front Street was completely submerged. In a more gruesome example of its impact, more than 2,000 caskets were unearthed from a historic cemetery in Luzerne County. Residents reported that some caskets and human remains floated down streets and avenues.

Pennsylvania's legendary and flamboyant Congressman Dan Flood (of the 11th Congressional District) commandeered a U.S. Department of Defense helicopter to fly him from Washington, D.C., to northeastern Pennsylvania. He required the pilot to fly at low altitude, beginning in Harrisburg, then following the Susquehanna River all the way to Wilkes-Barre. As with many others, Flood was stunned by the damage, commenting that many town and cities in eastern Pennsylvania looked like wastelands. Flood was known for

May 1976

his bravado and eloquent speech. He had been a Vaudeville-type actor prior to being elected to Congress and gave his speeches on the floor of the U.S. House of Representatives, garbed in a cape with a top hat and cane. When he arrived in Wilkes-Barre, he told the press that Agnes was one flood, he was the other. Flood was probably the single, most-visible commanding presence during the storm and its aftermath. Using his political influence, he ordered many of the vast resources from the federal government to combat the damage and aid in flood recovery efforts from Harrisburg to Selinsgrove to Wilkes-Barre. Governor Milton Shapp (1971–1979) did likewise with state government agencies and resources.

Television and radio stations provided round-the-clock coverage of the storm. For example, central Pennsylvania's public broadcasting station, WITF, informed the public of the track of the storm, rainfall amounts, and river and stream flooding, and the station carried interviews with state and local civil defense officials. Citizens were told when to evacuate, where they might seek assistance at temporary housing shelters, find medical care, locate fresh drinking water, and seek out volunteer assistance and aid from organizations such as The American Red Cross.

The Fish Commission was not immune from the impact of Agnes. Hundreds of miles of streams were irreparably damaged. These included Portage Creek, Kettle Creek, Tioga Creek, and Loyalsock Creek. Waterways Patrolman accompanied state and federal officials (and Abele in many instances) to inspect the damage. Numerous access areas on the Susquehanna River were in a state of disrepair. Fish kills were extensive as waterways receded leaving them on muddy land. Hatcheries lost 130,000 fingerlings, 50,000 yearlings, and 176,000 trout.

January 1977

And, to the great lament of Abele and PFC staff, municipal officials took advantage of disaster emergency declarations that waived state permitting which regulated waterway diversions. For example, numerous municipalities in eastern Pennsylvania contracted with heavy equipment operators to convert 50-foot wide stream beds into 100-foot wide flat ditches. Hundreds of miles were "reduced to straight, wide, shallow, featureless ditches with high unnatural dikes substituted for banks. Stone, shale, and gravel, taken from streambeds, have been piled six to eight feet above the original stream banks." Abele further noted, with a tone of disgust, that "the only way a fish could ever traverse these streams would be lying on its side."[14]

Just some of the streamside destruction in the aftermath of Tropical Storm Agnes.

To address these problems, the agency sought delegation of authority under the Water Obstructions Act from DER. The delegation made PFC an agent of DER to assist the department by issuing cease-and-desist orders where activities had gone far and above what was necessary to clear streams of obstructions deposited by flood waters. While some orders were issued, word got around, and numerous municipalities voluntarily complied with the provisions of the law. Abele later reported that, as a result of clearing obstructions, some habitat had been restored and "inspiring catches have been reported from the Juniata and the Susquehanna rivers, and we expect this to continue."[15] Trout Unlimited and other like-minded organizations

January 1977

Earth Day to the End of the Twentieth Century   **173**

also played a key role in flood recovery, as many of its volunteers assisted state and federal agencies in clearing debris from waterways. The clean-up from Agnes took years in some locales.

Cooperation, Legislation, and Operations

Not all was bad news, however. A few years prior to Agnes, the Commonwealth, along with Maryland, New York, and the U.S. Department of the Interior signed an agreement in 1970 with four power companies to address issues relating to migratory fish and, especially, the American Shad. Leading this effort was the Susquehanna Shad Advisory Committee (SSAC), formally created in 1969 to work with power companies to raise and hatch shad eggs and deposit the fish above the Conowingo Dam. Although Tropical Storm Agnes temporarily sidetracked the effort, the project later resumed.

Another major accomplishment was enactment of a statute granting PFC the authority over all cold-blooded creatures in the Commonwealth. While related legislation had been introduced in several sessions of the General Assembly, a bill presented to Governor Shapp was signed in 1974. The Commission already had authority over fish, frogs, tadpoles, and turtles. The new law extended its jurisdiction to aquatic organisms, amphibians, and reptiles, including the oft-dreaded rattlesnake. This new law also gave the agency authority to protect endangered species. Abele and the Commissioners had lobbied for the legislation and were quite pleased when it was enacted.

Despite its successes in flood recovery, shad hatching efforts, and new authority over amphibians and reptiles, in early 1973, PFC faced a serious problem: The agency had an operating deficit that amounted to $62,000, all of it in the Fish Fund that comprised nearly 67 percent of the agency's revenue. The Boat Fund remained solvent, reporting a surplus of about $550,000. While not insurmountable, the Fish Fund deficit had to be addressed. The problem mainly stemmed from increased operating costs that included pay raises required under Act 195 of 1970, known as the Public Employee Relations Act. This granted Commonwealth employees the right to collectively bargain and raised their compensation, although the law affected so-called "rank-and-file" employees, middle and upper management staff typically received pay raises and enhanced benefits that were consistent with union contracts.

To solve this problem, Abele proposed the following fees in House Bill 296 in March 1973:
- $2 increase in resident license fee,
- $2.50 increase in non-resident license fee,
- $2 new junior resident and junior non-resident license fee, ages 12-15, and
- $2 increase in non-resident tourist license fee to be valid for 7 days instead of 5 days.

The General Assembly and Governor Shapp didn't approve the proposal in its entirety. On July 24, 1973, Governor Shapp signed Act 47 to take effect on January 1, 1974. It established the following:
- Resident license fees increased from $5 to $7.50
- Non-resident license fees increased from $9 to $12.50
- Non-resident tourist license fee increased from $5 to $7.50 but remained valid for 5 days instead of the Abele's proposed 7 days.

Abele and the Commissioners were satisfied with Act 47 as it generated an additional $1.9 million in the Fish Fund revenue, which took care of the operating deficit and funded the salary, wage, and benefit increases required by Act 195 (Collective Bargaining for Public Employees), and then some. Though the Fish Fund was made solvent, the agency's comptroller warned that Commission management had to very carefully watch its budget in the future.

Despite increased fishing license fees, the public still got great enjoyment out of this leisure time activity. For example, Peg Rosato of Phoenixville reported that fishing "is a double pleasure; catching and giving." Mrs. Rosato went on to say that, because she and her husband were not big fish eaters, they gave most of their catches to neighbors and friends. And, Leroy "Shortie" Manning of Norwood reported that the youth-run Pine Creek Conservation Club removed debris and built several small dams along Straight Run to allow for deep pools of water where trout would gather. A total of 18 "juniors ranging from 8 to 17 years of age were involved in the project and many youths from the area enjoyed catching trout." Shortie was one of several adults who oversaw the work of the club. Apparently he was somewhat envious: "Wouldn't it be great if we older fellows had the present-day energy of these juniors!"[16]

Ralph Abele's "Bully Pulpit"

Robert Bielo had been somewhat outspoken. However, Ralph Abele took it to new and unprecedented levels. In his October 1975 Executive Director's article, titled "Will Fishing Be Next?," Abele took on what he dubbed as "do-gooders," which he attributed to the "Bambi Syndrome," emanating from a Walt Disney movie that showed a certain heartlessness among hunters. Abele pulled no punches when CBS aired a special titled "The Guns of Autumn" which cast hunters as "unfeeling, cruel, gross people." He accused "CBSers," such as Walter Cronkite and Eric Sevareid, of falling prey to the "do-gooder syndrome" and went on to express disgust that all hunters were portrayed as "slobs . . . whose children hand-fed black bears at a dump the night before opening day, while (their fathers) sat drinking beer and shooting down these same wild creatures which had lost their fear for humans." Abele said that such problems could easily be passed-off to the Game Commission. However, there were hints that anglers were beginning to be similarly tagged.

He cited a National Parks Association editorial that lamented so called "fish-for-fun" programs as nothing more than a free-for-all tantamount to "sticking pins in living cushions," which made fish suffer for the sake of fun. Moreover, he criticized National Humane Education Center literature, claiming that fish has similar feelings as humans when it came to pain, and that they preferred to "jump and play, just as we do when we are happy." The literature even crassly claimed that fishermen were cruel to worms, according to Abele.

While Abele admitted that some anglers and hunters may indeed be "slobs," the vast majority should not be painted as such. They were good, honest, and hardworking people who fished for pleasure, abided by laws and regulations, and seldom treated fish in any cruel manner. Abele warned that fishermen must be aware of prejudice, and that they had "better watch out, because the do-gooders are out to get us (especially) if we don't police our ranks, in some way weeding-out the insensitive minority of thankless boors!" While there is no direct evidence of any reaction to Abele's raucous commentary, it must surely have raised some eyebrows.[17]

On the other hand, Abele did not hold back when it came to the negative impact that corporations could have on the environment. In late 1977, he took-on Bethlehem Steel and its Johnstown mill. In the wake of the 1977 Johnstown Flood, Bethlehem Steel officials stated that the company would only reopen its plant if it were granted exemption from air and water pollution laws of the Commonwealth. If not, the plant would remain closed and 11,000 workers would lose their jobs. This amounted to nothing more than extortion and blackmail according to Abele. The truth was that the company wanted to permanently shutter the plant anyway, and blaming environmental laws was a convenient excuse. "Making one exception . . . is a nose under the tent that we will have to live with." Bethlehem was granted very few exceptions from state anti-pollution laws. Abele proved prophetic. Over the next decade, the company gradually shut down the mill, as was the case with most steel plants in Pennsylvania. By the late 1980s, Bethlehem Steel—once ranked among the largest steel producers in the world—was bankrupt.[18]

Agency Administration during Abele's Tenure

One of Abele's administrative undertakings was to issue comprehensive annual reports in *Pennsylvania Angler*. In his view, the public had a right to know this important information. The reports were very detailed and not only covered Commission finances, but they identified agency accomplishments and provided bureau-by-bureau reports.

Sometimes Abele or other Commission staff used *Pennsylvania Angler* to advance and summarize major policy issues. For example, in 1972, the Commission adopted a statement of policy that spelled out provisions for a cooperative trout nursery program where conservation, environmental, sportsmen's, and other like-minded entities raised and stocked fish. All provisions of the statement of policy were overseen by PFC Division of Fisheries. One of its most important requirements was that "no trout or trout eggs shall be obtained from any source other than those requested from the Pennsylvania Fish Commission, without the written consent of the Chief (of the Division of Fisheries)" and that the sponsoring organization was required to "maintain such records as may be required by the Fish Commission" pertaining to their nursery program. Soon, PFC released a list of organizations that participated in the cooperative nursery program. Nearly every county in Pennsylvania had at least one organization that raised and stocked trout, much to the pleasure of Commission staff. The policy was then chronicled in *Pennsylvania Angler*.[19]

By the mid-1970s, *Pennsylvania Angler* became quite detailed through Abele's direction. For example, the Commission reported that its operating budget was once again on firm financial footing, thanks to prudent management. Fish Fund revenues exceeded $9.3 million while Boat Fund revenues totaled $2 million in 1975. With a total revenue of $11.3 million, $10 million was charged in expenses: $4.7 million covered salaries and wages, $1.3 million was for capital investments, $483,000 for fish food, and $375,000 for printing (mostly for educational materials, including *Pennsylvania Angler*).

The Bureau of Fisheries and Engineering reported that combined state and federal stocking programs resulted in over 50 million fishes stocked throughout the Commonwealth: 6.2 million coldwater species and 44 million warmwater species. The Commission's law enforcement program, housed in the Bureau of Waterways, was at full complement with 69 Waterways Patrolman and 600 deputies who prosecuted 6,600 violations. Their work would only grow more important, especially when it came to industrial polluters.

April 1974– triple-header of trout (Brook Trout, Rainbow Trout, and Brown Trout).

The Office of Information was very productive, as well. Besides publishing *Pennsylvania Angler* and other educational material (that later included *The Pennsylvania Angler's Cookbook* which sold for $2.50 per copy), its educational programs also included the delivery of hundreds of slide presentations to schools, community groups, and other public audiences. In addition, the office instructed Waterways Patrolmen how to develop slide shows that enabled them to deliver a remarkable 3,000 educational programs during Fiscal Year 1974–1975. And, office staff continued to develop live and mounted exhibits for display at various venues such as the annual Pennsylvania Farm Show.

The Bureau of Fisheries and Engineering's major projects included renovations at the Oswayo Fish Culture Station (State Fish Hatchery) in Potter County at a cost of $1.3 million, a $1.9 million expansion and improvement program at Spring Creek and Benner Spring research stations, implementation of a new hatchery known as Fairview which produced salmon and steelhead for Lake Erie, and construction of new raceways at Huntsdale Fish Culture Station (State Fish Hatchery). The bureau's expenditures were augmented by Project 500 and federal Dingell-Johnson funds.

Besides issuing detailed internal reports, it was customary for staff and the Commissioners to deal with a wide range of issues and problems. For example, in early 1977, staff from the Philadelphia District of the U.S. Army Corps of Engineers complained to the Commission that boats were operating too close to the intake towers and a service bridge on Beltzville Lake, Carbon County. Corps of Engineers staff were concerned that the suction created at these intake towers would be very dangerous if a boat were to capsize or a person fall overboard in the vicinity of the intake and requested that vessels be prohibited within 100 feet of the area. In response, the Commissioners unanimously voted to amend Regulation 4.10, known as "Rules of the Road" to prohibit any vessel from operating within 100 feet of any water siphons, intake towers, and bridges on any dammed lake in the Commonwealth.[20]

Another issue was the mandatory retirement age for Special Waterways Patrolmen (present-day Deputy Waterways Conservation Officers) who were required to leave their post at age 65, pursuant to Commission personnel policy. Some Commissioners wanted to eliminate the policy but there lacked a consensus. After careful consideration, a compromise was reached. Special Waterways Patrolmen who were employed prior to January 1, 1976, would no longer be subject to a mandatory retirement age. However, new hires after January 1, 1976, were to retire on or before their 63rd birthday.[21]

Moreover, the Commissioners occasionally had to and continue to take official action to revoke the fishing privileges of law violators. At its meeting in October 1975, the Commission revoked the licenses of 13 anglers for one year, beginning January 1, 1976. Some cases took on a life of their own.

Such was the case with a 14-year-old angler from the northcentral Pennsylvania. On April 16, 1978, Special Waterways Patrolman Douglas Wyrich counted 19 trout on the young man's creel; six was the limit. On the advice of his parents, the boy signed an acknowledgement of guilt, and his father wrote a check for $150 to cover the fine. However, Wyrich made a paperwork error: In the "charge" section of his field report, he noted "13 trout over the limit," but under the nature of the offense, he noted "13 trout in his creel."

The boy's parents later caught the error and reported it to State Representative Tom Swift, who attended a meeting of the Commission at which he demanded that the fine be refunded. Moreover, he expressed his concern that the violation constituted "some form of criminal record" that would scar the Wyrich in the future. The matter was finally settled at the Commission's July 14, 1980, meeting. The Commissioners acknowledged that Wyrick had made a paperwork mistake, though

September 1970

April 1970

180   Chapter Six

they unanimously agreed the young man had violated the law. As a compromise, and on the advice of Commission staff and Legal Counsel Dennis Guise, the Commissioners voted to refund $90 to the parents and entered into the meeting minutes that "it does not consider (the boy) to have a criminal record and that his alleged violation, which involved no moral turpitude, is not considered by the Commission to be an adverse reflection on (his) character and reputation." Satisfied with the compromise, Representative Swift and the family did nothing more regarding the matter.[22]

With respect to conservation officer titles, in 1969 the name changed from Fish Warden to "Waterways Patrolman." Thereafter, a deputy was a "Special Waterways Patrolman." Because of the codification of the Fish & Boat Code in 1980, a deputy then became a "Deputy Waterways Patrolman." During 1984, the officer's title was changed again, this time to "Waterways Conservation Officer," and, since then, a deputy is a "Deputy Waterways Conservation Officer."

As previously mentioned, Abele used *Pennsylvania Angler* as a tool to take on tough issues and get his points across. Sometimes, his words were confrontational. On other occasions, they were written in a gentle storytelling style. However, such a writing style was not limited to him. In the September 1976 issue of *Pennsylvania Angler,* Joanne Haibach, a Special Waterways Patrolman in Erie, published a fictional account of a young girl's fishing experience. Though she was unnamed, the bored little girl was convinced by her father that fishing was fun. She went with him on a trip to Lake Erie. "Her mom tied her pigtails in blue ribbons and tucked her lunch under her arm." When the girl and her father arrived

May 1971

June 1972

Earth Day to the End of the Twentieth Century

at the Lake Erie boat launch, she was outfitted with a life vest and a fishing pole and tackle. Her dad had to show her exactly what to do with these strange gadgets. "She held on to her pole with both hands, eagerly waiting for the first bite." Though she lost her first bite, she was clearly excited when she reeled-in her first catch ever. Soon, their stringer was full, and they headed to shore as her father convinced her that her mom would cook the fish for supper. Demonstrating knowledge that belied her age, she asked her Dad, "Why do they say that Lake Erie is dead. We know better, don't we?"[23]

Examples of Waterways Patrolmen engaging with the public were many and were not only limited to the more negative aspects of issuing fines and making arrests. In one instance in 1978, Patrolman Raymond Hoover of Tioga County had a friendly conversation with a local resident who told him that, while night fishing, he felt a strong tug on his fly line, just as he cast into Pine Creek. Dave Brown was convinced it was a fish. When he reeled in the catch, it turned out to be a bat! Hoover informed Brown that this was the first time he had heard such a story and hinted that it might be just a tall tale.

During Abele's tenure, agency staff continued the practice of collaborating with many like-minded organizations about conservation and resources protection issues. One such collaborator was Trout Unlimited (TU), whose members monitored streams for pollution, testified at public hearings on natural resource issues, and conducted angling educational programs for all ages. Among its self-imposed mandates are to protect and preserve coldwater resources, educate the public regarding coldwater management practices, and teach children

February 1971

how to fish. The organization also continues to make efforts to protect wild coldwater fishes. TU's mission extends beyond Pennsylvania and across the nation.

Another organization is the Bass Anglers Sportsman's Society, or B.A.S.S., which sponsors bass fishing tournaments and other events. According to Ralph Abele, "these sportsmen are very much concerned about their image and fisheries resources."[24] Near the end of the 1970s, B.A.S.S. dedicated $12,000 to assist the Commission to undertake a bass research project on Kahle Lake in Clarion and Venango counties. The total cost of the study was $48,000 and helped to determine whether the minimum bass size limit could be raised to 12 inches from 9 inches and analyzed the impacts of competitive bass angling on the survival and recapture of the fish caught and released during competitive angling events.

Collaborative projects with youth were important, as well. In one instance, Pennsylvania's Youth Conservation Corps worked at the Reynoldsdale Fish Culture Station (State Fish Hatchery) in Bedford County during the summer months. Twenty young men and women, ranging in age from 15 to 18 years, worked 40 hours per week at the facility. Their assignments included cleaning up debris, assisting hatchery personnel, retrieving fish from low-water areas, and constructing a museum-quality exhibit about the common snakes of Pennsylvania. They also allotted eight hours per week to participate in educational programs conducted by Commission staff.

Among the most significant collaborations of the Abele era occurred when it came to restoration of American Shad. In 1976, the Susquehanna River Anadromous Fish Restoration Committee (SRAFRC) was formed and included state fishery agency representatives from Pennsylvania, New

November 1972

continued on page 188

Pennsylvania anglers and boaters in the 1970s

August 1974

July 1977

June 1975

January 1979

184   Chapter Six

October 1973

March 1976

January 1975

April 1975

Earth Day to the End of the Twentieth Century

Pennsylvania anglers and boaters in the 1970s

July 1977

April 1978

July 1977

April 1977

186 Chapter Six

March 1976

Almost as a fateful prediction of the mandatory cold-weather life jacket wear regulations (from November 1 through April 30) to occur in 2012, this boating safety poster produced by the Commission in 1976 educated boaters about the dangers of hypothermia and the life-saving importance of wearing a life jacket while boating

York, and Maryland, as well as the U.S. Fish and Wildlife Service, the Susquehanna River Basin Commission, and several power companies who operated hydroelectric dams along the river. As the successor organization of the Susquehanna Shad Advisory Committee (previously involved in anadromous fish restoration since 1963), SRAFRC worked with and used funding from operators of hydroelectric dams on the Susquehanna River to enhance restoration efforts. According to PFBC Fisheries Biologist Michael L. Hendricks (retired):

"The contributions of the operators of the Conowingo Dam has been the construction and operation of a fish lift at Conowingo. Each year since 1972, they have trapped adult shad below the Conowingo Dam and transported them by truck upstream to spawning areas.

shad fry

photo-Russ Gettig, PFBC

November 1977– Van Dyke Research Station hatch house

188 *Chapter Six*

December 1977– Angler Award Program

This 'trap and transport' of adults was the first real step in the restoration effort. The second step is hatchery production at PFBC's Van Dyke Research Station. Van Dyke, the world's first successful American Shad hatchery, produces 10 to 15 million 20-day-old shad fry and up to 100,000 four-month fingerlings each year. Other restoration activities include monitoring the downriver migration of juveniles using nets and special fish finders that use hydroacoustic equipment. Special studies have included radio tagging of adults, the extent of turbine morality, if any, and the experimental use of strobe lights to direct out-migrating juveniles around turbine intakes."

Hendricks reported that progress was measurable by the mid-1980s and would continue through the end of the twentieth century:

"Progress was slow, at first, but since 1985, with each new year the evidence is mounting that restoration is working. American Shad have been captured in the Conowingo Dam fish trap every year since 1972. Trap catches hovered at around 100 fish per year during the

photo-Russ Gettig, PFBC

In 1978, PFC Executive Director Ralph Abele (right) is shown pinning on President Jimmy Carter a Pennsylvania fishing license with the identification number of "1."

190   *Chapter Six*

1970s. In 1981, catches began to increase and, in recent years, have soared to a record of over 27,000 shad.

"In 1991, Philadelphia Electric Company, owner of Conowingo Dam, built a new lift capable of transporting 750,000 adult shad over the dam each year. In 1993, owners of the three upstream dams agreed to build lifts for their facilities. The agreements call for fish passage at Holtwood and Safe Harbor dams by 1997 and at York Haven Dam by 1999.

"These fish passage facilities will open up 210 miles of river habitat. By the turn-of-the-century, American Shad will once again roam unaided throughout most of their historical range."[25]

Shad restoration on the Delaware River occurred as well. Executive Director Abele proudly reported that, "on May 8, 1979, the Fish Commission participated in the dedication of the first completely successful fish ladder in our history in Pennsylvania at the Fairmount Park Dam on the Schuylkill River." The structure was built at a cost of $500,000, covered mostly by the City of Philadelphia. Design and engineering was a collaborative effort among the city, PFC, and the U.S. Fish and Wildlife Service. "Twenty-three species of fish have traversed the ladder and ascended into the next pool upstream. We saw American Shad, herring, and thousands of eels" said Abele.[26]

When it came to boating, one particular event in the early summer of 1975 drew widespread attention. Treasure Lake in Clearfield County was home to "Drag Boat Weekend" that drew "steely nerved

July 1978– PFC Law Enforcement patrol boat

Earth Day to the End of the Twentieth Century

devotees of raw power" from all over the eastern United States. Dozens of speedboats, powered by engines that could generate up to 2,000 horsepower, raced the waters for two days. The boats were capable of reaching speeds of 200 miles-per-hour. Elimination rounds meant that only the top competitors would move on to other races to be held elsewhere in the United States.

Marine Services Specialist Alan Mackay asked the question, "What could possess a man to set himself upon a tiny chip of glass bolted to a 2,000 horsepower machine, to challenge a clock? I couldn't get an answer . . . not even one as esoteric as, 'Because it's there.'" Mackay did take note that "the stillness is shattered and the air hangs heavy with the aroma of nitromethane and castor oil!"[27]

January 1979– State Record Fish exhibit

In a *Pennsylvania Angler* article a few months later, Mackay discussed "Noise—another pollution?" Specifically, Mackay was referring to the noise generated by a new generation of motorboats. Thanks to Pennsylvania's Motor Boat Law (Act 400 of 1963), boat engines were required to have mufflers, and manufacturers were building quieter more efficient engines by the mid-1970s. Thus, it wasn't so much that the average pleasure or fishing boat created noise problems. Rather, it was "a completely new element (that) has been introduced (in) the high powered ski boats, jet-propelled craft of all descriptions, and the drag boat with over or through the transom stacks." He continued, "One or two of these high-horsepower, high-speed boats taking off across a body of water is enough to draw the attention of everyone shoreside."

Measuring noise is a complicated science, explained Mackay. Factors such as hydrodynamic (the hull passing through the water), exhaust, air inlet, radiated mechanical noise, and noise transmitted to the boat hull through engine vibration were all part of the calculation. A normal conversation between two people generates about 60 decibels. Mackay noted that "some of the "hot dog" ski boats have been recorded at decibel levels exceeding 119." Decibel levels are calculated on a logarithmic scale meaning that each increase of six decibels doubles the volume. Thus, "a reading of 110 on a decibel scale is 16 times louder than a reading of 86."[28]

The solution was multifaceted, according to Mackay. Readers were reminded of the need to muffle engines; owners of these new types of watercraft should operate them safely and keep away from other boaters; boating while drinking was out of the question, and; the

January 1979– PFC law enforcement firearms training

Society of Automotive Engineers and Boating Industry Association were collaborating to develop a uniform set of noise standards that would apply to all such watercraft. The reality, though, was that such watercraft were here to stay, and regulating their noise output was easier said than done.

As the 1970s drew to a close, the Commission was in good condition, both financially and programmatically. Total Fish Fund revenue from July 1, 1978, to June 30, 1979, was a record $10.8 million, while Boat Fund brought in another $2.5 million for a total of more than $13 million. Fishing license purchases exceeded $1 million for the first time ever, while boat registrations were more than 200,000. These figures represented 25 percent and 35 percent growth, respectively, since the late 1960s. The agency's major expenditure was salaries, wages, and benefits that totaled nearly $8 million. Other major expenditures consisted of purchasing fish food that totaled $659,000, printing of educational materials at $210,000, and fixed asset costs of $603,000. Among the fixed assets was the purchase of numerous new vehicles that included additions to a special fleet best described by Executive Director Abele, "the harbinger of the new season (spring) is the sight of the Pennsylvania Fish Commission's Great White Fleet—those shining 44 white trucks with our own hand-built tanks carrying 16-month-old catchable trout, the products of our Fish Culture Stations—to over 900 streams and 96 lakes across the Commonwealth."[29]

In terms of the agency's programs, much had been accomplished. The Division of Fisheries reported that, in Fiscal Year 1978–1979,

June 1979

it had stocked 29.2 million fish of various species weighing a total of 1.9 million pounds. The Division of Engineering now cared for $100 million worth of real estate that included 13 fish culture stations, 60 lakes and dams, 232 boating and fishing access facilities, 23 dwellings, 13 administrative and storage buildings, plus many fish habitat devices and fish ladders. Among its major accomplishments was the total renovation of the Benner Spring State Fish Hatchery and Research Station along Spring Creek in Centre County. Over a three-year period, $2 million was spent on this project.

The Law Enforcement Division of the Bureau of Waterways reported an upswing of 13 percent in prosecutions. Moreover, the Pennsylvania State Police had trained and certified Commission officers and deputies in CPR and other life-saving methods. And, Waterways Patrolmen represented PFC with exhibits and educational programs at 319 sportsmen's club events, 120 city-county meetings, 29 fairs, 41 elementary and high schools, and appeared on 32 radio and television programs.

The Commission's Boating Safety Education program was expanded when two new vans were purchased for mobile exhibits and educational programs on boating safety. The vans traversed the Commonwealth, appearing at sportsmen's and boating club events, county fairs, various community events, and at schools. In recognition of its outstanding work when it came to boating safety, PFC received a Certification of Appreciation from the National Water Safety Congress in early 1979.

The Office of Information implemented a new program to certify notable catches of large fish at over 250 official measuring stations that included Commission sites, as well as those of other state agencies such as DER. Trophy-fish awards were given to over 800 anglers. In addition, the office published 20 booklets on numerous fishing, boating, and conservation subjects.

From time-to-time, studies were conducted as to whether the Fish Commission and the Game Commission should be combined as one agency. One such study took place during Abele's tenure. He vehemently argued that, as one of the few remaining independent natural resource agencies in the country, PFC should remain separate and distinct. There were several reasons, in his view. First, it was more efficient to have a smaller agency where staff were more close-knit, communication was more effective, and it was easier to supervise and train personnel.

Second, the technical expertise of staff was better concentrated in a single agency charged with protecting and enhancing fish species, reptiles, amphibians, and their habitats. Fish biologists, for example, should not have their work "muddied with that of wildlife specialists," Abele stressed. Third, when it came to so-called economies-of-scale, there was no evidence that a larger agency had any benefit. And, fourth, a single agency was much more effective than a larger agency that would be hampered with protection and enhancement of numerous species and resources. Fish expertise was better placed in an agency tasked only with related mandates. So-called multitasking didn't make much sense in Abele's view.

The Nuclear Accident at Three Mile Island

Ten months prior to the Commission issuing the aforementioned report, a major nuclear disaster was averted at Metropolitan Edison's Three Mile Island (TMI) nuclear power plant located on the Susquehanna River near Middletown, Dauphin County. In late March 1979, a series of system malfunctions and human errors resulted in the near meltdown of the Unit Two reactor (TMI had two reactors, Unit One was not impacted).

In a precautionary measure, newly inaugurated Governor Dick Thornburgh (1979–1987) ordered the evacuation of pregnant women and children who resided within a 10-mile radius of the plant. More than 200,000 central Pennsylvanians fled the area, many heading west to be upwind of any radiation fallout. Though the Pennsylvania Department of Health and the U.S. Nuclear Regulatory Commission (NRC) determined that radiation releases were minimal, public concern over the safety of commercial nuclear generating stations halted the issuance of permits for new reactors by the NRC for most of the remainder of the twentieth century.

Fish Commissioners took-up the matter at their April 9 meeting held in Ridgway. Of particular concern was that the operators of TMI had discharged 400,000 gallons of Xenon-laced water into the Susquehanna River. Abele reported that there was probably no cause for concern as Xenon is a noble gas with a half-life of 8 to 12 hours, and that it was quickly dissipated into the atmosphere. In a precautionary measure, the Commissioners agreed to dispatch two patrol boats and several officers to take downstream water samples and randomly collect

continued on page 200

March 1979– PFC float stocking of trout with early videography.

July 1979

Earth Day to the End of the Twentieth Century

March 1979– "Opening Day" cartoon by artist Nicholas Rosato

April 1979

March 1979 Pennsylvania Angler *back cover, photograph by Russ Gettig*

Earth Day to the End of the Twentieth Century **199**

fish to determine if there was any cause for concern.[30] By the end of May 1979, fish biologists and other PFC experts determined that there was no deleterious impact on the Susquehanna River's waters and fish. And, by the end of the year, PFC had begun expanding fishing and boating access at Gouldsboro in York County, within eyesight of TMI's four cooling towers.

Once again, however, Abele took no hostages in denouncing greed, exploitation of natural resources, and human carelessness in the wake of the TMI accident: "Throughout the weekend (of the accident) we saw Metropolitan Edison Company doing the predictable thing. They were lying. Left to their own devices, (Metropolitan Edison officials) would have said nothing or done nothing . . . or probably would have handed out lead coats to people . . . telling them that they were Easter presents!" Closely regulated and safe commercial nuclear power plants weren't necessarily a bad thing, according to Abele, especially if the alternative meant more reliance on polluting fossil fuels. But, nuclear operators had to be closely watched, he said. TMI left "coal producers rubbing their hands because the whole country . . . resolved not to have anything to do with nuclear power." Besides criticizing the carelessness of Metropolitan Edison, he cautioned against "complete captivity to a bunch of greedy, hungry, fossil fuel entrepreneurs who wouldn't miss (clean) water and clean air so long as they paid good dividends to their stockholders." Pennsylvanians had enough of that. Abele concluded his lecture-like editorial by chastising all Americans that they had to do more to conserve energy rather than continually want more of it: "I

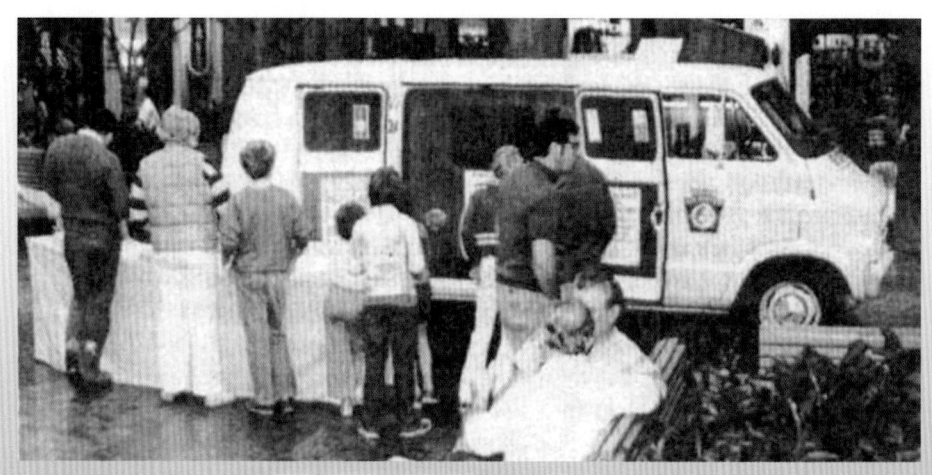

1979– PFC Mobile Education Van program

hope that the American people have had enough of living beyond their means with respect to our natural resources."[31]

. . . and other issues.

As previously mentioned, Ralph Abele's editorials in *Pennsylvania Angler* were typically titled with the issue or the problem that he discussed. In July of 1982, however, he permanently called the article "Straight Talk." Naturally, this title was consistent with his style. He continually expressed what he thought and seemed to care not who he might offend. There is no evidence that the Commissioners, any Governor, or anyone else in state government were offended by or tried to stifle his openness.

To the contrary, *Philadelphia Inquirer* reporter Susan Stranahan lauded Abele in an April 18, 1982, article in the paper's *Sunday Magazine*. The article was aptly entitled "Lord of the Fish." She interviewed Abele for the article and credited him with being a savior of the state's gamefish and champion of the environment whose conservation ethic permeated the Fish Commission.

With the full support of Abele, the Commissioners, and PFC staff, the codification of the agency's statutes was completed in 1980. The main result of this initiative was the consolidation of all related laws into a single Title 30. The legislation reworded several provisions of applicable laws for purposes of clarity, and, while it did not substantively alter the agency's statutory mandates, a section was added prohibiting disturbances of waterways, fish habitats, or streams that would cause damage to or kill fish.

continued on page 204

1979– line of PFC fish stocking trucks

Rainbow Trout

Golden Rainbow Trout

202   Chapter Six

**Brook Trout-
Pennsylvania's
State Fish**

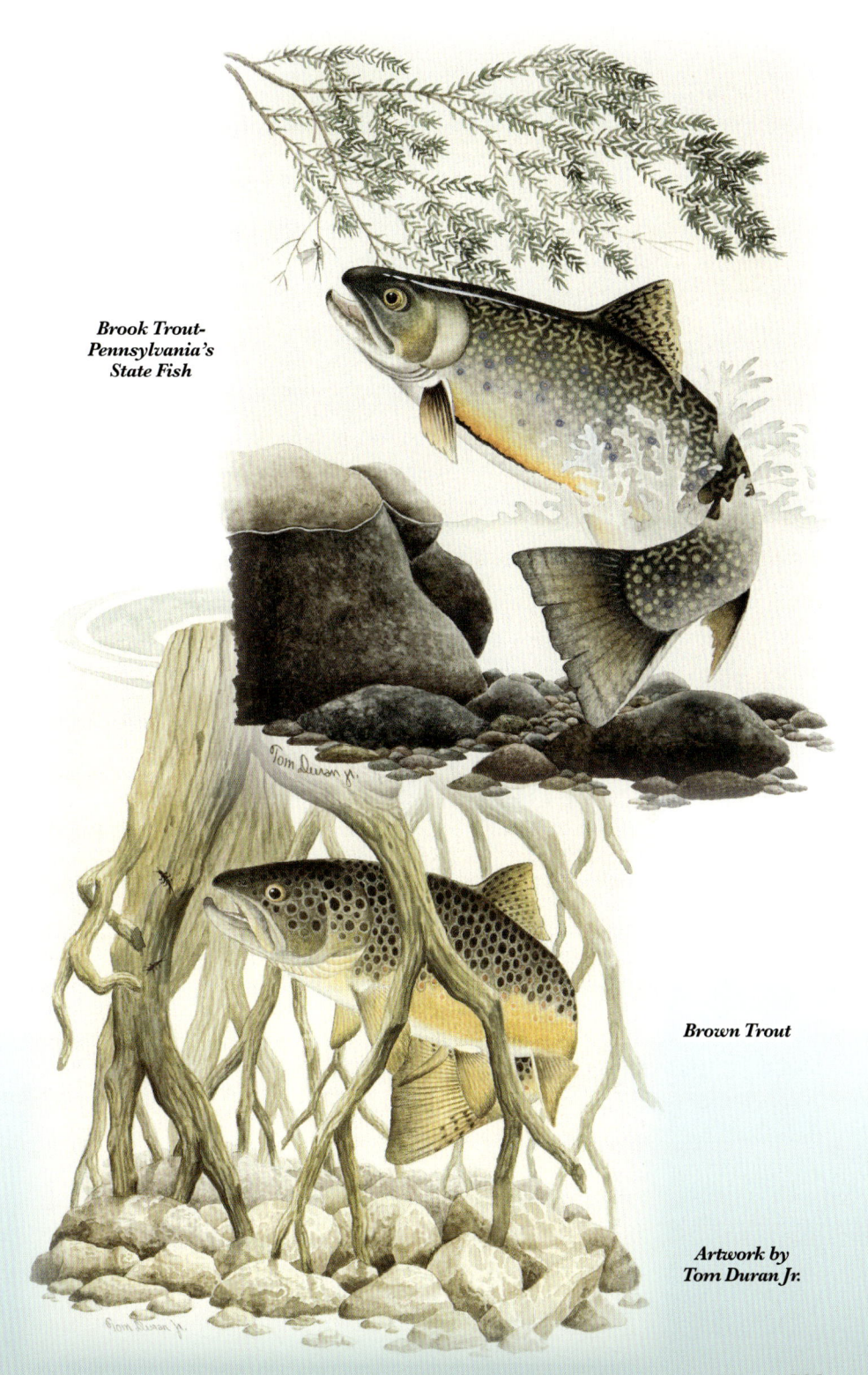

Brown Trout

*Artwork by
Tom Duran Jr.*

Earth Day to the End of the Twentieth Century 203

Codification was very important. So was PFC's interaction with the Federal Energy Regulatory Commission. In 1980, the federal agency issued long-term licenses to four hydroelectric plants. The PFC and other agencies intervened, demanding that fish passages be constructed and that shad eggs be nurtured and released upstream. To address this issue, a voluntary agreement was signed between agencies, the Federation of Sportsmen's Clubs, Pennsylvania Power and Light Company, the Safe Harbor and York Haven power companies, and the Philadelphia Electric Company which established a 10-year restoration program of $3.7 million to collect and pre-spawn adult shad and eggs, releasing them upstream of dams and construct fish passages at dam sites. In addition, 50,000 shad were to be transported each year above the Conowingo Dam. This was a major accomplishment for shad restoration.

Among PFC's big news items in the mid-1980s was a historic Susquehanna River shad restoration program signed by multiple state and federal agencies, including natural resources agencies in Pennsylvania and Maryland, the U.S. Department of the Interior, and

"By a quiet stroke of a pen..." Governor Thornburgh signed into law the Fish and Boat Code of 1980. Flanking Governor Thornburgh were: left, Leonard A. Green, President, Pennsylvania Fish Commission and right, Ralph W. Abele, Executive Director. Also in attendance were, standing, left to right: Peter J. Ressler, former Assistant Attorney General; Paul F. O'Brien, Director, Bureau of Administrative Services; Howard T. Hardie, Administrative Assistant; Gene Sporl, Assistant Executive Director, Bureau of Waterways; Edward W. Manhart, Deputy Chief of Law Enforcement; Dennis T. Guise, Chief Counsel; and John I. Buck, Chief of Law Enforcement.

several power companies such as Pennsylvania Power and Light and Safe Harbor Water Power Company. Ralph Abele was happy with both the agreement and the growing availability of shad in Pennsylvania: "Restoration of migratory fish in the Susquehanna (and Delaware) Rivers was the sole purpose for the establishment of the Pennsylvania Fish Commission (in 1866). The light at the end of the tunnel is bright, and we are past the end of the beginning" Abele wrote in the January 1985 issue of *Pennsylvania Angler*.[32]

Indeed, the taking of shad improved. Later in the 1980s, the Delaware River Shad Fishermen's Association conducted a nine-week study of shad fishing activities over 192 miles of the Delaware River from Hancock, New York, to Yardley, Pennsylvania. The results were impressive: 66,000 anglers spent nearly 300,000 hours fishing for shad in the survey area, most using boats. More than 56,000 shad were caught, many being released to increase fishing opportunities for others. Considering that, in 1965, a mere 5,318 shad were caught in the Delaware River, the improvement was quite remarkable.

The Delaware Shad Fishermen's Association took their volunteer work quite seriously. As shad were to be found in abundance in the 1980s, the Association set-up a phone service that was updated several times a week with recorded information on water temperature, school locations, and top-producing lures. Anglers simply had to call them by telephone. Anglers were also encouraged to purchase a $5 set of detailed maps of the river from the Delaware River Basin Commission. The maps were important for boaters, because the bottom of the Delaware was strewn with boulders and rock ledges. And, the river could sometimes be hard to navigate, particularly if currents were low.

May 1980– PFC staff dropping trap nets

A looming problem, however, was "acid rain" that was especially prevalent in the 1980s. Acid precipitation was a real problem for both fish and humans. Pennsylvania ranked in the unenviable position of being among the top four states in its production of acid precipitation. Incredibly, rainfall in Pennsylvania in the mid-1980s had pH levels of 4.0 to 4.1 or 1,000 times the acidity of neutral water. So toxic was its impact that many auto manufacturers agreed to repaint newly purchased automobiles whose finishes were harmed by acid fallout. The vehicle had to be returned to the dealer within a specified period of time following its purchase—usually one year. In one case in Scranton, a newly purchased 1983 Oldsmobile Cutlass had its dark lustrous brown finish turn a purplish color just a few weeks after it was driven off of the dealer's lot. The dealer repainted the car free-of-charge only to have the problem recur a year later. If acid rain could do this to a car's paint, what was it capable of doing to fish?

Unless acid rain was addressed by legislative restrictions on industrial air discharges, conservationists estimated that 5,000 miles of

photo-Russ Gettig, PFBC

In 1981, nine-year-old Donnie Ruth became the first youngster to enroll in the Fish Commission's new education program, the Pennsylvania League of Angling Youth (PLAY). Congratulating Donnie are his parents, Mr. and Mrs. Donald E. Ruth Jr., and Ralph W. Abele, Executive Director, Pennsylvania Fish Commission.

206 *Chapter Six*

trout waters would be lost by 1999, and 1.5 million anglers would no longer be able to fish for the popular species. Smallmouth Bass were particularly vulnerable to sulfur and nitrogen oxide emissions that fell to the ground when it rained. Moreover, wild trout losses occurred in the vulnerable egg and fry stages. Damage to the health of reptiles and amphibians had not even begun to be studied. In the 1980s, the Reagan Administration deferred any action on acid rain until the matter could be more fully studied.

Conscious of the impact of acid rain, more than 80 streams were subject to Commission trout stocking changes, including restricting pre-season stocking in affected streams. And, the Commission employed new technology to survey the health of trout. The new method was "shocking"—literally. One of the best ways for biologists to gather the needed objective data—hard facts about the trout actually living in Pennsylvania's streams—is by electrofishing. The technology is quite simple really. Fish naturally respond to an electrical field created in water. Either alternating current (AC) or direct current (DC) is put into the water through the use of a specialized electrical generator and one or more electrodes known as probes. The fish are either temporarily stunned (AC) or involuntary attracted (DC) to the current and can be scooped-up into a net and then handled, measured, weighed, and released unharmed back into the stream.

What were the biologists surveying? The general health and well-being of fish, their age, the water quality of a stream, and how water quality impacts various species. Moreover, this method aids biologists in estimating the fish population in a particular stream and helps staff

January 1980

manage streams by determining which ones should be more heavily stocked than others.

By the late 1980s and early 1990s, amendments to the Clean Air Act, as well as new policies issued by the U.S. Environmental Protection Agency, began to reduce the acidic level of industrial discharges. As a result, overall water quality improved in many locales, including Pennsylvania.

Policy Changes, OPERATION FUTURE, and "Resource First"

A major policy shift occurred in 1981, officially known as the "Policy for the Conservation and Management of Fishery Resources." According to the report *History of the Management of Trout Fisheries in Pennsylvania*, this policy "formally declared a shift in the philosophy and mission of the agency from recreation first to resource first," and "to achieve the objective of this policy the Commission will,

1. Establish and maintain a current database on the quality and quantity of the aquatic and fishery resources of the Commonwealth for effective environmental protection and resource conservation.
2. Develop statewide management programs to assure consistent treatment of all resources within any given class. Similar waters will be managed to meet the same objectives under the same philosophy on a statewide basis.
3. Manage self-sustaining fish populations as a renewable natural resource to conserve the resource and the angling it provides.
4. Use hatchery fish to provide recreation in those waters where fish populations are inadequate to sustain the fishery at desired levels.
5. Develop appropriate regulations and operational strategies to replace policies that are not compatible with management through resource classification."[33]

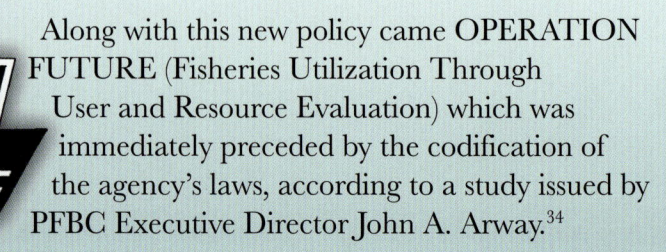

Along with this new policy came OPERATION FUTURE (Fisheries Utilization Through User and Resource Evaluation) which was immediately preceded by the codification of the agency's laws, according to a study issued by PFBC Executive Director John A. Arway.[34]

FUTURE resulted from the work of a task force established by Abele in 1983. The task force "systematically evaluated Pennsylvania's fish population and the recreational anglers who fish for them."[35] It resulted in an interdisciplinary approach to carry out Abele's vision of "Resource First." And, it further defined PFC's conservation and management of fishery resources.

At its heart, FUTURE changed the way that trout were allocated throughout the Commonwealth. Following the science, PFC professionals determined that 268 streams and 24 lakes were to receive 25 percent more fish, more than 180 waterways previously unstocked were to receive trout, and nearly 99 different stream sections managed for wild trout would not be stocked, as there was no need to do so. Why the change? From the late 1970s to the early 1980s, agency biologists had conducted a thorough survey of the Commonwealth's streams and determined that this was a better strategy.

OPERATION FUTURE was another Abele innovation. However, Arway points out that Resource First wasn't simply a slogan or motto. It was a way of doing business. The philosophy was to protect, conserve, and enhance the quality and diversity of fishery resources, including reptiles and amphibians, as well as to inventory, classify, and manage these resources. The philosophy, Abele thought, would be of great benefit to anglers. They would become more aware of the variety of

The 1981 Seventh graduating class of law enforcement cadets: Front row, left to right: James Ammon, Guy Bowersox, Jan Caveney, David Corl, George Gerner, Ronald Hoffman, Wayne Imler, Gregory Jacobs. Second row: Edward Lavsa, Gary Moore, Barry Pollock, Kim Pritts, Keith Small, William Snyder, Lee Tilton, Michael Wheale. Back row, class instructors: Virgil Chambers, William Hartle, Kerry Messerle, Paul Swanson, Perry Heath, and Edward Manhart.

these resources in the Commonwealth. It was also beneficial to the agency's staff. It made it clear that their job was to protect and conserve natural resources.

Operation FUTURE was implemented in 1981. Resource First went into effect in 1987. Ralph Abele's vision was now officially on the books.

One outcome of the new way of doing business was to ensure better fishing in lakes. As a result, the Division of Fisheries Environmental Services entered into a partnership with DER on a new fish management practice of sinking bundled Christmas trees and tires in Pymatuning Reservoir, Crawford County. Making such artificial reefs was also assisted by the Pennsylvania Conservation Corps and the Shenango Sportsman's Club. The results were quite impressive as anglers reported higher catches of crappies when fishing near the reefs. And, more anglers were attracted to the lake.

Another practical way to protect and conserve environmental resources occurred when the General Assembly and Governor Thornburgh agreed to establish a new Pennsylvania Wild Resource Conservation Fund in 1982. The program was consistent with Resource First and was supported by the Commissioners, other state agencies, and a number of groups involved in conservation and outdoor recreation. When completing their annual state tax returns, taxpayers could check

photo-Russ Gettig, PFBC

February 1981

Office of Information Director Will Johns is shown here in 1981, manning the PFC booth at a sportshow.

210 *Chapter Six*

a box and write-in an amount that they wanted to contribute. Their contribution was deducted from the monies they received in their tax refund. Or, residents could write a check and send it to the fund's comptroller in Harrisburg. Monies were used to reintroduce the Bald Eagle, Osprey, and Peregrine Falcon to Pennsylvania. To directly address an issue of concern to Abele and the Commissioners, funding was also allocated for the development of nesting and feeding habitats of turtles, reptiles, and amphibians.

Fish biology and species management were, no doubt, aided by a major contribution to the field, detailed in a new book issued in 1983, titled *Fishes of Pennsylvania and the Northeastern United States* by Edwin L. Cooper.[36] No similar study had been conducted since 1956 when some species were collected by the Academy of Natural Sciences and described in its various publications and works by other authors.

Cooper's exhaustive study familiarized readers with an explanation of the geological factors that determined Pennsylvania's ridge, valley, and plateau topography. Stream drainage has largely been unchanged over several million years. Some areas of the Commonwealth were impacted by glacial advances and contractions that spanned hundreds of thousands of years. Cooper detailed how and why the present distribution of fish was influenced by the Mississippi lowlands, Southern Appalachians, and Atlantic Coastal areas. He also explained how the state was impacted, not only by glaciers, but by other natural features such as erosion,

PFC boating instructor Virgil Chambers is shown in 1981 providing a boating safety class.

variations in water levels in the Atlantic Ocean, and changes in climate. Favorable watersheds, diverse chemical and physical environments, the composition of soils and rocks, and temperate climatic conditions that offer cold and warmwater habitats made Pennsylvania hospitable to fish. Commission staff used the study to better understand the historical development of waterways, fish migration patterns, and fish biology.

While understanding the history and biology of various species was very important, educating the public remained high on the Commission's agenda. As more boaters traversed Pennsylvania's waterways in the early 1980s than ever before, the Commission's Bureau of Waterways recognized the need to educate municipal and regional river rescue teams on safe boating practices. The statistics were alarming. Drowning was the second leading cause of accidental death in the nation. According to the National Safety Council, most victims were engaged in recreational boating and fishing when they lost their lives. In Pennsylvania alone, the Commission estimated that an incredible 85 percent of people who died in boating accidents would not have perished had they been wearing a life jacket. *(See page 353 for additional statistics.)*

PFC boating instructor Virgil Chambers is shown, in 1983, leading a class in river rescue involving low-head dams. Chambers was critical to the establishment of the Commission's Water Rescue program which currently serves as a national model of water rescue training.

In response to this troubling trend, the Bureau of Waterways held a River Rescue Conference in Harrisburg in mid-September 1983. One hundred and twenty attendees learned about various rescue techniques in high and cold waters, as well as at dam heads, at night, and in situations where the individual was unconscious. CPR was part of the training. Several individuals from the Reading Fire Department brought a special land and water rescue vehicle (sometimes referred to as a "duck") and demonstrated how it was used to rescue individuals in the Schuylkill River.

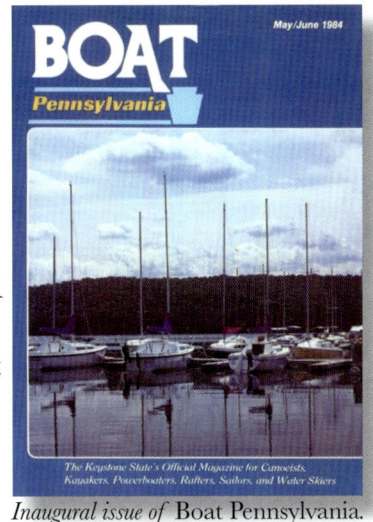

Inaugural issue of Boat Pennsylvania.

Reaching out to boaters with education and safety information also took the form of a new publication issued by the Fish Commission entitled, *Boat Pennsylvania*. The first issue appeared in May/June 1984. Executive Director Ralph Abele welcomed readers by pointing out that the publication "is designed to provide you . . . with information to help you enjoy your sport more" and that "*Boat Pennsylvania* is geared toward the water recreationists who are beginners, who are beyond the novice stage, and who are highly proficient." Included in the magazine were articles on where boaters might go to find recreational waters from tranquil to "the explosive waters of the Yough; specific how-to information on all aspects of boating; regular columns (featuring) the latest information on Pennsylvania waterways; safety information, and; conservation matters affecting your water environments."[37]

Waterways Conservation Officer K. Derek Pritts is shown in 1984 conducting water sampling in conjunction with a pollution investigation. photo-Russ Gettig, PFBC

Earth Day to the End of the Twentieth Century 213

One of the Commonwealth's most popular waterways is the Youghiogheny River which stretches for 17 miles through the laurel canyons of southwestern Pennsylvania. The waters of the "Yough," as it is called, range from a gentle flow to turbulent, Class III and IV boulder-filled rapids. The water level is dam controlled, making it accessible 12 months per year. Spring and summer remain the most popular months on the river.

As a result of its popularity, the Yough—part of which is adjacent to Ohiopyle State Park—was Pennsylvania's first waterway featured in the inaugural issue of *Boat Pennsylvania*. Central Pennsylvania Kayak School instructor and founder of Pennsylvania Women Outdoors Inc., Leann R. Diehl, described the river in detail including its numerous rapids, put-in and take-out points, and travel directions. Diehl warned that the majority of the Yough was not for beginners, and that careful study of the river's maps and inquiry of river guides, experts, and state park staff were essential for those with less than expert experience. The most eye-catching read is where Diehl describes the Class III and IV rapids and how to best maneuver them:

> "Dimple Rapid is . . . one of the most difficult . . . on the Yough. As you move around a sharp left bend in the river, you'll see what looks like a wall of rocks. Stay close to the left bank, keeping right of the Pinball Rock. The water is very pushy here and jams against Dimple Rock, creating a turbulent foam pile. You want to ride the end of the eddy behind Pinball and just skirt that dangerous white water. (Then) catch your breath in the big eddy behind the large boulders."[38]

WCOs Emil Svetahor and James Wagner are shown in 1984 at a PFC exhibit booth during the busy sportshow season of January through March of each year.

photo-Russ Gettig, PFBC

214   Chapter Six

Added to informative articles such as Diehl's, *Boat Pennsylvania*'s feature known as "Currents" gave residents the opportunity to write-in with various practical questions and to express their points of view. For example, one boater asked if they may use their boat in Pennsylvania even though it was registered in another state. The answer was "yes," that reciprocal boating privileges are granted to boats registered in other jurisdictions with numbering systems that are approved by the U.S. Coast Guard.[39]

And, boater Charles Abent of Avoca wrote, "It makes me sick to go boating in the Susquehanna River and see all the garbage along the banks. We must protect the environment for future generations. Our charge is to leave the world better than we found it." In response, Abent was informed that he "may be interested in the activities of the Susquehanna River Watch Coalition, a newly formed group coordinated by the Luzerne County Federation of Sportsmen. (The group) is concerned with the abuse of the Susquehanna and . . . concentrates its efforts in the area of solid waste disposal."[40]

Later issues address the problems of Boating Under the Influence (BUI) (also called BWI or Boating While Intoxicated). As reported in the mid-1980s, about 100 BUI citations were issued each year. No one at the Fish Commission expected the number to decline. In fact, arrests for BUI were expected to increase during the 1980s, since state legislatures, including Pennsylvania's, enacted tougher drunk-driving laws that lowered blood-alcohol content thresholds that are required for arrests. Thus, while the Commission had a responsibility to educate boaters on many issues, the effects of

1984

photo–Russ Gettig, PFBC

Earth Day to the End of the Twentieth Century   **215**

alcohol on boaters topped the agenda. For example, *Boat Pennsylvania* featured an article by Dr. Marcelline Burns, a research psychologist at the Southern California Research Institute in Los Angeles. Burns was a known expert on the effects of alcohol on human performance in a variety of tasks, among them navigating a boat. Dr. Burns informed readers . . .

> "An alcohol consumer who operates a boat . . . is at greater risk than the individual who has not consumed alcohol, because his ability to process sensory information and to respond in a timely and appropriate manner has been impaired by the drug. Alcohol . . . increase(s) the probability of an accident. Poor decisions, bad judgement and increased risk-taking are the result. What can be concluded about alcohol's effect on boating skills?
>
> "Performance is impaired because alcohol affects central nervous system processes. Judgement is impaired and risk-taking is increased. There is no question that the right decision, good judgement, and an accurate perception of are crucial to safety in a boating environment."[41]

In addition to launching *Boat Pennsylvania* in 1984, PFC began its annual Fish-for-Free Day that continues to be a mainstay of the Commission's public outreach efforts in the twenty-first century. Commissioners designated two days when both residents and non-residents could fish without a license. All other fishing regulations applied. The program was well received by the public. Take young Jake Hornicak from Pittsburgh, for example. His father wrote that:

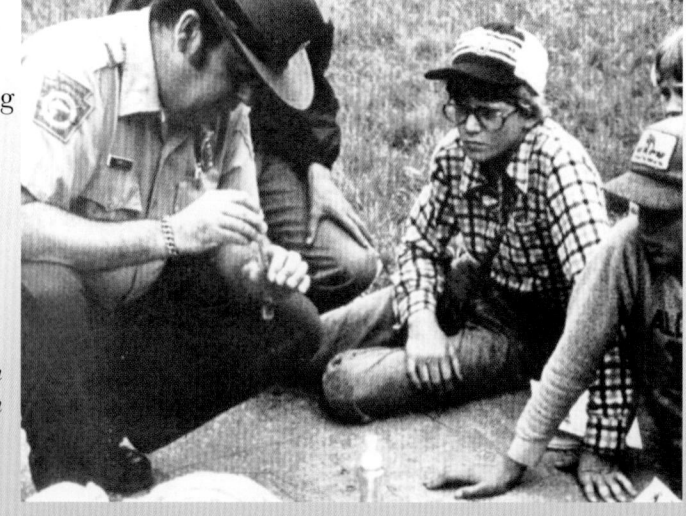

Waterways Patrolman Don Parrish is shown in 1984 instructing youth.

"My son . . . is 4-years old and possesses a growing passion for fishing and the outdoors. (We) were fishing along the banks of the Ohio River on Fish-for-Free Day. Within 10 minutes of Jake's first catch, he felt a big tug on his line that almost pulled him off his feet! After 10 seconds we realized that Jake had a fight on his hands, so I wrapped my arms around him and the rod for added support. With a little help, he got the fish to the bank and his uncle helped him handle and release the fish—a 19.5-inch Freshwater Drum that weighed about 4 or 5 pounds. This fish was Jake's first catch. Jake said that the fishing trip was 'awesome' and that the fish was 'cool!'"[42]

Within the Fish Commission, an important title change occurred when, on May 24, 1984, Governor Thornburgh signed Act 66 changing the title of Waterways Patrolman to Waterways Conservation Officer. The PFC advocated for the change. Conservationists and the Commission had previously adopted a new definition of conservation: a wise use of natural resources. Changing the name and image of the agency's law enforcement officers better portrayed PFC's focus on conservation.

In addition, their duties were expanded and made more complex. Paul Swanson (retired), then manager of the Commission's Northcentral Law Enforcement Region, laid-out the increasingly complex work of WCOs in an *Angler* article "WCOs and Protecting Water Quality."[43] According to Swanson, WCOs spent a good deal of their time reviewing permit applications for stream encroachments or other activities where water quality would be affected. Applications for permits for construction sites, roads, bridges, and pipelines were just a few examples. The goal was to prevent waterway pollution.

In 1986, then and current Area 6 Fisheries Manager Michael Kaufmann samples a stream's water for analysis.
photo-Russ Gettig, PFBC

Earth Day to the End of the Twentieth Century

With regard to these activities, WCOs worked with the Division of Fisheries's Environmental Services to conduct stream studies and take water samples to ensure minimal damage.

WCOs became more involved in monitoring water quality impacted by coal mining, especially acid mine drainage and siltation. Though the damage was much less in the 1980s as it had been in previous decades (in part because less coal was mined), there were, nevertheless instances that required attention such as the discharge of pollutants from the Butler Mine Tunnel on the Susquehanna River, north of Wilkes-Barre. WCOs also monitored oil and gas drilling operations and gathered information on so-called "brine" discharges that could harm fish species. They also monitored: logging operations to ensure that loggers use proper stream crossings and road placements to protect streams, bridge sandblasting, and repainting to ensure that proper measures were used to minimize paint spillage into streams, and municipal sewage treatment plants to ensure their proper operation. WCOs were called to testify as expert witnesses where industrial polluters were prosecuted by county district attorneys. Like Abele and his reference to The Thin Green Line, Swanson likened WCOs as the front-line defenders of clean waterways in Pennsylvania. "The WCO must be prepared at all times to (address) many different problems."[44]

PFC's finances were looking-up by mid-decade. Total Fish Fund and Boat Fund revenue exceeded $19 million, while expenditures were nearly the same in 1984. Wise stewardship of accumulated fund balances from previous years brought the total available revenue to over $30 million, leaving a healthy fiscal year-end surplus.

In 1986, then, Area 8 Fisheries Manager Blake C. Weirich uses a pH test kit in sampling. Weirich went on to help establish the Commission's KARE (Keystone Aquatic Resource Education) program in the 1990s in the Bureau of Education and Information.

Stocking numbers were impressive, as well, with a record 85 million trout, salmon, panfish, forage fish, and other gamefish being placed into Pennsylvania's waters at a total of 2.6 million pounds.

Though a relatively small portion of Commission revenue, $350,000, came from the Law Enforcement Division, its work was critically important. More than 100 citations were issued in Fiscal Year 1985–1986 for BUI, alone. All of the violators pled or were found guilty. The first conviction for homicide by watercraft was secured against a man who was operating a motorboat while under the influence of alcohol and killed a person. He was sentenced to three to six years in a state correctional institution (between 1970 and 1990 more than 430 people died in boating accidents in the state). Besides routine arrests for fishing and boating without a license, other prosecutions included arrests of two individuals who used dynamite to take fish from a York County stream. Their combined fines were $4,600, and the sentencing judge also mandated community service hours.

Anglers were particularly pleased with the work of the Commission. Take lakes and streams in Huntingdon County, for instance. By the mid-1980s, more than 64,000 trout were stocked in 13 streams. And, popular Raystown Lake became one of the fishing hot spots in Pennsylvania. Despite some reticence on behalf of anglers when the lake was being constructed by the U.S. Army Corps of Engineers between 1968 and 1973, by the 1980s bass, perch, crappies, Walleyes, and Muskellunge were caught in abundance. Bass were stocked in this inland reservoir to take

March 1986– mechanical feeder on a hatchery truck

photo-Russ Gettig, PFBC

Earth Day to the End of the Twentieth Century **219**

advantage of a Gizzard Shad forage base. In April 1985, one weighing 28 pounds was caught from the lake. A year later, a 30-pounder was caught. PFC fingerling stocking programs played an important role in the lake's abundance of various species.

Young anglers weren't left out of the picture. A new program titled Pennsylvania League of Angling Youth or PLAY was formed during the Abele era, formally in 1981 *(see page 206)*. The program enticed fourth through sixth graders to learn to fish. For $2 per year, youngsters received a special license and membership card, plus a jacket emblem and easy-to-read publications that provided fishing tips and explained various species. The program was marketed mainly through school districts and was expanded to include youth of all ages by late 1985. By the end of the decade, youth enrollment topped-out at 7,000.

Getting the word out to schools about the PLAY program was part of the responsibility of the Commission's new Volunteer Education and Information Corps. According to Steve Ulsh (retired), at the time Commission educator and manager of the Corps, "the Volunteer E & I

This 1986 photo shows most of PFC's Bureau of Education and Information staff at the time. Shown from left to right are Ted Walke, Steve Ulsh, Cheryl Riley (Bureau Director), Dave Wolf, Larry Shaffer, and Art Michaels. Not shown and responsible for the photograph is staff photographer Russ Gettig.

Corps currently (includes) 16 men and one woman who give classroom talks to school groups, speaking to church and civic organizations and . . . man Commission exhibits and assist in writing materials used in the Commission's aquatic resources education program." Ulsh also noted that Corps staff conducted educational programs at summer youth conservation camps. They were an eclectic bunch, according to Ulsh: "two members are retired from college teaching, one is a retired automobile travel service executive, four (are) secondary school teachers," and among the others was a municipal police officer and a housewife.[45]

In the area of boating safety education, a grant program was developed by the Bureau of Boating and approved by the Commission in January 1989. It made monies available to school districts to implement education programs and purchase equipment such as personal flotation devices (life jackets), canoes and throw bags, and to develop visual aids and films about boating safety. The total grant program costs were estimated to be $50,000 per year with not more than $3,000 awarded to each school district through a competitive application process. The program was piloted following Commission approval and, at the end of Fiscal Year 1988–1989, three grants totaling $8,500 were awarded to Schuylkill Valley, Spring Grove, and Upper Adams school districts.

While they were encouraged to learn about and enjoy fishing and boating, youth were also warned that there was a downside. A common problem that "caused tears in the eyes and blood on the body" was when a fish hook punctured the skin. Fingers were the usual puncture sites, and the problem most often occurred when a hook was baited.

PFC educator Steve Ulsh is shown here in 1987, during PFC's "Day at the River" event. photo-Russ Gettig, PFBC

Earth Day to the End of the Twentieth Century

Young anglers were advised to get the help of an adult and that "if only the point of the hook enters (the skin) it can be easily pulled out. If the hook goes deeper, past the barb, the wisest thing to do is to have a doctor remove it." However, if medical help was not readily available, "remove the hook by pushing it through until the barb is showing (then) use a cutting tool at either the barb or shank end and remove it. Clean the wound and cover it. As soon as possible see a doctor to avoid the danger of tetanus."[46]

There were many important achievements during the Abele years. And, there were many issues that remained on PFC's agenda for years to come. All-in-all, however, 1972 to 1987, were some of the best years in the agency's history. Clearly, it was not "business as usual."

The Abele Era Comes to an End

After many years of service to the citizens of Pennsylvania, Ralph W. Abele retired on May 27, 1987. Known for his prose that usually addressed larger environmental, conservation, and social issues, he didn't leave the Commission without using the bully pulpit one more time. In his departing "Straight Talk" article, Abele opined:

> "It's tough to write this "Straight Talk" column because it will be my last one. It is natural to leave behind something that is noteworthy and worth remembering. Looking around us we can find the evidence of a throwaway society. There are those who get a great feeling of . . . satisfaction in feeling that you can afford to throw things away and easily find something even better. The expansion of America was seeded in such an ethic.
>
> "I think that this is wrong. The unique power bestowed on each individual human being to do good and even change the course of history is quite often underestimated.
>
> "All the greed and shortsightedness of the exploiters . . . will not prevail if just one individual rises-up and says, "why should we put up with this?" I insist that if one is stubborn enough . . . he can and will prevail over those misanthropes who were obviously born out of wedlock.
>
> "The trail will be long and full of frustrations. Good and ill must be accepted together. We have to reconcile ourselves to the mysterious rhythm of our destinies. "Rest! Cries the chief sawyer, and we pause for breath."[47]

Symbolic of the transfer of leadership, Ralph W. Abele (left) is shown with the new PFC Executive Director Edward R. Miller in 1987, during Abele's retirement celebration.

April 1988

Abele seldom rested. At heart, he was a conservationist. And, he never gave in. Of course he was recognized and given awards by several organizations. Perhaps among his proudest was a mounted shad presented to him by the Susquehanna River Anadromous Fish Restoration Committee at its annual meeting held in Baltimore, Maryland, in March 1987. He was given the award by Howard Larsen,

Earth Day to the End of the Twentieth Century

Northeast Regional Director of the U.S. Fish and Wildlife Service. It was quite an honor. Abele beamed at its presentation.

Prior to Abele's retirement, his replacement was selected by the Commission. A special executive session was called on April 12, 1987, at the Holiday Inn in State College. Three individuals were interviewed including Edward R. Miller. At the general Commission meeting on the following day, Commissioner Ross Huhn made a motion to name Edward R. Miller as Executive Director. Commissioner Marilyn Black of Venango County made a motion to postpone a vote on hiring a new Executive Director at least until the day's agenda could be covered. Her motion was defeated by a 6 to 4 vote. Miller was then selected by a majority voice vote. Miller thanked the Commissioners for the confidence that they had placed in him.

Marilyn Black-first female Commissioner, appointed in 1983.

At this last meeting with the Commission, Abele reported that "I have considered it a great honor to have (had) the best job in the world for 15 years, being able to work with some of the finest people in the world that includes this beautiful staff." He continued, "I can tell you without any exaggeration that the Pennsylvania Fish Commission is considered by its peers and by others who know of our work to be among the top, if not THE finest of such organizations in the world." Abele concluded that the

Ralph W. Abele shown in 1987 with a class of school children.

224 *Chapter Six*

Fish Commission was a "resource first agency that is the envy of all others" and that the Commission "has a conservation ethic exuding from every pore. Defend these precepts with your very lives—let alone your careers." At the conclusion of his remarks, Abele received a standing ovation. Some thought that they observed a tear or two in his eyes.[48]

To honor Abele, the Commissioners created the Ralph W. Abele Conservation Heritage Award in 1991, the highest honor the agency could bestow on

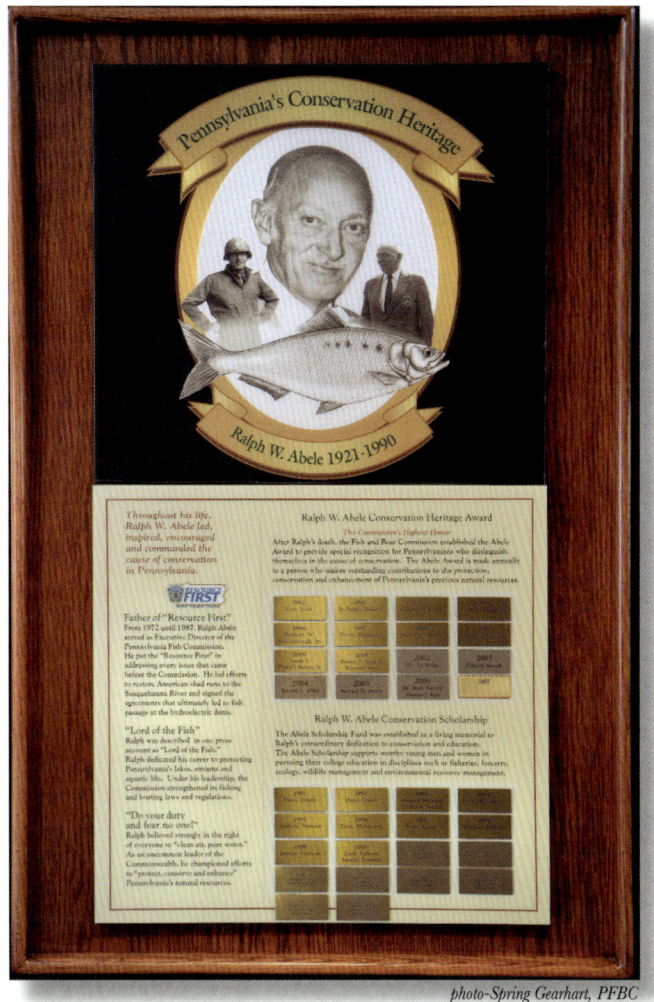

photo-Spring Gearhart, PFBC

Ralph W. Abele Conservation Heritage Award plaque, residing in the lobby of the PFBC Harrisburg headquarters building.

a person who distinguished themselves in the cause of conservation. Recipients were recognized for dedicating their time and energy to the conservation of the state's natural resources and, specifically, aquatic resources. The first awardee was Kenneth L. Sink of Indiana, Pennsylvania, who was an enthusiastic Commission volunteer and a past President of Trout Unlimited. And, in honor of Abele, the Penns Creek Catch-and-Release Project near Weikert was renamed as the Ralph. W. Abele Memorial Glen. The property contains 450 acres of pristine woodlands and 3.5 miles of Penns Creek. The site was one of Ralph's favorite. Ralph Abele passed away on June 15, 1990.

continued on page 240

Earth Day to the End of the Twentieth Century 225

September 1987 **Pennsylvania Angler** *cover by Russ Gettig*

226 *Chapter Six*

May 1986– A group of youth anglers at a PFC event.

photos-Russ Gettig, PFBC

1987– A young angler at a PFC event.

May 1984– A parent secures his child's life jacket.

Earth Day to the End of the Twentieth Century

April 1981– Miniature railroad car used for stocking trout along Muddy Creek.

August 1987– WCO Tom Kamerzel (future PFBC Bureau of Law Enforcement Director) is shown with a team of young stocking helpers in southeastern Pennsylvania.

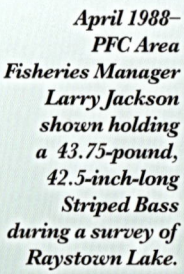

April 1988– PFC Area Fisheries Manager Larry Jackson shown holding a 43.75-pound, 42.5-inch-long Striped Bass during a survey of Raystown Lake.

228 *Chapter Six*

April 1989– Linesville State Fish Hatchery Open House

Commission artist Tom Duran Jr.

Tom Duran Jr. began his career as an artist and taxidermist for the Carnegie Museum of Natural History before spending 12 years as a staff artist for the Commission in the 1980s and 1990s.

Duran started with the Commission during a a time when the agency was focused on increasing its printed publications and educational materials. He was also a three-dimensional artist and taxidermist, so he literally knew most of his subjects from the inside-out.

Tom Duran Jr., 2014

During his time with the Commission, in addition to the fine art he produced for *Pennsylvania Angler & Boater* magazine's "Profile" series *(see the trout species paintings on pages 202–203)*, Duran produced a series of large fine art paintings of the Commonwealth's fish, amphibian, and reptile species. These paintings, shown on the next 10 pages, established the series of educational wall charts that the Commission has produced and distributed for more than 40 years and continues today—truly, a lasting legacy of both environmental education and artistry.

Earth Day to the End of the Twentieth Century

"Pennsylvania's Coldwater Fishes" artwork by Tom Duran Jr.

1. Lake Trout
2. Kokanee Salmon
3. Steelhead Trout
4. Rainbow Smelt
5. Landlocked Atlantic Salmon
6. Coho Salmon
7. Chinook Salmon
8. Rainbow Trout
9. Brook Trout
10. Brown Trout
11. Golden Rainbow Trout

For up-to-date species status and regulations, visit the Commission's website at **www.fishandboat.com**. *For fish species scientific names, current status, and watershed location, see tables appearing in the appendix of this book.*

230 *Chapter Six*

"Pennsylvania's Coolwater/Warmwater Fishes" artwork by Tom Duran Jr.

1. Largemouth Bass
2. Redfin Pickerel
3. Smallmouth Bass
4. Muskellunge
5. Northern Pike
6. Chain Pickerel
7. Grass Pickerel
8. Sauger
9. Tiger Muskellunge
10. Walleye
11. Amur River Pike

Earth Day to the End of the Twentieth Century   231

"Pennsylvania's Migratory Fishes" artwork by Tom Duran Jr.

1. American Shad
2. Gizzard Shad
3. Hickory Shad
4. Striped Bass Hybrid
5. American Eel
6. Striped Bass
7. Blueback Herring
8. Alewife
9. Shortnose Sturgeon

"Pennsylvania's Miscellaneous Fishes" artwork by Tom Duran Jr.

1. Longnose Gar
2. Freshwater Drum
3. Common Carp
4. Quillback
5. Channel Catfish
6. Bowfin
7. Brown Bullhead
8. White Catfish
9. Flathead Catfish
10. Burbot

Earth Day to the End of the Twentieth Century   233

"Pennsylvania's Panfish" artwork by Tom Duran Jr.

1. White Bass
2. Yellow Perch
3. White Perch
4. Redear Sunfish
5. Pumpkinseed
6. Black Crappie
7. Bluegill
8. White Cappie
9. Rock Bass
10. Redbreast Sunfish
11. Green Sunfish
12. Shorthead Redhorse
13. Northern Hogsucker
14. White Sucker

Chapter Six

"Pennsylvania's Forage Fishes" artwork by Tom Duran Jr.

1. Spottail Shiner
2. Spotfin Shiner
3. Fallfish
4. Golden Shiner
5. Banded Killifish
6. Common Shiner
7. Satinfin Shiner
8. Logperch
9. Emerald Shiner
10. Creek Chub
11. River Chub
12. Streamline Chub
13. Eastern Blacknose Dace
14. Redside Dace
15. Longnose Dace
16. Rosyface Shiner
17. Rainbow Darter
18. Fantail Darter
19. Fathead Minnow
20. Central Stoneroller
21. Greenside Darter
22. Shield Darter
23. Cutlips Minnow
24. Johnny Darter
25. White Sucker
26. Mottled Sculpin
27. Stonecat
28. Margined Madtom

Earth Day to the End of the Twentieth Century   235

"Pennsylvania's Turtles, Lizards, and Skinks" artwork by Tom Duran Jr.

1. Northern Coal Skink
2. Five-lined Skink
3. Eastern Fence Lizard
4. Broadhead Skink
5. Spotted Turtle
6. Eastern Box Turtle
7. Blanding's Turtle
8. Eastern Musk Turtle
9. Wood Turtle
10. Map Turtle
11. Bog Turtle
12. Snapping Turtle
13. Eastern Spiny Softshell
14. Redbellied Turtle
15. Painted Turtle
16. Eastern Mud Turtle

For up-to-date species status and regulations, visit the Commission's website at www.fishandboat.com.

236 Chapter Six

"Pennsylvania's Frogs" artwork by Tom Duran Jr.

1. Mountain Chorus Frog
2. Northern Cricket Frog
3. Easter Gray Treefrog
4. Spring Peeper
5. Western Chorus Frog
6. Northern Green Frog
7. Wood Frog
8. Bullfrog
9. Pickerel Frog
10. Northern Leopard Frog
11. Eastern American Toad
12. Fowler's Toad
13. Eastern Spadefoot

Earth Day to the End of the Twentieth Century

"Pennsylvania's Salamanders" artwork by Tom Duran Jr.

1. Green Salamander
2. Jefferson Salamander
3. Spotted Salamander
4a. Red Eft
    (Immature Eastern Red-Spotted Newt)
4b. Eastern Red-Spotted Newt
5. Wehrle's Salamander
6. Marbled Salamander
7. Northern Slimy Salamander
8. Four-Toed Salamander
9. Allegheny Mountain Dusky Salamander
10a. Eastern Redback Salamander
10b. Lead-backed color phase of
     Eastern Redback Salamander
11. Seal Salamander
12. Northern Dusky Salamander
13. Mudpuppy
14. Northern Red Salamander
15. Eastern Hellbender
16. Northern Spring Salamander
17. Northern Two-lined Salamander
18. Longtail Salamander

238   Chapter Six

"Pennsylvania's Snakes" artwork by Tom Duran Jr.

VENOMOUS SPECIES
1. Copperhead
2. Eastern Massasauga
3. Timber Rattlesnake (yellow phase)
4. Timber Rattlesnake (black phase)

NON-VENOMOUS SPECIES
5. Northern Redbellied Snake
6. Eastern Garter Snake
7. Shorthead Garter Snake
8. Northern Brown Snake
9. Eastern Kingsnake
10. Eastern Ribbon Snake
11. Eastern Ratsnake, with young
12. Eastern Worm Snake
13. Eastern Milksnake
14. Northern Black Racer
15. Northern Ringneck Snake
16. Eastern Hognose Snake
17. Queen Snake
18. Northern Water Snake
19. Kirtland's Snake
20. Mountain Earth Snake
21. Rough Green Snake
22. Eastern Smooth Green Snake

Earth Day to the End of the Twentieth Century

A New Executive Director and New Initiatives at the End of the Millennium

Edward Miller stepped-in as Executive Director when Ralph Abele retired. An engineer by training, Miller was not new to the Commission. He began working for the agency at a young age. Ed learned to fish from his father who was a butcher and grocery store owner in Pleasant Gap; Ed's father also held public office as both treasurer and sheriff of Centre County in the 1940s. Their favorite spot was Spring Creek, where his father introduced his 17-year-old son to Dewey Sorenson, who supervised several fish hatcheries. Dewey offered Ed a summer job in 1951 as a general helper at the Spring Creek Hatchery for 75 cents per hour for a five and one-half day week. Ed jumped at the chance and soon began cleaning ponds, brushing screens, and working on deferred maintenance tasks. He saved most of his earnings for college.

Ed also worked at the hatchery during the summer of 1952, between high school graduation and his first year of engineering studies at Penn State University. In the summer of 1953, Ed again worked at

In April 1988, Fish Commission Executive Director Edward Miller (second from right) presented Governor Robert P. Casey (center) with a framed poster depicting the Commission's watchwords, "Resource First." Accompanying Miller for the presentations were Joe Greene (left), Commission legislative liaison; Cheryl Riley (second from left), Bureau of Education and Information Director; and Dave Wolf (right), Commission Media Relations. The award-winning poster depicted Cherry Run, Centre County, with photograph by Russ Gettig, staff photographer, and design by Ted Walke, staff graphic designer. The poster received the Izaak Walton League of America's 1987 Outdoor Ethics Communication Award for "Best Graphics." Photo by Russ Gettig, PFBC.

"Take a Break in '88!" was a marketing tagline used throughout 1988 at PFC-attended sportshows and in printed publications such as this March 1988 Pennsylvania Angler *back cover. Photograph by Jim Bashline. Logo design by Ted Walke, PFBC.*

the hatchery. This time he had a more substantive role in assisting to develop plans and design the Benner Spring Research Station. When construction got underway, Ed worked as a laborer for $1.25 per hour.

Following graduation from Penn State with an engineering degree in 1956, Ed worked for U.S. Steel at its Homestead Works in Pittsburgh,

Earth Day to the End of the Twentieth Century

the U.S. Army Corps of Engineers, and Pennsylvania State University, where he also pursued a graduate degree. His stint at Penn State barely lasted a year before he came to work for the Commission. He joined its staff in 1960 as Assistant Chief of Engineering. He graduated to chief engineer, then to Bureau of Fisheries and Engineering Director, Assistant Executive Director, and was sworn-in as Executive Director on June 1, 1987.

At times, Abele was prophetic. Miller, on the other hand, was more the pragmatist. In the July 1987 issue of *Pennsylvania Angler*, he clearly and simply stated his vision: "The Pennsylvania Fish Commission is special, because it cares about people and wants to do its very best for all Pennsylvanians and our welcomed visitors." He further opined that the agency's "attitude (is to) represent all the people fairly and to provide fishing and boating opportunities for all." He, too, believed in Abele's motto of Resource First.[49]

Under Miller, PFC set out in a new direction, while, at the same time, remained somewhat on the path that Ralph Abele had set. And, like Abele, Miller wanted the public to know that Pennsylvania boasted outstanding fishing opportunities. For example, not long after he took the helm he encouraged freelance writer and photographer Jeff Mulhollem to publish an article in *Pennsylvania Angler* aimed at reminding readers that there were many great fishing spots within "An Hour From Altoona." Trout were to be had in Canoe Creek and Lake near Hollidaysburg, Brown Trout and Rainbow Trout could be caught in Yellow Creek in Bedford County, as with the Bald Eagle Creek in Centre County, and the Frankstown Branch of the Juniata River was a favorite spot for anglers who preferred to use salmon eggs for Rainbow Trout. In short, the message was that "ordinary people could enjoy the outdoors, fish, and recreate within a short distance from wherever they resided."[50]

And, Miller, like Abele, believed employee excellence was a hallmark of PFC. Quite simply, he knew that employees were dedicated to their work and that they should be recognized for that. In late 1989, Miller instituted a new employee recognition program that made awards in four categories: outstanding service, lifesaving, cost savings, and special projects. The first award was presented to Waterways Conservation Officer Gerald Greiner who was "officially commended for lifesaving action on August 7, 1988, when a race boat veered out of control during the Pittsburgh Three Rivers Regatta and injured 23 people. His immediate action (was) to assist in administering first aid (and) was a contributing factor in saving lives."[51]

Western Pennsylvania again became the focus of PFC's work in 1988. This time it was in response to a major catastrophe. Ashland Oil Company owned a facility near the Monongahela River in Jefferson, not far from Pittsburgh. On January 2, 1988, a 3.5-million-gallon diesel oil tank collapsed spilling more than one million gallons into a storm sewer that led to the Monongahela. It was later discovered that a dime-sized flaw on the 45-year-old tank caused the rupture.

The spill made its way to the Ohio River and contaminated drinking water for over one million people in Ohio, West Virginia, and Pennsylvania. Thousands of Pittsburghers were without water for more than a week. It was among the largest inland oil spills in U.S. history. Thousands of fish died, and it was estimated that anywhere from 2,000 to 4,000 waterfowl were killed. An irate Governor Robert P. Casey (1987–1995) went to the site where he told reporters and onlookers that Ashland would be held fully accountable for what he termed as nothing less than an environmental disaster. Casey dispatched numerous state agencies to the site to measure the spill's impact and mitigate further damage.

Numerous federal agencies also had staff at the locale, as did environmental agencies from Ohio, West Virginia, and Kentucky. Various methods were used to contain and clean up the spill, ranging from deflection booms to river barges that collected oil from the water. Cold weather hampered efforts as single-digit temperatures affected equipment operation and put workers at risk for hypothermia. Ashland eventually paid out over $18 million in clean-up fees and to settle civil lawsuits. The company was charged with violating the federal Clean Water Act and was fined $2.25 million.

On a brighter note, during Miller's tenure, the computer era had taken hold at the agency. Cheryl K. Riley, Director of the Bureau of Education and Information, reported to the Commissioners that "this year (1989) all of our staff will be equipped with personal computers, which is helping us to better accomplish our objectives. One staff member is *even beginning to type* so he can become part of the new age." Cheryl also noted that computer technology was having its greatest impact in the "Graphic Services Section (where) computer typesetting and art layout are allowing Ted Walke to save money, time, and create improved publications. Several recent publications . . . have all been produced using computer typesetting and art." In 1996, a new color

continued on page 246

September 1990 **Pennsylvania Angler** *cover • photograph by Wally Eberhart*

244   *Chapter Six*

March 1991 **Pennsylvania Angler** *cover • photograph by Doug Stamm*

printer was purchased, and the Graphic Services Section began printing all posters in-house, resulting in an average savings of $9,500 per poster run. The average poster cost $12,500, when contracted to a printer, while, in-house, the cost was about $2,500 per run.[52]

And, the Bureau of Education and Information's 15 employees (plus 20 volunteers) published two new brochures, *Let's Go Trout Fishing in Pennsylvania* and *Let's Go Fishing in Pennsylvania's Lakes*. Staff also conducted "A Day at a Hatchery" program at the Linesville Fish Culture Station (State Fish Hatchery) that attracted 8,000 people, who learned about fish egg cultivation, lake surveys, and fish filleting and cooking fish. Of course, tasty samples were provided!

Moreover, collaboration efforts continued. For example, DER had begun to gather survey data for the development of its statewide recreation plan, and it yielded some enlightening news for PFC. Thirty-percent of Pennsylvania's 12 million residents fished in 1989, and 27 percent participated in boating recreation. DER estimated that, for every dollar spent on fish and boat programs by the Commission, $150 in economic benefit was generated. Citizen interest in fishing was also reflected by the raw numbers: The total of all fishing licenses sold in 1990 grew by 33,807 during 1989. DER's finding appeared to be true, at least when it came to PFC budget. According to the agency's comptroller, who had begun subjecting its accounting to professional standards known as GAPP or Generally Accepted Accounting Principles, Fish Fund revenue was nearly $20 million in Fiscal Year 1988–1989, an increase of eight percent from the previous fiscal year.

1990

246 Chapter Six

At the same time, the Bureau of Fisheries stocked 83 million species, comprising a total weight of 2.6 million pounds. The Division of Environmental Services was quite busy. Division staff had reviewed 4,000 DER and Federal Energy Regulatory Commission projects, as well as numerous permit applications and had been involved in quite a few enforcement cases, the biggest of which was the Ashland Oil spill.

The PFC's Boating Safety and Education Division expanded its youth safety education program by conducting educational workshops for 20 schools and 26 conservation and scout clubs, reaching a total of 2,000 youth. And, the Bureau of Property and Facilities Management reorganized the Adopt-a-Stream habitat improvement program, resulting in 130 waterways being "adopted," that included 46 stream layout projects and 22 stream fish enhancement initiatives. The original program was inaugurated in the 1970s, along with its sister program called Adopt-a-Lake. Both programs provided funding and technical support for habitat improvement projects

In the early 1990s, Commission established a $5 fee for a trout and salmon permit, the revenues of which were dedicated to the agency. The regulation pertaining to the permit requirement went into effect on January 1, 1991. As of July, 1993, $10.4 million in revenue was already generated by the trout and salmon permit. The goals of the program were multifaceted.

1990– Water Rescue training with PFC instructor Dan Martin (yellow pants).

Earth Day to the End of the Twentieth Century

One was the allocation of $4.6 million for major improvements at nine state fish hatcheries, including Pleasant Gap, Tionesta, Corry, Huntsdale, and Big Spring (Big Spring was taken out of production in 2001 due to pollution problems). Facilities for wastewater treatment, chemical containment, and oxygen generation were either constructed or upgraded. In a major initiative, 40 new trout stocking trucks were purchased. They had diesel engines and fiberglass tanks that extended vehicle life and reduced operating costs. In addition, the agency acquired numerous coldwater streams and access points, expanded its Adopt-a-Stream program to include 100 stream projects using mainly voluntary labor, expanded the complement of WCOs by 10, and grew the Keystone Aquatic Resource Education (KARE) Program to educate 3,000 schoolteachers, who then reached 200,000 students with fishing and aquatic resource education programs.

One of the agency's biggest changes occurred in 1991, when Governor Robert P. Casey signed Act 39 into law on December 12. The Pennsylvania Fish Commission was now officially the Pennsylvania Fish & Boat Commission (PFBC). The name change reflected the fact that the agency has been mandated to enforce boating laws since the 1930s. Public perception of the Fish Commission was that the agency had little or nothing to do with boating unless, of course, one was a boat angler.

Over time, many Commission programs and materials reflected the name change. Readers of the long-popular *Pennsylvania Angler* witnessed a new name for the magazine in 1997. *Pennsylvania Angler* became *Pennsylvania Angler & Boater*. Why the change? The agency wanted to

As shown from 1991, not all waterway surveys conducted by Bureau of Fisheries are in the daytime. Many are conducted into the late hours of the evenings. At right, WCO Tom Kamerzel is shown obtaining a water sample for a pollution investigation in 1990.

photo–Art Michaels, PFBC

better address the interests of boaters since a survey revealed that a higher percentage of boaters than anglers actually read the magazine. Data noted that 30 percent of Pennsylvania boaters read *Pennsylvania Angler* as compared to 23 percent of resident anglers. And, obviously, the name change was consistent with the agency's new name in 1991 and cessation of *Boat Pennsylvania* magazine in fall of 1995.

An important initiative in 1993 was implementation of the new Keystone Recreation Park and Conservation Fund Act, also signed into law by Governor Casey. The program was funded by a publicly approved $50 million bond issue, plus a small percentage of the Commonwealth's annual revenue from realty transfer taxes. The fund provided monies to, among other agencies, the Pennsylvania Historical and Museum Commission for historic site maintenance, DER for state park maintenance, and $1.5 million over three years to PFBC for planning, acquisition, development, and rehabilitation of fishing and boating access areas and natural areas, as well as for technical work. "Key-93," as it was known, was a signature element of the Casey Administration's efforts to financially support cultural and recreational infrastructure.

In early 1994, Ed Miller completed his 35 years of service. Of course, few accomplishments could have been registered without the hard work of the agency's 445 permanent staff, 65 seasonal employees, plus its countless volunteers. There were many major achievements during Miller's tenure. Perhaps the largest feather in the agency's cap

photo-Ted Walke, PFBC

During the Commission's commemoration of its 125th anniversary in 1991, the agency's Harrisburg headquarters building was adorned with a large graphic banner, visible to all traffic on Walnut Street.

was that it "gained national recognition among its counterparts as having its fishing programs determined to be 'the best in the nation.'"[53]

When Ed Miller retired in 1994, Lawrence W. Hoffman was appointed as Acting Executive Director. He then served as Executive Director from March 1994 until Peter Colangelo was appointed to the post on October 3, 1994. Pete came to the agency from the Pittsburgh District of the U.S. Army Corps of Engineers, where he had served for 34 years, mostly in senior management positions. Prior to his employment with the Army Corps, Pete earned a degree in civil engineering from the University of Pittsburgh. The next year, Dennis T. Guise was promoted to Deputy Executive Director.

Guise was the agency's Chief Counsel beginning in 1978. Guise had an impressive and diverse career. He graduated from the University of Pennsylvania's law school in 1972 and had received his undergraduate degree in political science at Gettysburg College, where he was salutatorian. He had served in the U.S. Air Force and remained in its reserves where he held the rank of Colonel. During his military duty, Dennis earned the Meritorious Service Medal and the Air Force Commendation Medal. He was also presented with the Commonwealth's Management Performance Award from Governor Dick Thornburgh in 1984.

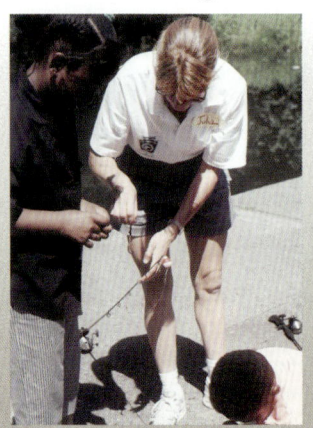

Lawrence W. Hoffman

Peter A. Colangelo

PFC's Urban Fishing and Education Program–first piloted in 1990.

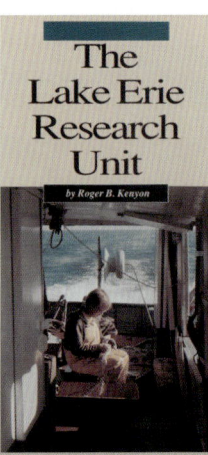

December 1990– magazine feature

July 1992– WCO John Sabaitus on patrol.

photos-Art Michaels, PFBC

250   Chapter Six

Strategic Planning: An Agency First

Under the leadership of Colangelo, the agency announced its first-ever strategic plan. It straightforwardly stated the agency's mission: "To provide fishing and boating opportunities through the protection and management of aquatic resources." Buffering this mission were several goals including:

1. Protect, conserve, and enhance aquatic resources.
2. Provide for the protection of aquatic resource users.
3. Meet the expectations of anglers and boaters.

Resource categories defined in the plan were: coldwater streams, warmwater streams, large rivers, impoundments, tributaries watersheds, wetlands, and Lake Erie. Commission staff held eight regional public meetings to gather input on the plan.

Strategic planning wasn't the only item on the agenda. For example, Colangelo oversaw the full implementation of the Conservation Acquisition Partnership (CAP). The program solicited tax-deductible, private monetary contributions for use in acquisition of public lands, mainly for recreational purposes and PFBC was authorized to match contributions on a dollar-for-dollar basis. The overall goal of the program was to grow the Commonwealth's water resources.

Colangelo and the Commissioners also had to grapple with Fish Fund inflationary erosion. Increasing license fees was necessary for the fund to remain solvent. To address the problem from a management standpoint, Colangelo implemented a hiring freeze, reduced overtime costs by 15 percent, agency-wide, and significantly reduced fixed asset expenditures. In 1996, the Commissioners agreed that resident annual license fees be increased from $12 to $16.25, non-resident annual license fees be increased from $20 to $34.25, and seven-day tourist annual license fees go from $15 to $29.25. Governor Tom Ridge (1995–2001) signed legislation granting the fee increases.

Interestingly, the new fees were implemented at a time when anglers and boaters clearly saw the need for the Commission to not only have a firm presence in the Commonwealth, but to enhance its programs, as well. Colangelo chaired nine public meetings across the Commonwealth in the mid-1990s. Attendees included some members of the general public but mostly boaters and anglers along with a few public officials. When presented with the statement, "There is a need

continued on page 254

photo–Art Michaels, PFBC

Judges and other Commission dignitaries surround Robert Kray's painting of a Brook Trout, the winning artwork in the 1994 trout stamp competition (see page 256), held in June 1993. Left to right are Division of Fisheries Chief Delano R. Graff, Chief Counsel Dennis T. Guise, Commissioner Leon H. Reed, Commissioner Paul J. Mahon, Executive Director Edward R. Miller, Game Commission Bureau of Information & Education Assistant Director J. Carl Graybill, print contractor George Lavanish, Bureau of Administrative Services Director Allison J. Mayhew, Graphic Services Section Chief Ted Walke, and Bureau of Education & Information Director Stephen B. Ulsh.

photo–Russ Gettig, PFBC

Then, Division of Environmental Services Chief, John Arway (left) is shown in 1996 conducting water analysis of a waterway with the assistance of WCO Gary Slutter of Schuylkill County. Arway would then go on to become PFBC Executive Director in 2010.

252   *Chapter Six*

Pennsylvania anglers and boaters in the 1990s

May 1997

July 1994

August 1990

Earth Day to the End of the Twentieth Century

to promote/increase education programs," 82 percent either agreed or strongly agreed.

In addition, when asked whether the agency should increase its law enforcement presence, 78 percent agreed or strongly agreed, and, when asked whether the Commission should increase and enhance its environmental protection and conservation activities, 67 percent agreed or strongly agreed. Boaters and anglers saw the agency as central to resource enhancement and protection, concomitant with the Commission's mantra of Resource First that had started with Ralph Abele. In partial response to the public's demonstrated concerns, 20 new WCO cadets were hired in the summer of 1995. All completed PFBC's nine-month mandatory training program. The class was the largest up to that time.

More officers were needed to ensure that laws and regulations were enforced, particularly since angling remained big business in the Commonwealth. One study by the American Sportfishing Association concluded that fishing alone generated $1.34 billion in economic activity in 1996. The industry supported 16,000 jobs, and fishing also generated $49 million in state tax revenue, besides fees collected by the Commission. Big business translated into additional big accomplishments for PFBC. Similar to the Department of Conservation and Natural Resources's (DCNR's) Rails-to-Trails programs, in 1997, the agency partnered with various organizations to begin developing water trails on streams and rivers, especially the main stem of the Susquehanna River. This initiative, largely funded by DCNR grants to water trail organizations, would become what is known today as the Pennsylvania Water Trails program. Currently with 25 water trails established across the state, the Commission's role in this development was not just recreational but an advisory one that ensured that boating safety principles, especially life jacket wear, were incorporated into the guidance to partnering organizations and trail users. From 2000 through 2007, an estimated 5 million water trail guides, free to the boating public, were produced by the Commission's Educational Media Section and its print shop. These printed guides, specific to each water trail, contained maps, trail amenities, boating laws, and safety guidance. The guides were a provision by PFBC in concert with DCNR's grant funding.

As the end of the millennium drew nearer, the Commission was quite pleased with a Pennsylvania Superior Court decision. The decision upheld the ruling of the Court of Common Pleas of Luzerne County that the Lehigh River is a navigable water of the Commonwealth that is held in trust for public use, including fishing and boating. The 1999 ruling resulted from an incident that occurred in 1995.

During the spring of 1995, angler John Andrejewski waded into a portion of the Lehigh River and gradually—and unknowingly—moved downstream and ended up adjacent to land leased by The Lehigh Falls Fishing Club. He was confronted by one of the club's members and told that he could not fish in the river at that specific location, as it was private property. Andrejewski believed the river to be within the public domain, so he refused to leave.

The club subsequently instituted a legal action seeking a declaration that the two-mile portion of the Lehigh River, located through its land, is not navigable and thus not owned by the Commonwealth. The trial court determined that the Lehigh River is indeed a navigable water of the Commonwealth in which the public has the right to fish.

The club appealed the decision to the Superior Court, which affirmed the ruling of the lower court. The Superior Court's decision was based in large part on its analysis of prior opinions in which earlier courts described the Lehigh River as one of the principal rivers of Pennsylvania and a navigable waterway in which the right of fisheries "is vested in the state, and open to all."[54] The Commission, together with DCNR, the Department of Environmental Protection (DEP), and The Pennsylvania Federation of Sportsmen's Clubs, filed amicus curiae (friend of the court) briefs with the Superior Court, supporting the conclusion that the Lehigh River is a navigable waterway.

Increasing license fees, hiring new WCOs, and ensuring that the public could fish all of the Lehigh River were significant matters. Yet, seemingly trivial issues had to be dealt with as well. For example, in late-1990, the Commissioners agreed to amend part of the agency's property regulations that dealt with parking. The amended regulation made it clear that "vehicles properly registered in conformity with the Vehicle Code, Title 75 of Pennsylvania Statutes are permitted on Commission property" but that it was unlawful to park a vehicle "in any manner so as to obstruct or impede free public access to driveways, access roads, and launch ramps." The new rule also made it clear that parking was permitted only in designated parking slots. It seemed that complaints

continued on page 260

Trout/salmon stamp art appearing on Pennsylvania Angler covers

1993 Trout/Salmon Stamp Artwork by Roger Cruwys.

1994 Trout/Salmon Stamp Artwork by Robert Kray.

256 Chapter Six

1995 Trout/Salmon Stamp Artwork by Terry Doughty.

1996 Trout/Salmon Stamp Artwork by Robert Kray.

Earth Day to the End of the Twentieth Century

The beginnings of Pennsylvania Angler & Boater magazine

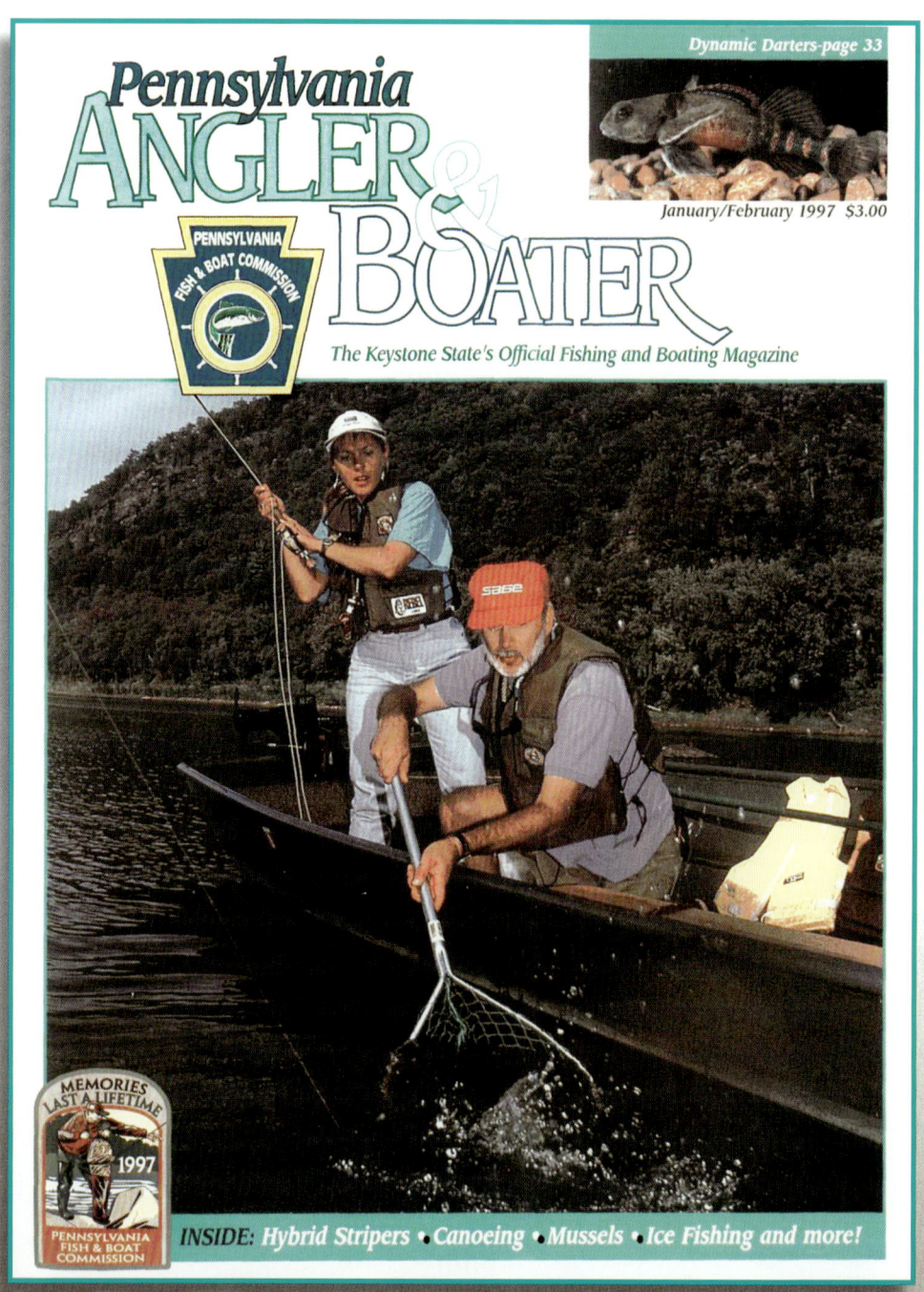

January/February 1997 **Pennsylvania Angler & Boater** *cover • photograph by Barry and Cathy Beck*

258 *Chapter Six*

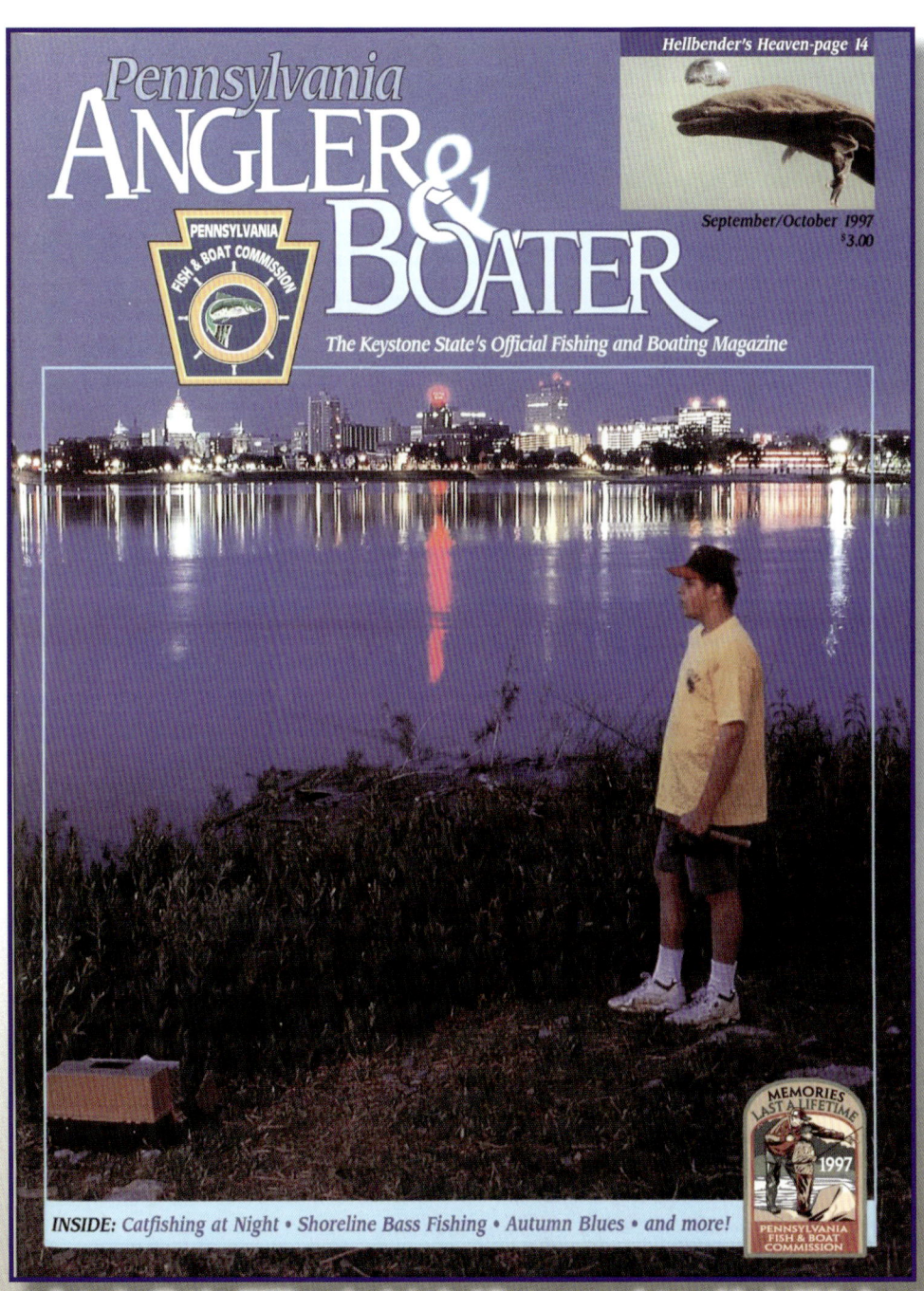

September/October 1997 **Pennsylvania Angler & Boater** *cover • photograph by Art Michaels*

Earth Day to the End of the Twentieth Century   259

photo-Art Michaels, PFBC

Committing the Commission to breaking ground for its new Harrisburg headquarters building and bright future on May 12, 1999, PFBC Executive Director Colangelo invited children of the Commission's staff to join in the ceremony to demonstrate that this new building will benefit future generations of anglers and boaters. The children included (from left) Shannon Ford, Ben Walke, Chelsea Covage, Kelsy Richardson, Cassandra Covage, John Morgan Seifert, Tericka Clark, Kikeya Holton, Natasha Gaston, and Joe Martin.

from anglers and boaters prompted the change, especially when callous individuals blocked access to launch ramps.[55]

A New Headquarters for PFBC

In addition, plans were finalized for a new headquarters building to be constructed along Elmerton Avenue in Harrisburg, not far from the Pennsylvania Farm Show Complex and across the street from the Pennsylvania State Police Headquarters. PFBC had managed the 35-acre tract for a number of years and constructing a new building on the site had been discussed for a long time. In 1992, Act 188 granted the Commission capital budget authorization to construct its new administrative headquarters in Dauphin County. It was eight years from the time that Governor Casey signed the authorizing legislation until the grand opening of the new facility on July 22, 2000.

The dedication ceremony was quite impressive. Numerous dignitaries were on hand, including State Senator Jeff Piccola, State Representative Mark McNaughton, and Dauphin County

Commissioner John Payne. Governor Tom Ridge (1995–2001) sent greetings, as did several other state officials. WCOs Steven Boughter, Terence Deibler, David Kaneski, Mark Pisko, and James Stout comprised the honor guard. Following the official ceremonies, more than 500 people toured the new facility.

Naturally, educational programs emanated from staff at the new headquarters. However, the Commission wasn't the only educator. Sometimes angler education came from the grassroots. Take Howard Wagner of Fombell, northwest of Pittsburgh, for example. Known as "Mr. Muskie," Wagner operated a fish education center at his home where he conducted various seminars and ran a guide service for 40 to 50 anglers each year. Howard caught his first Muskellunge in 1967, and, from that point on, he realized that "Muskie fever is real." On a fishing trip to Canada, Howard watched a muskie grab the lure and pull his fishing partner "halfway out of the boat." After seeing its streamlined shape and beautiful markings, he knew that muskies were his fish of choice. Wagner estimated that he fished for muskies 200 days per year and caught more than 1,500 of them since 1967. His best year was 1986, when he landed 85 fish that were more than 30 inches in length with another seven that exceeded more than 50 inches. "I fish for muskies, because I think they are the king of freshwater fish. They are evasive and big—tough and difficult to catch." He admitted, though, that he never even came close to catching the state's record muskie: 54 pounds taken on Conneaut Lake in 1924.[56]

During the May 12, 1999, ground-breaking ceremonies for the new headquarters building, Deputy Executive Director Dennis Guise is shown addressing the attendees of the event with Commissioner Enoch "Inky" Moore; PFBC Executive Director Peter Colangelo; and Representative Bruce Smith, Chairman, House Game and Fisheries Committee seated.

photo-Art Michaels, PFBC

Earth Day to the End of the Twentieth Century

Conowingo Dam, Susquehanna River

Back in the eastern part of Pennsylvania, the combined efforts of the Delaware River Shad Fishermen's Association; the Lehigh River Preservation, Protection, and Improvement Foundation; other eastern Pennsylvania sportsmen's organizations; and the Commission resulted in many American Shad returning to the Lehigh River for the first time in 170 years. By the late 1990s, more than 1,000 shad swam in the river. Other fishes which passed upstream included sunfish, bass, carp, trout, Muskellunge, and the American Eel. Two million dollars-worth of passageways had been constructed at the Easton, Hamilton Street, and Chain dams to allow fish to move upstream. The Commission pitched-in with a spawning program that released upwards of 200,000 shad annually. Estimates were that shad would attract more than 100,000 anglers per year.[57]

Other collaborations yielded positive results, as well. Thanks to cooperative work between PFBC and DCNR and DEP, Pennsylvania's state parks were "ranked high on the list of the best family fishing vacation spots" by *Pennsylvania Game and Fish* magazine in 2001. Nockamixon State Park in Bucks County was known for bass, crappies, Walleyes, and Hybrid Striped Bass pulled from its 1,450-acre lake; the 63-acre Hopewell Lake in French Creek State Park in Berks and Chester counties attracted Northern Pike and pickerel anglers; Ohiopyle State Park in Fayette County was known for the abundance of trout in the Youghiogheny River; and Gifford Pinchot Lake at Gifford Pinchot State Park in southcentral Pennsylvania offered bass, hybrid stripers, and panfish. Each of these parks—plus many more—offered camping, cabins, boat rentals, restroom facilities, hiking trails, and even recreational games such as disc golf.[58]

photos-Ted Walke, PFBC

Safe Harbor Dam fish elevator on the Susquehanna River, 1999.

Near the end of the 1990s, Commission staff undertook some unusual investigations. In one case, there was an 18-month special inquiry into the illegal trafficking of Pennsylvania reptiles and amphibians. WCOs arrested an Allegheny County resident when he attempted to purchase bog turtles, a Pennsylvania endangered species. His plan, of course, was to sell the turtles at a premium to willing buyers. However, he wasn't quite able to pull it off. WCOs obtained a search warrant and found more than 100 illegally obtained turtles, snakes, and reptile eggs. He was charged with 21 law violations and paid a hefty fine.

All in all, it was a remarkable century for the Pennsylvania Fish & Boat Commission. There was much change. To cite just a few examples, the agency's name went through a few iterations; its budget grew substantially, as did its staff. Science was increasingly applied to propagation and habitat improvement. And, species management and new laws and regulations enhanced its powers to protect, conserve, and enhance. Yet, there were constants as well. Chief among them were the continuing need to combat water pollution and to propagate specific species, especially shad.

Change and perpetual issues extended into the twenty-first century.

Chapter Seven: 2000–2015

"Many of the 'old' problems are today's problems. Water pollution is one."

John Arway, Executive Director
Pennsylvania Fish & Boat Commission
2010–Present[1]

The Pennsylvania Fish & Boat Commission entered the twenty-first century with its second strategic plan, titled *Enhancing Fishing and Boating in Pennsylvania: Strategies for the 21st Century.* Some of the policies and strategies that the plan addressed included:

- **Conserving Pennsylvania Aquatic Resources:** promoting watershed-based resource protection, sustaining the Commonwealth's non-game aquatic resources, ensuring migratory fish species restoration, enhancing fishing and boating access partnerships, and public outreach and educational programs.
- **Promoting and Managing Recreational Fishing and Boating:** increasing boating safety outreach and ensuring compliance with fish and boat laws and regulations.
- **Addressing the Expectations of Resource Users:** developing and implementing management plans to protect and enhance native species and coordinate zoning access, regulation, education, and awareness programs with partner organizations.
- **Investing in the Future:** linking license fees to inflation and expanding voluntary contribution programs.

Commissioners and staff also adopted four agency-wide goals:

- To protect, conserve, and enhance all aquatic resources.
- To provide for the protection of aquatic resource users.
- To address the expectations of anglers and boaters.
- To advocate the wise, safe use of Pennsylvania's aquatic resources.

photo-Spring Gearhart, PFBC

PFBC's strategic plan recognized the economic benefits of angling and boating. To meet demand, the Bureau of Fisheries raised and stocked more than 3.8 million adult trout in 2002, plus an additional one million fingerling trout. Moreover, one million steelhead were distributed in Lake Erie. And, to improve access to the Ohio River in Allegheny County, agency crews constructed the Kilbuck Access concrete launch ramp and 32 parking spaces. In Northampton County, anglers had access to a new launch ramp adjacent to the Lehigh River, and improvements were made to access points in Bradford, Pike, and Beaver counties.

Consistent with the new plan, boating safety was high on the agenda. In 2000, a boating safety education program consisted of eight videotaped courses that were made available to the public, sportsmen's organizations, and, particularly, schools, teachers, and summer camp youth. A test was given at the end of each video, overseen by a proctor who was, sometimes, a Commission staffer. Other educators included professors at colleges and universities, high school teachers, and members of boating and sportsmen's associations. Upon successfully completing the curriculum, students received a Boating Safety Education Certificate from PFBC.

Extensive educational programs were also implemented for users of high-speed watercraft, such as personal watercraft (PWC), better known as jet skis, which were becoming increasingly popular in the waning decades of the twentieth century. These courses were required, beginning in 2000, when the Commission instituted a regulation mandating that all persons wishing to operate a PWC to first receive a Boating Education Certificate. One such program consisted of eight hours of instruction completed with a 50-question test. Upon successful completion, participants earned a Commission-issued certificate (credit-card format). In 2000, alone, more than 30,000 boaters successfully completed these programs.

In addition to watercraft safety, operating a reliable boat requires proper maintenance. According to *Pennsylvania Angler & Boater* magazine author Alex Zidock Jr., "like the human circulatory system, unless your marine engine is kept clean of impurities, and if its flow is not restricted, it will contribute to long engine life." Here, Zidock was referring to engine oil. He advised that engine oil be changed regularly. As "engines used for boats receive a lot more punishment than automobile engines," Zidock provided advice on types of oils that should be used in particular types of engines and advised that used motor oil be disposed of properly.[2]

Humans weren't the only ones protected when it came to being on the water. K-9s figured into the picture as well. Take Stella, a Golden Retriever, who modeled a Kurgo Surf-n-Turf doggie life jacket. In 2000, there were four life jackets on the market for dogs. Ten years later eight models were available. Most were made of foam. Some were inflatable models. Life jackets for the pooch ranged in price from $20 to $100. When selecting life jackets for dogs, boaters were encouraged by PFBC to look for ease of fit and adjustment, comfort when worn dry, adjustment needed when wet, and the swimming characteristics of the dog.

When it came to the work of WCOs, January and February were usually slow months in terms of enforcement problems, at least according to WCO David Kaneski of northern Wayne County. In fact, he anticipated that the winter of 2000–2001 would be so slow that he occasionally ice fished on a nearby lake to garner a sense of how the fish were biting in the cold weather. However, the so-called slow season proved to be not too slow after all for Kaneski. On one occasion he attended the trial of a man who was accused of shooting at a fellow

WCO. "This would prove to be quite a learning experience," according to Kaneski. The defendant was found not guilty of any criminal charges but was guilty of two lower-level charges for which he paid fines. Moreover, Kaneski tallied 14 summary cases, three criminal cases, served two warrants, was in court for four days, and gave dozens of warnings.[3]

The work of WCOs wasn't always serious. In fact, it could sometimes be humorous. On one occasion WCO Martha Mackey of southern Allegheny County reported in 2000 that . . .

> "While patrolling a lake in a neighboring district, I came upon a path that led away from the lake into the woods to a secluded fishing spot. As I began to move farther into the wooded area, I could hear a woman shouting "hit me, hit me!
>
> "Intrigued, I continued to move cautiously along the path toward the lake, expecting—I'm not sure—what or worse. As I came nearer to the lake, I spotted a woman holding a fishing rod with the line in the water. With relief and amusement, I observed from a distance. Each time she was unsuccessful and the bobber broke the surface, she called out "hit me, hit me!"[4]

Marlene Gilmore-Luben, former front-desk secretary for the Northwest Region, in 2003, had an unusual experience when she received a phone call from a woman regarding her pet Wood Turtle. "This woman was quite concerned that her pet turtle was constipated. She had been feeding it lettuce and hamburger and was at her wit's end. How about letting the turtle go, I suggested. But she wanted no part of that. Then I suggested putting some vegetable oil in the hamburger." The trick must have worked. The woman never called again. Similarly, Gail Burkholder (currently in the Harrisburg Headquarters), then of the Southeast Law Enforcement Region, recalled in 2003 that "someone once called and wanted me to line them up with a list of fishing guides in Africa. I said, 'here, yes. But Africa, no.'"[5]

Citizen-anglers reported other unusual stories as well. Angler John Keller of Dover, York County, reported the following rare occurrence.

> "While fishing the York Haven Dam catwalk on the Susquehanna River, I had caught a 14-inch Largemouth Bass. But, as I was reeling it in, about 20 feet to my left was another angler yelling that he had also caught one. After a small tug-of-war, we realized that

we had the same fish. We noticed that I had hooked the bass on the right side of the mouth, and the other angler had hooked him on the left side of the mouth. How strange was that?

"As if I thought I had seen it all . . . I then hooked a rock bass on a shiner. As I reeled it in, I noticed that someone else had already caught the fish before but had cut the line because the fish had swallowed the hook. I had hooked the loop on the line, not the fish, and had reeled this fish in by the loop! What are the chances of that happening? I've been fishing about 15 years, and I never had either one ever happen to me. Yet, I had both happen all in one day!"[6]

In 2003, PFBC again faced conflict over the public's rights in another Commonwealth waterway. Along with DEP and DCNR, PFBC staff filed a complaint with the Court of Common Pleas of Huntingdon County, seeking a declaration that the Little Juniata River is a navigable river, that the lands below the ordinary low water mark are submerged lands owned by the Commonwealth, and that the public has the right of use and enjoyment of the river, including the right to fish, boat, wade, and recreate. The Commonwealth agencies also requested that the court enjoin the defendants from interfering with the public's rights in the Little Juniata River.

This litigation was initiated after the Commonwealth agencies received numerous complaints that the defendants verbally and physically harassed members of the public seeking to lawfully use a 1.3-mile section of the river and after the defendants hung cables with

January/February 2003

In 2002, Coldwater Unit Fisheries Technician Bob Weber shows one of the large Brown Trout caught while surveying Cedar Run, Tioga County. Summer intern Susan Avau assists in recording information on each fish.

photo-Art Michaels, PFBC

268   Chapter Seven

signs at the upstream and downstream ends of the section in dispute and posted other signs on the riverbanks warning the public not to trespass. The defendants were various individuals and entities associated with the operation of a private, for-profit, fly-fishing guiding business located on riparian property along the Little Juniata River at Spruce Creek.

In 2007, the trial court ruled in the Commonwealth's favor and found that the Little Juniata River is, indeed, a navigable water that is held in trust for the benefit of the public. In addition, the court permanently enjoined the defendants "from interfering with the public's rights in the Little Juniata, including the posting and/or hanging of signs, advertising the Little Juniata River as private waters and threatening, harassing, and otherwise attempting to exclude the public from fishing, boating, wading, and/or recreating on and in the Little Juniata River and the submerged lands owned by the Commonwealth."[7] The defendants initially appealed the decision to the Commonwealth Court of Pennsylvania. However, they later withdrew that appeal.

Pete Colangelo was pleased with the work of PFBC during his watch. When he decided to retire in mid-2003, a nationwide search was undertaken to find his replacement. Deputy Executive Director Dennis Guise filled the vacancy during the search process that took six months.

A Change in Leadership

The Commissioners then hired Douglas J. Austen Ph.D., who was sworn in as Executive Director at the Commission's quarterly meeting on January 27, 2004.

Waterways Conservation Officer Dawn Sapp checks an angler's license in southern Lancaster County in 2002.

He had 25-plus years of experience in natural resource and fisheries management. Austen had served as head of the Technical Support Section of the Illinois Department of Natural Resources and taught for the Natural Resources and Environmental Science program at the University of Illinois. In 1992, he earned a Ph.D. in Animal Ecology from Iowa State University and was recognized by the American Fisheries Society as a Certified Fisheries Professional. Austen continued the agency's mantra of "Protect, Conserve, and Enhance."

Austen's main message was: "there is no such thing as separate and conflicting environmental and conservation communities or agendas. Certainly there is a spectrum of opinions. The Fish & Boat Commission has been an active part of the Commonwealth's conservation and environmental movements. In my tenure as Executive Director, I hope to build upon this energy and forge new coalitions with the many entities that share the same common purpose, as well as to work collegially with those who don't. We all have a place at the table."[8]

Under Austen's leadership, the Commissioners and staff agreed that it would be a good idea to survey trout anglers to garner their views on various related matters. The Commissioners hired Virginia-based Responsive Management, which ranked among the nation's top consulting firms that engaged in such work. The findings were enlightening. with 1,500 anglers surveyed and 92 percent reporting contentment with fishing regulations. Moreover, most had a positive opinion of PFBC, as 74 percent ranked the agency excellent or good. About half of those surveyed were dissatisfied with the costs of a license and trout stamp,

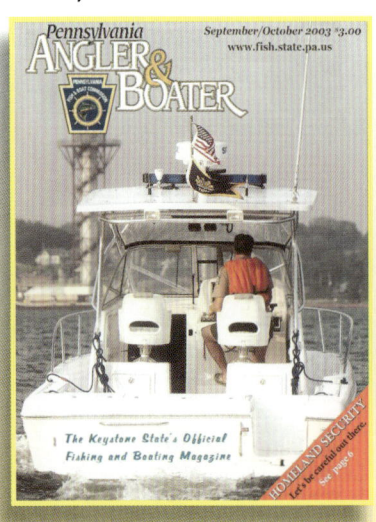

Hatchery fish stocking truck in 2003.

Chapter Seven

while the remainder thought that the price was fair. The majority thought that PFBC should be doing more to restore and protect water quality for wild trout (72 percent). And, 41 percent opposed stocking hatchery trout in streams where there were wild trout. This information was used to inform PFBC's new strategic plan that went into effect in the summer of 2005.

The three-to-five-year strategic plan reiterated the agency's mission:
- The encouragement, promotion, and development of fishery interests.
- The protection, propagation, and distribution of fish.
- The management of boating and operation of boats.
- The encouragement, promotion, and development of recreational boating interests.

The plan further delineated six specific strategies to accomplish and maintain its mission. In order to do as such, the plan stated that the Commission…

- Will position itself as an organization known for serving the fishing and boating public and the resources it protects.
- Will invest in activities, resources, and programs to increase boating and fishing participation in the Commonwealth.
- Will explore and implement methods to increase traditional and non-user, fee-based revenue.
- Will enhance relationships leading to partnership opportunities with stakeholder groups, corporations, natural resource agencies, non-governmental organizations, and others.
- Will develop the internal structure and processes needed to effectively protect and manage aquatic resources and fishing and boating activities.

Examples of the Bureau of Law Enforcement patrol fleet vehicles in 2004—The Thin Green Line.

- Will develop a coordinated agency-wide approach to aquatic resource management, protection, and conservation.

This was a tall order, but, not long after its adoption, PFBC staff and Commissioners began to take action. Consistent with PFBC's new strategic plan, working with municipalities to develop, rehabilitate, or improve boat access launches was high on the agenda. PFBC staff awarded $1.8 million in grants during the summer of 2005. This initiative was an important collaborative partnership, as many municipalities lacked funds to do so on their own. Some examples included:

- Harborcreek Township, Erie County: awarded $300,000 to provide a breakwall, launch ramps, and walking trails along Lake Erie.
- Ohioville Borough, Beaver County: garnered $190,000 to develop a community park with access roads, boat launches, and restrooms along Little Beaver Creek at the mouth of the Ohio River.
- Steelton Borough, Dauphin County: awarded $150,000 to complete the Susquehanna River Park and Boat Launch, a project already under construction.
- Hunlock Township, Luzerne County: received $30,000 to construct a launch ramp and stone parking lot for better access to the Susquehanna River.

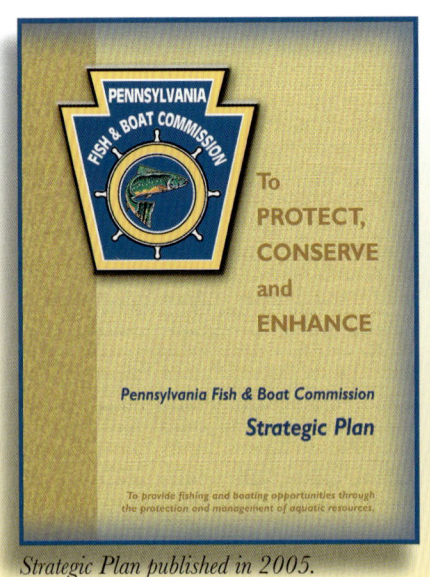

Strategic Plan published in 2005.

Muskellunge fingerlings stocked by PFBC in 2005.

Moreover, in 2008, the Commission awarded grants totaling $50,000 for sportfishing, boating, and aquatic resource educational programs. Grants were awarded to:

- Mount Lebanon School District: $5,000 for a program to introduce youngsters to fly fishing, including hands-on lessons and streamside field experiences.
- Perseus House Charter School of Excellence: $5,000 for its Fisheries and Aquatic Science Teaching Program to education children on aquatic life in the Great Lakes.
- Pennsylvania Trout Inc. (Pennsylvania Council of Trout Unlimited): $5,000 to fund Trout in the Classroom, an educational program on conservation, habitat and species protection, and stream ecology.

Similarly, the agency awarded $1.5 million to various municipalities through the Boating Facility Grant Program. Among the awardees were the Borough of Susquehanna in Susquehanna County, which received $54,000 to construct a new boat launch on the North Branch Susquehanna River; $185,000 to the Borough of Sharpsburg in Allegheny County to rehabilitate a boat launch facility along the Allegheny River; and $80,000 to Lehigh County to construct two new vault toilets at PFBC's Leaser Lake.

Beginning in the mid-1990s and provided free-of-charge, PFBC has produced a regularly updated series of region maps that contain prime fishing and boating locales across the state.

At right, beginning in 1988, the Commission started using portable backwall exhibits at sportshows it attended. The "Pennsylvania State Record Fish" exhibit was one of the most popular exhibits produced.

photo-Spring Gearhart, PFBC

March/April 2005
*Pennsylvania
Angler & Boater
cover by artist
Mark Susinno*

*Winter 2005 PLAY
newsletter
25th anniversary
edition
cover art
by Ted Walke*

274   *Chapter Seven*

Another important grant initiative was the Wild Resource Conservation Program (formerly the Wild Resource Conservation Fund). Monies from the U.S. Fish and Wildlife Service were matched with state funds derived from sales of Conserve Wild Resource license plates, donations, and the Commonwealth's Growing Greener programs. The program supported research, protection, and educational initiatives relating to Pennsylvania's natural heritage. Specific examples were fish surveys and inventories, acid mine drainage studies, and a habitat protection program for rattlesnakes. From 2005 to 2007, 30 projects were undertaken by organizations, such as nature conservancies, museums, colleges, and universities with funds totaling $1.2 million.

Educational Programs

When it came to educational programs, an important initiative was launched just prior to the implementation of the strategic plan. In 2004, the Youth Bass Anglers School (YBAS) was launched as a residential camp operated by the Commission in collaboration with DCNR and the Pennsylvania Bass Federation. The program targeted 14-to-17-year-olds who came to Penn State University's Stone Valley Recreation Area Civil Engineering Lodge along Perez Lake in Huntingdon County during July of each year. Youth were selected through a competitive application process that required them to write an essay on the importance of conservation. More than a dozen students comprised the first class and learned about fisheries biology and management, habitat improvement, watercraft safety, and the basic principles of conservation and

photos-Art Michaels, PFBC

environmental stewardship. Another education program started by the Commission was KARE or Keystone Aquatic Resource Education. This initiative was also provided to youth and taught fishing skills, safe fishing, and aquatic resource conservation.

Youth also assisted cooperative nursery programs. One was led by students from St. Mary's Area Middle School in Elk County. In 2004, science faculty members Murray Neeper and Wayne Fondoski worked with students and then Commission Cooperative Nursery Chief Cecil Houser to develop such a program. To raise funds, students founded the Helping Hands for Habitat Club raising $1,000, plus other in-kind contributions from organizations such as the Pennsylvania Army National Guard, to establish three raceway tanks that held 500 trout each, a pumphouse, waterlines, and a cistern.

Once other Commission fish-raising standards were met, Houser officially sanctioned the St. Mary's Middle School group as a member of the Commission's Cooperative Nursery Program in late 2004. Fish typically arrived at the nursery at the end of May or early June of each year. Of course, this posed a bit of a challenge as school wasn't in session during summer months. Weyerhaeuser Corporation stepped up to the plate. Company staff ran its own cooperative nursery program in nearby Johnsonburg, Elk County, and oversaw the St. Mary's project when school wasn't in session.

Another Commission initiative was the implementation of ice fishing clinics. With this program, anglers learned the basics of ice fishing, long a tradition in the Keystone State. In one instance, in

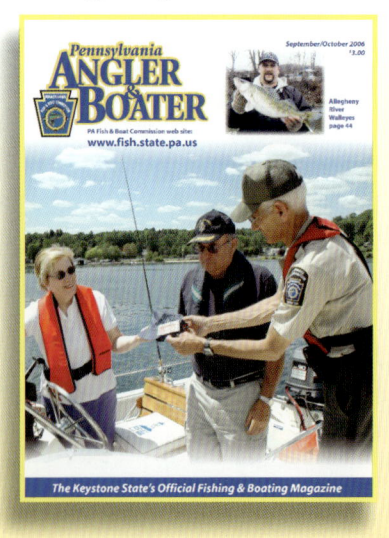

276   Chapter Seven

January 2004, WCO Thomas Edwards Jr. conducted a clinic for youth on the East and West Basin Ponds in Presque Isle State Park:

> "Arrangements were made with a local cooperative nursery to plant 300 fish in the East Basin, and we waited to see what would happen. We had coffee and hot chocolate and, more importantly, we had ice in which to drill holes. About 50 young, hard-water anglers participated. Unfortunately, the fish were not very cooperative and the catch was poor, but all participants seemed to have a good time."[9]

Edwards worked with WCO Edward Stuart to conduct another such clinic in February 2006.

In addition to educating youth about ice fishing, informing youth about reptiles and amphibians was part of PFBC's educational goals. For example, *Pennsylvania Angler & Boater* regularly featured articles about amphibian and reptile species and, in the Fall 2006 edition of the Pennsylvania League of Angling Youth (PLAY) newsletter (included as part of *Pennsylvania Angler & Boater* magazine), PFBC Southcentral Region Aquatic Resources Program Specialist Alice Stitt authored an educational group of articles for the newsletter about "Pennsylvania's Turtles."

> "Turtles are wonderful reptiles. They are easily recognized because of their protective shells. This great form of shelter, defense, and shielding has helped them survive for thousands of years. In Pennsylvania, we have 14 different turtle species. Some live on land

Beginning in 1997, PFBC's involvement in the Pennsylvania Water Trails program spurred the collaborative creation of more than 20 such trails by the end of the following decade.

photo-Art Michaels, PFBC; logo design-Ted Walke, PFBC

(terrestrial), some live in water (aquatic), and some live on land and in the water (semi-aquatic).

"All turtles have a shell. Each shell has a top, called a carapace, and a bottom called a plastron. The shell is made up of large, hard scales called scutes.

"Most turtles have 13 scutes on the top shell . . . (which) can come in many shapes, colors, and sizes. A turtle's skin is dry and scaly. All turtles lay eggs. Since a turtle is a reptile, it is cold-blooded, or ectothermic.

"In the winter, turtles need to hibernate. People who study turtles are call herpetologists."

Seal Salamander-
photo-Tom Diez

Redbellied Turtle-
photo-Andrew Shiels

Broadhead Skink-
photo-Tom Diez

For up-to-date species status and regulations, visit the Commission's website at **www.fishandboat.com.**

278   Chapter Seven

Stitt's article went on to describe various types of turtles, including those that are endangered:

"Pennsylvania has several threatened and endangered turtles. Candidate species are those that could become threatened or endangered (Blanding's Turtle). Threatened species (Redbellied Turtle) are those that may become endangered or extinct. Endangered species (Bog Turtle) are those that are in danger of extinction. These turtles are protected by federal and state laws and regulations. If you see or find one of these turtles, you should respect the laws and leave it alone."[10]

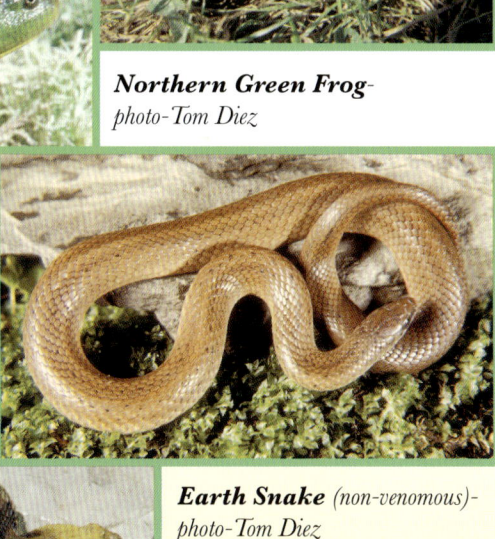

Northern Leopard Frog-
photo-Tom Diez

Northern Green Frog-
photo-Tom Diez

Earth Snake *(non-venomous)-*
photo-Tom Diez

Timber Rattlesnake-
yellow phase (venomous)
photograph by Tom Diez

As previously discussed, by the mid-to-late twentieth century, angling was no longer just a man's sport. Women increasingly fished (perhaps they always did so, but they just received less attention). *Pennsylvania Angler & Boater* editor Art Michaels featured one such angler, Misty Rotigel, in the July/August 2006, issue:

> "Misty Rotigel's ultimate Pennsylvania Fishing Adventure includes 'catching a bunch of steelhead by mid-morning, landing several monstrous Northern Pike by mid-afternoon with an occasional Smallmouth Bass, and topping off the day with sizeable Walleyes. As long as I am catching fish, I am happy. My father's teaching me to fish at a young age was an excellent introduction to the sport. I encourage women . . . to go fishing. Another useful way for women to try fishing is through the Fish & Boat Commission. Visit the Commission's website . . . and on the left side of the main page, click on Education. On that page click on Aquatic Resource Program Specialists (ARPS) and contact your regional ARPS for information on educational programs."

Misty's largest fish included a 20-inch Smallmouth Bass, a 22-inch Striped Bass, a 20.5-inch Walleye, a 19.5-inch Largemouth Bass, a 27-inch Northern Pike, and a carp of about 25 pounds.[11]

The "big business" nature of angling continued well into the twenty-first century, as it had for the better part of the twentieth century. Recreational fishing generated $1.65 billion per year in the Keystone

Angler Misty Rotigel is shown here in 2005 with a prize steelhead catch.

State, supported more than 14,000 jobs and generated $55 million in sales and income taxes. License sales in 2007 increased by 2.1 percent during 2006, while trout and salmon stamps increased by 1 percent. Total sales were nearly $25 million in 2007. At the same time boat registration and titling transfers increased by 2.4 percent with 222,765 transactions. In recognition of the important economic and recreational benefit of angling, newly inaugurated Governor Edward G. Rendell (2003–2011) purchased "fishing license no. 1" at the Pennsylvania Farm Show in 2003.

Besides implementing the strategic plan, numerous challenges remained for Austen and PFBC staff. One problem was deferred maintenance, especially at hatcheries and boating access sites. A related matter was the additional revenue needed by the Commission to meet day-to-day operating costs. Moreover, habitat improvement was needed, as 29 species of fish were on the threatened or endangered list maintained by PFBC. To address these issues, the Commissioners urged Governor Rendell and members of the General Assembly to enact House Bill 2155 to modestly increase license fees. Numerous organizations supported the legislation, including the Federation of Sportsmen's Clubs, the Boating Association of Southeast Pennsylvania, the Coalition of Concerned Anglers, and the Unified Sportsmen of Pennsylvania. Governor Rendell signed the bill into law in November 2004. Under Act 159, the resident annual fishing license fee increased to $21, while non-resident annual license fee went to $51. Trout stamps became $8, while the senior resident annual license fee was increased to $10.

Former Boating Education Safety Manager Dan Martin is shown in 2006 at Harrisburg's Garden Expo, where PFBC had an exhibit. While the show did not directly involve fishing and boating, it did involve much of the backyard habitat that were homes to many species of amphibians and reptiles.

WCOs remained quite busy at mid-decade. In 2005, alone, they issued (and courts adjudicated) 4,317 summary citations for fishing law violations and 3,486 citations for boating law violations. They also issued a record 34,000 warnings pertaining to watercraft safety and law compliance warnings. And, they conducted safety checks of 32,700 recreational watercraft.

To keep up with the need to enforce fishing and boating laws, the 2005 Waterways Conservation Officer Class graduated six individuals who were assigned throughout the Commonwealth. However, numerous vacancies remained and several retirements were on the horizon. Thus, in 2006, the Deputy Waterways Conservation Officers Class graduated 22 new officers. As with past programs, classes were held at the H. R. Stackhouse School of Fishery Conservation and Watercraft Safety in Centre County. Their agendas were quite full over the 16 days of formal training. To graduate, each individual had to complete 40 hours of lethal weapons training, as well as courses in constitutional law, fish identification, armed and unarmed self-defense, boat accident response and investigation, hazardous materials identification, and CPR and first aid. Once this training was complete, they were placed on probationary status until they successfully logged 150 hours of on-the-job training within one year.

Probably the most difficult task of any WCO is to investigate deaths resulting from boating accidents on Pennsylvania's waters. Nine fatalities were reported in 2005. While they were all tragic, the most striking was the case of a 20-year-old young man who was inebriated when he

PFBC educator Ryan Walt is shown in 2007 providing a child with a "Pennsylvania Fishes" poster. This and many other publications are provided free to attendees at sportshows.

photo-
Spring Gearhart, PFBC

282 *Chapter Seven*

jumped overboard from his paddleboat on Acre Lake in Susquehanna County. It was about midnight on July 7th. The boat had no lights, flotation devices, or other safety equipment. There were three others on the boat who heard the young man cry out for help as he was drowning. They couldn't see him and, soon, he fell silent, making it impossible to find him in the darkness. He was found floating, face down, a short while later. Alcohol and boating clearly don't mix. An earlier tragedy involved a 13-year-old boy who was struck by a propeller of a 19-foot motorboat. The boy was in the water behind the boat when its operator, a 15-year-old friend (accompanied by his father), thrust the engine in reverse. His friend's body was badly mangled.

In the spring of 2008, WCO Mark Sweppenhiser of the Southcentral Region investigated a complaint regarding a discarded home heating oil tank floating in the Yellow Breeches Creek in Cumberland County. When he arrived at the scene he found a campsite littered with rubbish that included drug paraphernalia and empty beer cans. When he further explored the area, he also found young marijuana plants still in their cultivation containers. It was clear to him that the site was occupied quite frequently, by whom, however, remained a mystery. Sweppenhiser contacted the Pennsylvania State Police Vice Unit who agreed to take over the investigation. The State Police knew all-too-well that remote locales on stream banks were prime spots for cultivating marijuana plants: the sites were secluded, soil was usually rich, and there was ample water supply. One of the tactics used by the State Police was to conduct helicopter fly-overs of suspected areas.

In 2007, Commission biologists surveyed some of Marsh Creek Lake's bounty, including many Yellow Perch like the one shown.

photo-PFBC staff

Based on Sweppenhiser's tip, they did as such along the Yellow Breeches and found numerous marijuana patches which were later destroyed. The culprits were never caught.

As the 2006 trout season approached, PFBC implemented new policies with regard to stocking the popular species. One change was that several new waterways were added to the streams for dispatching 4.2 million adult trout. These included Sandy Creek in Venango County and Tulpehocken Creek in Berks County. Each would be stocked with preseason and inseason fish. Because of poor water quality, Schrader Creek in Bradford County was removed from the stocking list. Yet, on the bright side, Lyman Lake in Potter County and Mix Run in Cameron County were to be once again stocked after being off of the Commission's list for several years due to flood damage on embankments of Mix Run and concerns over dam safety on Lyman Lake.

In 2006, PFBC educational programs and efforts were quite impressive as well:

- More than 78 Family Fishing Programs took place that provided family-friendly fishing opportunities to 1,628 people.
- More than 340 teachers participated in PFBC workshops on a variety of resource and conservation topics. Most workshops were for graduate-level credits.
- More than 1,000 classrooms received the PLAY newsletter.
- PFBC partners offered angling education programs for 700 participants.
- PFBC staff spoke at more than 400 conferences and events.
- PFBC boating courses were taken by 12,000 residents, and 11,000 passed PFBC's online and correspondence boating courses.

One of the Commission's most innovative education-related initiatives was the Fishing Tackle Loaner Program. More than 40 sites across the state provided tackle to the public, free of charge. Residents could borrow rods, reels, and tackle boxes full of fishing items, much the same way as they could borrow a book from a library. PFBC partnered with anglers associations, tackle manufacturers, and several state parks to provide the programs. Keystone State Park in Derry, Black Moshannon State Park in Philipsburg, and Ricketts Glen State Park in Benton were among the tackle loaner sites.

One item of fishing gear that PFBC didn't loan was the bow. Harkening back to a time when tackle was not all that sophisticated (and even further back, considering that Native Americans bowfished), some anglers liked this "low-tech" form of fishing, according to *Pennsylvania Angler & Boater* contributor Linda Steiner:

> "Some bow anglers pursue their sport with technologically advanced equipment. But others prefer their bowfishing low-tech. No wheels on their bows or motors on their boats. Just stick bows and canoes. Nearly any stick bow is suitable for bowfishing. What's a stick bow? In archery phraseology, it's an old-style bow . . . that doesn't have the cables and wheels of the modern compound bow."

Steiner noted that carp were the best species for bowfishing, because they are large, easily visible, and usually swim near the surface. They were easy to strike with an arrow shot from a good, old-fashioned bow. But, "if the shot is missed, bring in the arrow and line and recoil it, cleaning the weeds away. Get the bow in hand again, give the paddler the nod, and move on toward your next low-tech bowfishing opportunity."[12]

Another unique way of angling was the use of a so-called "belly boat" or, simply, a tube. According to the Fish & Boat Commission, "tubing gives you access to that narrow band of water just offshore, which is too deep for wade fishermen and too shallow for boat

As shown in 2007, these wooden porcupine cribs, which are sunk in a lake to provide fish-spawning structure, continue to be popular devices for lake habitat improvement with PFBC and its partners.

photo-PFBC staff

2000–2015　285

fishermen." It was the preferred way to fish for Bob Johns and his wife Dorothy, who used tubes to fish for bass, panfish, and steelheads at Presque Isle Bay. They were quite good at it: "Bob's office is lined with Commission Angler Awards for trophy steelhead and Brown Trout . . . all taken from tubes."[13]

However, catastrophe was never far off. In June 2006, 31 Norfolk Southern rail cars derailed near Gardeau, in McKean County. Liquid sodium hydroxide spilled into wetlands and Big Fill Run, a tributary of the Sinnemahoning-Portage Creek. Besides polluting the water, soils, sediments, and groundwater were impacted, and thousands of fish and other aquatic life were destroyed. Eventually, Norfolk Southern paid a record $7.35 million to the state with $3.675 million allocated to PFBC and the remainder to DEP.

An ongoing challenge was cleaning-up the Chesapeake Bay and the Susquehanna River that flowed into the Bay. As part of an agreement between Pennsylvania, Maryland, and Virginia, Pennsylvania undertook a major effort to reduce its pollutant load. In 2006, Pennsylvania was ahead of each state in planting riparian buffers—600 miles in all—along the Susquehanna River and its tributaries. The benefits of such buffers were many as they provided shade trees to reduce water temperature in summer, stabilize stream banks to reduce erosion, and help to trap pollutants. Pennsylvania received a grade of "B+" for its efforts in developing buffers. However, cleaning-up the Chesapeake remains a significant challenge.

photo-Art Michaels, PFBC

286   Chapter Seven

However good Pennsylvania's efforts might have been, the overall health of the bay remained seriously impaired. According to the Chesapeake Bay Foundation, in 2007, the Chesapeake Bay scored a mere 28 points out of 100 as a result of assessing 13 different measures used to monitor its health. These measures were divided among the three major categories of pollution, habitat, and fishing. As Austen put it, "a score of 100 reflects the pristine state of the bay about the time of Captain John Smith's 'discovery.'" There was, however, some good news. Besides Pennsylvania's grade of B+ for stream bank improvements, higher numbers of Striped Bass were found in the bay than in previous decades, and at least some clean-up efforts were underway. However, Austen warned, "the state of the bay might as well be the state of the Susquehanna. Invasive species and pollutants that we are just learning to measure (such as household products including antimicrobial soaps) . . . would create a report card for the Susquehanna that may not be positive."[14]

Another very important issue was mercury levels in waterways and fish. Mercury often occurs naturally in the environment and is released by natural sources such as volcanoes and soils. Dental fillings usually contain trace amounts. The human body typically processes and

Dock Street Dam, Susquehanna River at Harrisburg: Also known as "drowning machines," low-head dams, such as this, and others across the state are marked with danger buoys and signs administered through PFBC.

eliminates mercury. However, industrial facilities and processes caused the greatest threat to humans and the environment, as mercury can be found in fossil fuels, medical and hazardous waste, and pulp and paper milling. It is not uncommon for mercury to find its way into waterways where it accumulates in fish tissue and affects reproduction, hinders growth, and decreases the ability to avoid predators. To address this matter, PFBC issued an advisory suggesting that pregnant women and those of childbearing age, young children, and individuals who consumed fish on a regular basis, should limit fish intake to once per week.

During Austen's tenure, the agency faced its critics, as it always had. One was that the agency should exercise caution in stocking trout in streams where wild trout could be found. In fact, one critic argued that this policy would cause Ralph Abele to "turn in his grave." Austen's answer was simple. "Nonsense" that echoed Abele's rubber stamp apparatus that imprinted "Bullshit" on correspondence with which he disagreed. Consistent with Operation FUTURE, which was enacted during Abele's tenure, stocking of hatchery trout was a common practice in streams where wild trout were in very limited supply. Austen pointed out that "determining desirable fishing levels and taking action to attain such levels are the foundation of fisheries management" and that "in many of the wild trout waters that are stocked, we are creating a fishery in a stream that simply doesn't have the environmental conditions to

Nothing can replace the excitement or fun of an angler's "first catch." As many remark, you're then "hooked for life"!   *photo-PFBC staff*

288   *Chapter Seven*

photos-PFBC Photo Contest

support natural reproduction." This was good policy, he concluded. And, Ralph Abele would not only support such policy. He advocated for it during his time as Executive Director.[15]

As Austen's tenure came to an end, overall, the agency was in good shape financially, the majority of anglers and boaters were pleased with recreational opportunities that Pennsylvania had to offer, and the Commission was fully embracing the new technology of the twenty-first century: a Twitter account was launched in early 2010 and PFBC pioneered the use of a Geographic Information System (GIS) to spatially organize natural resource information.

continued on page 292

photo-Spring Gearhart, PFBC

photo-PFBC Photo Contest

2000–2015   **289**

July/August 2009 **Pennsylvania Angler & Boater** • *photograph by Chris Gorsuch*

2009 Fishing License promotion • *photograph by Spring Gearhart*

"John is a Doer"

John A. Arway was appointed to the job of Executive Director on March 2, 2010. John is a graduate of the University of Pittsburgh and earned a master's degree in aquatic biology from Tennessee Technological University. Initially, he had thoughts of becoming a physician. Rather, he dedicated his career to protecting and enhancing Pennsylvania's aquatic resources and conservation.

John's interest in nature and fishing began in his childhood when he frequented a cottage on Cranberry Glade Lake in Somerset County. The cottage was owned by his Aunt Ann and Uncle Nick. John had free range of the lake and woodlands. He caught his first Bluegill when he was five-years-old and "one summer my uncle offered me a quarter for every Bluegill I caught. I brought him a stringer of 25. That was the last time he offered to pay me!"[16]

His tenure with the Commission began during the Abele era. John's first post was as a semi-skilled laborer, right out of graduate school. In

In 2010, Bureau of Law Enforcement Assistant to the Director Lt. Colonel Donald L. Lauver (left) and Executive Director John A. Arway (right) are shown at the steps of the State Capitol Building in Harrisburg with the Nineteenth WCO Class: (from left) Richard Daniels Jr., Aaron Lupacchini, Eric Davis, Daniel Nietupski, Anthony Beers, and Chad Doyle.

photo-Spring Gearhart, PFBC

292   Chapter Seven

1981, he was promoted to a biologist position, then to Division Chief of Environmental Services, where he served for 20 years. Ralph Abele was his mentor who, to Arway, was a visionary likewise committed to conservation and resource protection. "John is a doer," said former Commission President Tom Shetterley, "He doesn't just talk about problems, he solves them. He's not a 'paperwork' person. He's someone who gets things done."[17]

Throughout his career with PFBC, Arway has remained a staunch advocate for conservation and environmental protection for the public's benefit as spelled-out in Article 1, Section 27 of the Pennsylvania Constitution *(see page 157)*. In addition, John has testified as an expert witness in more than 100 cases before civil, criminal, and administrative courts, and he has published many papers and given innumerable talks discussing the impact of pollution, habitat disturbances, fish biology, and many other topics. He's an expert, and those who know him can attest to that.

Arway remains an angler and especially enjoys fishing for panfish, Walleyes, trout, bass, and steelhead. As Executive Director, he remains committed to managing both wild and stocked fish. "Pennsylvania has a variety of waters that can support both. They don't have to be competing fisheries." He also remains committed to Abele's mantra of "Resource First" and "Protect, Conserve, and Enhance." In fact, he went "back to the future" when he renamed his feature introductory article in *Pennsylvania Angler & Boater*, "Straight Talk," as did Ralph Abele.[18]

This is one of the many award-winning photographs submitted for more than a decade to PFBC's Annual Photography Contest. This photo, submitted for 2010's contest, is by James Gilson of Port Royal. His photo won first place in its category and "Best of Show."

Arway remained committed to the idea that PFBC should spend only what it earned. Quite simply, the budget must balance and surpluses were to be carefully guarded for the proverbial "rainy day." When Arway took the helm, PFBC had a complement of 432 full-time staff positions and more than 100 seasonal and temporary employees. Moreover, a major project that was already underway was $27 million worth of upgrades to its hatcheries and other agency infrastructure. Total fishing license and boat registration revenue when he took office in Fiscal Year 2010–2011 was $54.5 million.

John touted the need to diversify PFBC's funding base and lobbied for a variety of alternative funding sources, such as using a portion of the Commonwealth's six-percent sales tax for conservation and environmental-based programs (this would be based on the amount that anglers and boaters spend every year); implementing a consumptive water-use fee; dedicating a substantive portion of the Oil Company Franchise Tax derived from gasoline boater use; and for PFBC to share in a Marcellus Shale impact fee and severance tax (at the time of this writing, Pennsylvania does not have a severance tax for Marcellus).

Among Arway's first major tasks was working with staff and the Commissioners to develop a new strategic plan for the agency. The five-year plan had a simple mission: Resource First. The plan set the vision of improving fishing and boating opportunities and for conservation of the Commonwealth's natural resources. Core values in this strategic plan included good stewardship of the Commonwealth's aquatic resources and working collaboratively as a team to effect positive change.

John expressed pride that shad fishing continued to improve, especially on the Delaware River. Agency staff confirmed the improvement. "Contrary to what you may hear" said PFBC Fisheries Biologist Michael Hendricks, "shad fishing in the Delaware River has been excellent, but many anglers seem to have abandoned shad fishing. (My son) Nick and I fished out of a popular boat ramp and we were the only anglers there. (Many) young shad were documented in 2005 and 2007, resulting in a large number of five-year-old fish returning in 2010 and six-year-old fish returning in 2011." As a result, Hendricks concluded, "In 2012, I expect good numbers of large, seven-year-old fish."

Hendricks further described the experience of his young son Nick: "A few years ago, Nick caught a shad that ate the dart three times before he hooked it on the fourth try. When you see a shad eat the dart, the tendency is to strike quickly, but often you are too quick. The shad will turn away, then do a complete 360-degree turn, and strike again. On the fourth try, Nick was able to control his adrenaline and wait until the shad had taken the dart!"[19]

On September 30, 2011, Commissioners and staff participated in a public ceremony dedicating Spring Creek Canyon in Centre County as a Cooperative Management Area. This was a significant collaborative event. Nearly 1,900 acres of land adjacent to Spring Creek were dedicated for public recreational use. The process to make the land public began in 2005 when DCNR hired a private consulting firm,

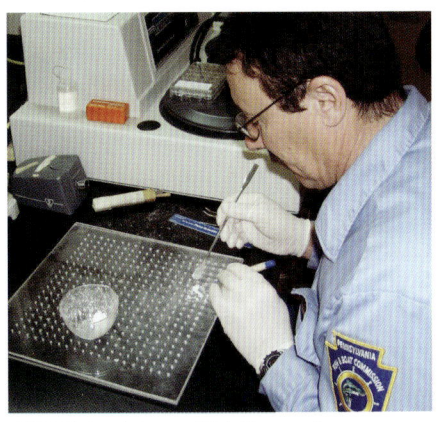

PFBC Anadromous Fish Restoration Unit Leader Mike Hendricks

On September 30, 2011, a dedication and ribbon-cutting ceremony was held at Spring Creek Canyon Cooperative Management Area, Centre County, near Benner Spring State Fish Hatchery. Pictured (left to right) are Commissioner David J. Putnam, Pennsylvania Game Commission; Commissioner David W. Schreffler, Pennsylvania Game Commission; Bruce A. McPheron, Ph.D; Commissioner G. Warren Elliott, Pennsylvania Fish & Boat Commission; State Representative Michael K. Hanna; Division of Outreach Chief Ted Walke, Pennsylvania Fish & Boat Commission; State Representative Kerry A. Benninghoff; John Elnitski; Marirosa Lamas; Bureau of Wildlife Habitat Management Director William Capouillez, Pennsylvania Game Commission; Barbara J. Christ, The Pennsylvania State University; Secretary John E. Wetzel, Pennsylvania Department of Corrections; and PFBC Executive Director John A. Arway.

Environmental Planning Designs Inc., to gather public input, develop a feasibility study, and present a master plan for responsible management of the land, water, and natural resources of the beautiful canyon that is also home to PFBC's Benner Spring and Stackhouse facilities. With legislative support, the Department of Corrections ceded 141 acres (Rockview State Correctional Institution is nearby and owned the land), the Pennsylvania Game Commission 1,211 acres, Pennsylvania State University 451 acres, and Benner Township 25 acres for public use. Spring Creek is widely recognized as a premier wild Brown Trout fishery with a portion of the creek having a rich heritage as Fisherman's Paradise.

Another milestone was reached on January 31, 2012, as the Pennsylvania Fish & Commission held its 100th quarterly business meeting. Over the course of the agency's history, these meetings were held to discuss various issues ranging from budgets and finances to propagation and engineering projects. Following Arway's recommendations, at this meeting, the Commissioners allocated $4,000 to purchase a public fishing access site and conservation easement along Fishing Creek in the Upper Susquehanna-Lackawanna watershed. Commissioners also voted to increase the number of commercial seine licenses for Lake Erie from 10 to 40 and approved a $270,000 grant for the Wildlands Conservancy to develop a water trail and access area along the Lehigh River in Carbon, Northampton, and Lehigh counties.

In May 2011, state legislators, U.S. Coast Guard, boating organizations, and PFBC participated in "Ready, Set, Inflate!" at the State Capitol Complex. As part of this special event highlighting the importance of life jackets, attendees were asked to wear and simultaneously activate an inflatable life jacket in order to be counted in a national record-setting campaign. In addition, attendees had the opportunity to sign a "Wear It Pennsylvania!" pledge indicating their personal commitment to wearing a life jacket while boating.

photo–Spring Gearhart, PFBC; logo design–Ted Walke, PFBC

296   Chapter Seven

Awards were presented as well. The Pennsylvania American Water Company was recognized for opening five reservoirs in Lackawanna County for public fishing while PFBC Northeast Region WCO Walter Buckman received an Outstanding Service Award for his efforts in working with the company to provide access to its reservoirs. The meeting was topped-off by an evening program celebrating the Commonwealth's fly fishing heritage. Expert fly anglers from organizations such as Pennsylvania Trout Unlimited and its Cumberland Valley Chapter demonstrated their techniques and discussed fly tying and other aspects of the sport for an audience of 130.

As in previous years, Trout Unlimited remained a consistent partner with PFBC. Consider, for example, the contributions of the Chestnut Ridge chapter in the Laurel Highlands counties of Fayette and Somerset. The organization was founded in 1995 by anglers concerned about the water quality of the Youghiogheny River and its tributaries. Watershed restoration and educational programs headed their agenda. Using monies collected from various fundraising events and by partnering with the Western Pennsylvania Coalition for Abandoned Mine Reclamation, as well as the Miller Brewing Company's Friends of the Field Program, the chapter built a permanent anoxic limestone treatment facility on the headwaters of Glade Run. Soon after, Brook Trout were distributed in the stream with the help of PFBC. By 2010, water quality improved as did the abundance and diversity of aquatic life.

photo–Spring Gearhart, PFBC

Family Fishing Festivals

In 2011, PFBC began hosting Family Fishing Festivals at locations across the state. First, in May, and then May and June in subsequent years. The festivals are held in conjunction with "Take Me Fishing in PA" month and help new anglers prepare and look forward to the two annual Fish-for-Free Days held on or near Memorial Day and on Independence Day, July 4. "Family Fishing Festivals are free educational events designed for families with little or no fishing experience," said

GIFFORD PINCHOT STATE PARK • May 5

KEYSTONE STATE PARK • May 12

CORE CREEK COUNTY PARK • May 19

Carl Richardson, manager of the Education Section. "Participating families learn basic fishing skills and have the opportunity to practice those skills while fishing together during the program." As shown in the photos below from the festivals held in 2012, learning fishing skills is definitely a family affair.

Fish-For-Free Days
Your Fishing Holidays!

logo design-
Ted Walke, PFBC

photos-Spring Gearhart

photos-Jeff Decker

photos- Ted Walke

2000–2015 299

Arway's Passion

Like Ralph Abele, Arway can be outspoken when he finds an issue about which he was passionate. For example, in late 2012, he began to take on the very public issue of pollution and impairment of the Susquehanna River, especially in regard to Smallmouth Bass. "The river . . . is in very serious trouble," he said. Its main problems included rising temperatures and oxygen levels and pH that exceed protection criteria for warmwater fish. Moreover, "dissolved phosphorus levels are increasing at exponential rates while total nutrient load is gradually declining—a good thing for the Chesapeake Bay but not for our river," according to Arway.

Some young bass had "gross lesions and sores from bacterial infections which cause them to die, and we have started seeing those same types of lesions on the older adult bass." It was "even more frustrating that those who are in the position to do something about it won't even admit that there is a problem." As a result, PFBC restricted fishing on the river "contrary to our very mission." Arway concluded that "we need to take action now and not wait until the last bass is caught from the river to realize that we have a problem."[20]

Arway attempted to convince DEP of the problem in the spring of 2012. He wanted the river to be declared impaired under provisions of the Clean Water Act. This would mean that the river would be subject to certain federal criteria which regulate discharges of pollutants and would require studies to determine and prioritize the causes of fish diseases. Much to Arway's frustration, DEP refused to do so and

For more information and photographs about the Susquehanna River impairment issue, visit **www.fishandboat.com/susq-impairment.htm**.

argued that the science was inconclusive. More study was needed and definitive conclusions spelled-out.

This wasn't a new problem. In 2009, PFBC learned that Smallmouth Bass were negatively impacted by trace chemicals and pharmaceuticals that pass through waste water treatment facilities. In fact, from 2006 to 2009, a staggering 68 percent of total Smallmouth Bass died from Sunbury to York Haven. A variety of pollutants were the likely culprits. In 2009, PFBC allocated $200,000 to further study the problem in collaboration with the U.S. Geological Survey and DEP.

The Rendell Administration wasn't entirely convinced of the severity of stream pollution in the Commonwealth, especially in the Susquehanna River. Officials wanted more studies. The same remained true following Rendell's tenure. Though it remained difficult to convince the administration of Governor Tom Corbett (2011–2015) that the Susquehanna River had its problems, Corbett himself enjoyed the outdoors, and he and his staff annually took kayak trips during the summer on various rivers of the Commonwealth. Arway and PFBC staff joined him on numerous occasions. He and the Governor frequently discussed serious matters, such as the importance of fishing and boating for the Pennsylvania economy, the problems of invasive species, and the potential risks posed by the expanding Marcellus Shale natural gas development across the state.

Arway also seized such opportunities to "coach" the Governor on less serious matters—such as the basics of fly fishing: "I had the personal opportunity to give the Governor a lesson in fly casting. After explaining the basic methods of what fly casting is all about—casting a line to carry an object which imitates some form of food that a fish wants to eat and allowing gravity and river currents to do the rest—the Governor tried his hand at it and remarked that he may want to become a more serious angler one day." Arway concluded that, "Once he feels the tug at the end of the line, he'll be hooked on fishing!" Corbett was "hooked" before getting lessons from Arway. He officially purchased a fishing license at the January 2011 Farm Show in Harrisburg.[21]

Yet, the impact of pollution on fish in the Susquehanna River persisted. On Election Day in November 2014, Arway was fishing with a friend who caught a Smallmouth Bass that had a tumor on its lower jaw. The story was reported by many media outlets and was a sign that . . .

> "the river is calling for our help with yet another sign of abnormality. Lesions and sores on young of-year bass continue to appear annually in our collections since 2005, blotchy bass syndrome appearing and now spreading throughout the (Susquehanna River) basin, high rates of intersex in bass caused by exposure to endocrine disrupting chemicals (EDCs) coming from sewage treatment plant outfalls and other anthropogenic sources, unprecedented algae blooms fueled by dissolved phosphorus, and low dissolved oxygen and high pH conditions exceeding protection limits for warm water fish."[22]

Insufficient forest buffers, agricultural runoff, outdated sewage treatment plants, herbicides, and even runoff from suburban lawn fertilizers added to the problem. In late 2015, DEP issued a report that concluded that herbicides and endocrine disrupting compounds (EDCs) are likely causes contributing to the Smallmouth Bass population decline. The report also identified parasites and pathogens as likely causes. "The report . . . confirms what we've said all along, that the Susquehanna River is sick and needs our help before it's too late. The next step is to identify the sources of the herbicides and EDCs and to develop plans to reduce them in the river."[23]

PFBC launched its "Save Our Susquehanna" or S.O.S. campaign to save the river on June 2, 2015, by announcing that a portion of license sales and proceeds from a $10 S.O.S. fishing license button would be dedicated to funding water and soil conservation projects along the river, where young Smallmouth Bass population had been plagued through the last decade by illness and elevated mortality rates. To kick off the campaign, PFBC pledged $50,000 in matching funds. By the end of the year, concerned citizens have raised more than $29,000 for the S.O.S. campaign, including a $1,000 donation from the Enola Sportsmen's Association in

poster design-Andrea Feeney, PFBC

S.O.S.
SAVE OUR SUSQUEHANNA!

BUY and DISPLAY a 2015 PA "S.O.S." Fishing License Button TODAY!

Help to raise funds through the Pennsylvania Fish & Boat Commission (PFBC) to help the Susquehanna River and its Smallmouth Bass fishery.

$10.00 PER BUTTON

All PFBC profits contribute to funding projects to reduce known sources of pollution in critical areas where diseased bass have been found in the Susquehanna River in Pennsylvania.

The purchase of an Alternate Fishing License Button is optional in order to fish in Pennsylvania and is only available to current adult and youth fishing license holders who possess a valid Pennsylvania fishing license that enables them to fish the entire year. Use of a current button meets the fishing license display requirement as long as the angler has a license certificate in their possession while fishing. Reference the 2015 Fishing Summary or visit www.GoneFishingPa.com for additional information.

You can order your S.O.S. license button online
GoneFishingPa.com

Cumberland County and a $5,000 donation from the Fishing Creek Sportsmen's Association in Columbia County.

In addition, in December 2015, the Commission announced a partnership with the non-profit Ralph W. Abele Conservation Scholarship Fund to launch an online "FirstGiving" fundraising site for the Susquehanna River, broadening the agency's efforts to save the ailing river. Individuals can donate through the agency's website. According to John Arway:

> "Direct fundraising is an unusual step for a state government agency, but we thought that there are many people who care

about the river and would want to be able to contribute to our 'S.O.S.—Save Our Susquehanna' campaign. The connection to the Ralph W. Abele Conservation Scholarship Fund was the perfect step in expanding the reach of the campaign, since Mr. Abele was a leader in conservation and loved the river. The fund was set up to provide for tax-deductible contributions to the campaign with the funding being used by the Commission for projects to improve the water quality of the Susquehanna and its tributaries. This is an opportunity to carry on Mr. Abele's legacy by further raising awareness of the issues plaguing the Susquehanna River. At the same time, the online site will help deliver a conservation message to a far greater audience and provide a mechanism for others to contribute to a fund to help the river.

"The 'Save Our Susquehanna' message is resonating with anglers, with sportsmen's clubs, and with others who care about the river. I'm optimistic that with the new FirstGiving site, we will raise and exceed the $50,000 from anglers, other conservationists, and anyone who cares about our natural resources and supports our efforts to do everything in our power to protect and conserve them. Once we raise $50,000, the S.O.S.—Save Our Susquehanna! campaign will have its first $100,000 to begin working on projects to fix the river."[24]

Marcellus Shale

Drilling for natural gas extraction from Marcellus shale is extant in Pennsylvania. Drilling has proceeded at a lightning pace with several thousand wells drilled between 2010 and 2015, alone. Marcellus represents yet another major wave of resource extraction in the Commonwealth's history, preceded by the extraction of other fossil fuels such as coal, oil, and natural gas. Marcellus Shale is a fine-grained rock formation left behind by ocean sediments that were deposited some 390-million years ago. Natural gas formed within the sediment in a 50- to 300-foot-thick rock layer usually located about a mile underground. State-of-the-art drilling techniques are employed to bore vertically, then horizontally, followed high-pressure, water-sand mixtures to "frack" or fracture the rock formations to release natural gas. Incredibly, the so called "fracking" process uses three to six million gallons of water per well, much of it trucked-in from off-site supplies. Less than a quarter of the water is recovered. Marcellus well pads are typically five acres in size. Some sites can have several wells.

Marcellus gas well drilling has been consistently controversial in Pennsylvania. Environmentalists and conservationists express concerns when it comes to the large quantities of water needed for drilling and the pollution potential of ground water supplies. On the other hand, the industry points to its safety record and its use of state-of-the-art safe drilling methods. And, public policymakers remain divided on the extent to which the industry should be regulated and taxed.

Drilling is mainly regulated by DEP rules regarding well permitting and development, disturbances to habitat and the environment, and waste disposal. Moreover, because large quantities of water are withdrawn from Pennsylvania's major rivers, the Susquehanna River Basin Commission and Delaware River Basin Commission each regulate such withdrawals. PFBC works closely with these agencies to ensure habitat and species protection. Like other agencies, PFBC has its concerns when it comes to the cumulative impact of drilling and well pads that tend to cluster in resource-rich areas of the Commonwealth, such as northcentral Pennsylvania; water pollution which may occur as a result of sedimentation and the release or spill of chemically-laced fluids; land and stream disturbances caused by heavy equipment; and reduced water quantity especially during low-flow or drought periods.

The Commission faced a critical decision when the industry approached Executive Director Arway asking him to consider entering into water access agreements on Commission-owned or controlled lakes and properties. As indicated, drilling for shale requires enormous amounts of water. Better access to local water sources enables the industry to be more productive. The Commissioners granted Arway the authority to consider case-by-case water access and natural gas leasing requests and granted full autonomy to PFBC staff to make professional decisions as to whether there would be a negative impact on aquatic resources and water quality (there would be no wells or well pads on PFBC sites). This was a huge move for the agency, but, as Arway put it, "the reality is that this industry is here to stay, (and) I did not reach my decision without much thought, analysis and consternation."[25]

However, Arway didn't shy away from expressing his concerns. Excessive consumption of water is a serious threat to the Commonwealth's waters and fisheries. John called it "Highway

Robbery." "My dad always taught me that if you borrowed something, you should always return it in a better condition than when you received it. Unfortunately, this isn't the case for some of our Commonwealth property. We haven't paid much attention to those using our water resources, because they are so abundant." He continued, "In 2003, it was estimated over 10 billion gallons per day were being withdrawn from surface and ground waters. Activities such as power plant use, bottled water withdrawals, Marcellus natural gas well drilling, and other industrial activities take water directly from our streams, lakes, and rivers, and it is not returned." Natural resources, such as water, are held in trust for the public. However, "water is literally being taken without compensation, and it makes me mad." The culprit is an industry—mainly Marcellus—where "water that is being borrowed . . . every day for industrial processes and is returned to our streams in a degraded condition."

Pennsylvania's water protection regulations made it entirely legal to do as such so long as industries received a National Pollutant Elimination System Permit from DEP. However, water quality was still degraded. "Our streams, rivers, and lakes are being taken advantage of, and we should demand just compensation. Some of this cost is currently being borne by many of us when we pay our water bills." However, degraded water flows downstream and, when it enters a public water supply, additional purification treatment costs are passed on to the public. "Speak out and let your elected officials know that you are mad and expect to be compensated for the damages. The fish are depending on it."[26]

From 2005 to early 2011, DEP permitted the drilling of 21,075 gas wells. There were some environmental issues. In 2010–2011, DEP cited 43 drilling companies for a total of 1,435 violations. Because of the growing threat that Marcellus Shale poses to waterways and the natural environment, PFBC partnered with several colleges and conservation groups—such as King's College in Wilkes-Barre and the Western Pennsylvania Conservancy—to visit and assess headwater tributaries to determine which ones merited the greatest protection. Water temperature, dissolved oxygen, pH levels, the wild trout population, as well as the impact of suburban sprawl and agricultural runoff were assessed in these streams, the majority of which had never before been analyzed.

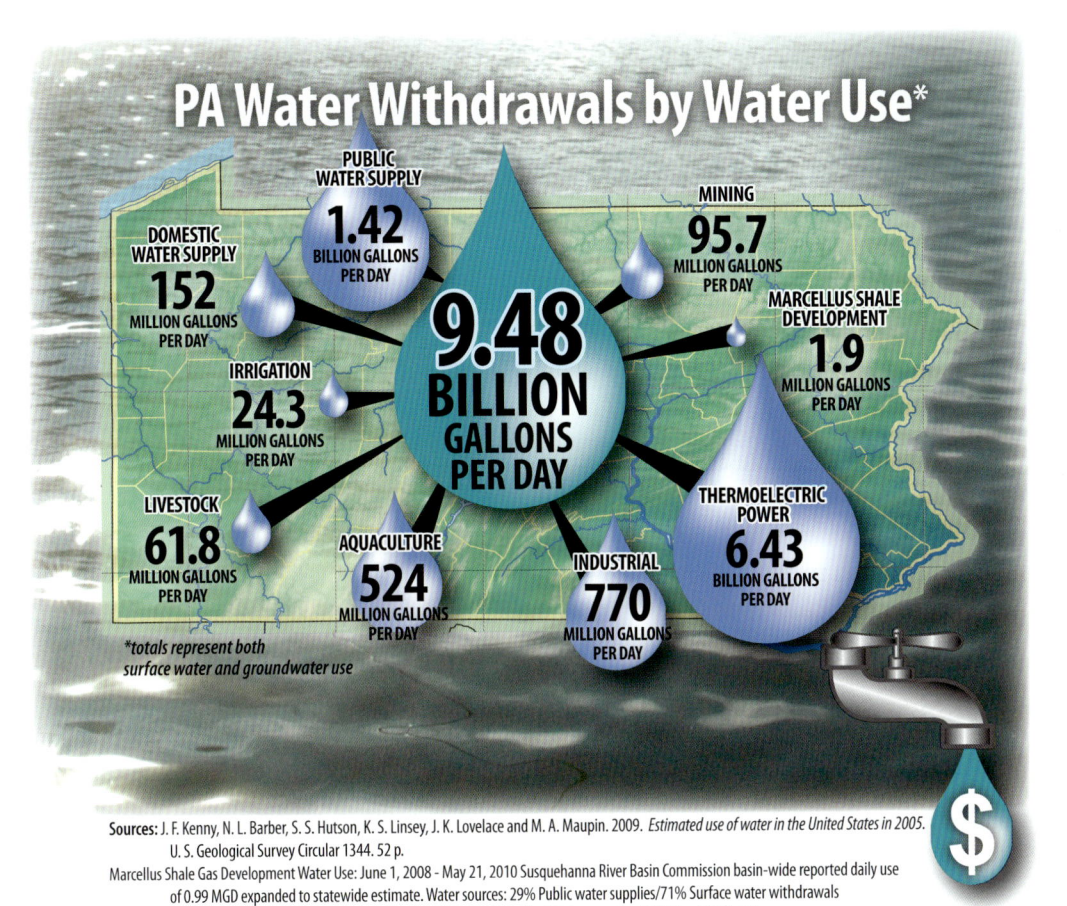

PA Water Withdrawals by Water Use*

9.48 BILLION GALLONS PER DAY

- **PUBLIC WATER SUPPLY** — 1.42 BILLION GALLONS PER DAY
- **DOMESTIC WATER SUPPLY** — 152 MILLION GALLONS PER DAY
- **IRRIGATION** — 24.3 MILLION GALLONS PER DAY
- **LIVESTOCK** — 61.8 MILLION GALLONS PER DAY
- **AQUACULTURE** — 524 MILLION GALLONS PER DAY
- **INDUSTRIAL** — 770 MILLION GALLONS PER DAY
- **THERMOELECTRIC POWER** — 6.43 BILLION GALLONS PER DAY
- **MARCELLUS SHALE DEVELOPMENT** — 1.9 MILLION GALLONS PER DAY
- **MINING** — 95.7 MILLION GALLONS PER DAY

*totals represent both surface water and groundwater use

Sources: J. F. Kenny, N. L. Barber, S. S. Hutson, K. S. Linsey, J. K. Lovelace and M. A. Maupin. 2009. *Estimated use of water in the United States in 2005.* U. S. Geological Survey Circular 1344. 52 p.
Marcellus Shale Gas Development Water Use: June 1, 2008 - May 21, 2010 Susquehanna River Basin Commission basin-wide reported daily use of 0.99 MGD expanded to statewide estimate. Water sources: 29% Public water supplies/71% Surface water withdrawals
1 MGD daily use in Susq. Basin ÷ wells drilled in Susq. Basin/wells drilled statewide=1 MGD ÷ (765/1428)

Statistical graphic (above) and photograph (right) from John Arway's editorial titled "Highway Robbery," which appeared in the January/February 2011 Pennsylvania Angler & Boater. *The editorial highlighted use of the public's water supply and subsequent degradation by entities through withdrawals.*

graphic-Ted Walke, PFBC
photo-Spring Gearhart, PFBC

By early 2011, this "boots on the ground" Unassessed Waters Initiative surveyed approximately 300 streams and found wild trout in more than half of them. The study resulted in more accurate characterizations of these waters and allowed DEP to properly classify them with the appropriate water protection designations. Another result was that DEP placed restrictions on the construction of a pipeline until after the

2000–2015

November 2010 trout spawn. DEP worked with PFBC to classify stream habitat and assess water quality to aid in making decisions about their protection when it came to permitting gas drilling and other related activities. For example, some waterways received High Quality (HQ) or Exceptional Value (EV) classifications which meant that they are of the highest quality and are conducive to natural reproduction of coldwater species. Thus, DEP and PFBC more closely guarded these streams when considering Marcellus Shale well permits.

Habitat Impairment in the Twenty-first Century

*"Rock Snot," or didymo (*Didymosphenia)
photo-Tim Daley, DEP

There is no shortage of problems when it comes to habitat impairment in the twenty-first century. Some problems were man-made, as Arway indicated. Others weren't. These included aquatic invasive species (AIS). So called "Rock Snot," or *Didymosphenia* germinate, took up residence in Pennsylvania waters. Zebra Mussels and Quagga Mussels and viral hemorrhagic septicemias (VHS) in the Great Lakes were other concerns. VHS is a fatal fish disease that can be carried to inland streams by anglers who catch and release infected fish, especially from Lake Erie. A regulation was put in place to prevent the transportation of infected fish and fish eggs beyond the lake's watershed. Zebra Mussels "hitch-hiked" on boats, waders, and other fishing gear.

Round Goby
photo-Andrew Shiels, PFBC

308   Chapter Seven

poster design-Jeff Decker, PFBC

PREVENT THE SPREAD OF DIDYMO!

Didymo alga, or "rock snot," has recently been discovered in various waterways across Pennsylvania. Anglers, boaters, swimmers and tubers can unknowingly spread didymo. Didymo can survive outside a stream in a cool, damp environment—like boots, waders, boats, nets, etc.—for 40 days or more.

Didymo creates thick mats of white, tan or brown cotton-like material on the bottom of rivers and streams. These mats can completely cover the substrate, engulf a stream bottom, smother aquatic plants, insects and mollusks, and reduce fish habitat and food. Take appropriate steps to clean and disinfect your gear to prevent the spread of didymo.

CLEAN YOUR GEAR!

Check these areas: Clothing, Fishing rod, reel & line, Fishing vests, Shoes or boots, Nets & tackle

Check for and remove any visible plants, mud and aquatic life from all equipment before transporting.
Dispose of unwanted bait in the trash, not on land or in the water.
Drain water from all equipment before transporting elsewhere.
Clean gear with **hot** water, or
Dry everything for **at least** five days.
Never release plants, fish or animals into a body of water unless they came out of that body of water.

Great Lakes RESTORATION | pennsylvania | Sea Grant Pennsylvania | pennsylvania

STOP AQUATIC HITCHHIKERS!™
Prevent the transport of aquatic invasive species.
Clean all recreational equipment.
www.ProtectYourWaters.net
For more information: www.fishandboat.com/AIS.htm

Cleaning them with bleached, soapy, hot water was the only solution.

PFBC posted signs on many of the Commonwealth's streams informing anglers of the problem and how it could be prevented and encouraging them to "practice good gear hygiene." Wooly green algae, or didymo, could also be prevented from spreading. One method of transport is waders, especially those that are felt-soled. Fly shops were encouraged to inform anglers to thoroughly clean their waders, and the PFBC posted informative signage.[27]

In addition, a by-product of any hatchery operation is the generation of suspended solids that consist of uneaten fish feed, fish waste, and other particles being carried in the hatchery water flow or effluence. PFBC's Bureau of Hatcheries staff has worked to improve the aquatic environment downstream of its hatcheries for several decades. In addition to improved hatchery management practices, the installation of state-of-the-art microscreen filtration systems has resulted in a substantial decrease in the amount of suspended solids exiting hatchery waters.

In the early twenty-first century, there were positive results of this important work. The Tylersville, Pleasant Gap, Bellefonte, Benner Spring, and Huntsdale State Fish Hatcheries were all equipped with microscreen filtration systems between 2007 and 2010. Since the beginning of their

These carp, collectively referred to as Asian Carp, are the latest aquatic invasive species (AIS) threat to Pennsylvania's waters.

Bighead Carp — Dark blotches along back — No scales on head / No barbels on nose / Low set eyes

Silver Carp — Small scales — No scales on head / No barbels on nose / Low set eyes

Black Carp — Large scales — Pointed, shaped face / No barbels on nose / No scales on head

operation, these filter systems, along with the implementation of best hatchery management practices, have resulted in an average decrease of 50 percent in the amount of total suspended solids released into the aquatic environments downstream of these five hatcheries. The improvement of the receiving water below the Tylersville State Fish Hatchery was sufficient enough to allow DEP to remove Fishing Creek from the list of impaired Commonwealth waters.

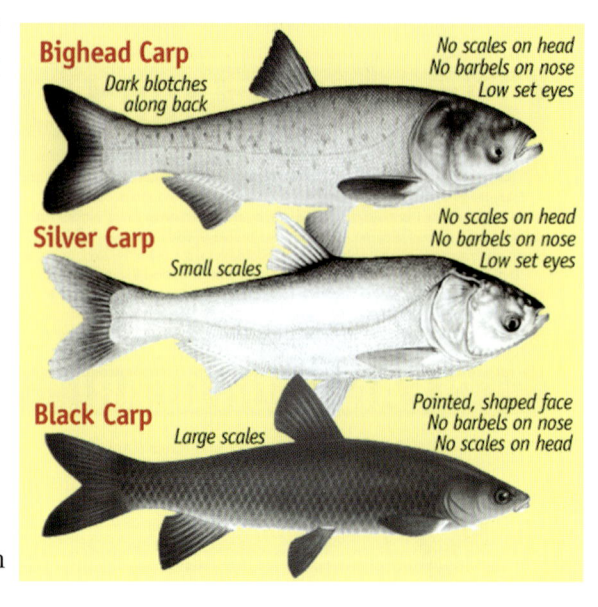

Many conservationists participated in occasional Susquehanna River sojourns that dated back at least to the 1980s and 1990s, when Pennsylvania DER Secretary Art Davis and his wife "Neen" took frequent trips on the Susquehanna (Davis was appointed to the post by Governor Robert P. Casey and served from 1987 to 1995). The sojourners typically highlighted both the negative and positive aspects of the river and its water quality. For example, conservationist and long-time *Pennsylvania Angler & Boater* contributor Mike Bleech wrote about one experience in 2010:

> "The Susquehanna River seemed relatively small when we launched the flotilla of canoes (in Bradford County). The nature of the river would change: gravel riffles and pools (and) slow moving sections. The float trippers would stop occasionally along the sojourn, so more notable members of the group could talk to the new media. Throughout the 1970s and 1980s . . . agreements were made to remedy the problems that were occurring in the Chesapeake Bay. These problems were brought about by nutrients that were entering the Susquehanna from municipal drainage, agricultural runoff, and other causes. Sojourns have helped focus attention on

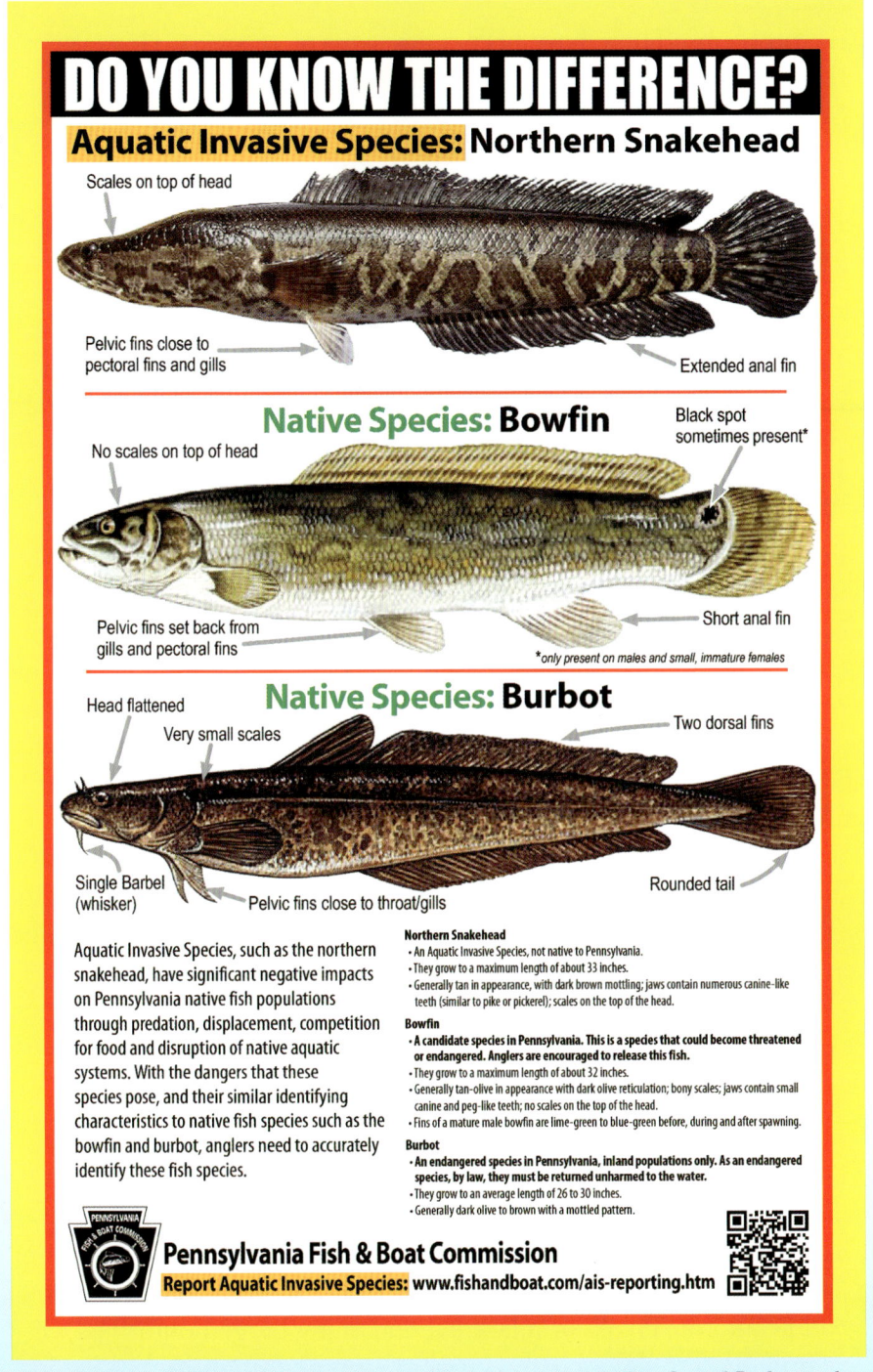

As shown in this PFBC-produced poster, native fish species such as the Bowfin and Burbot can be mistaken for AIS species like the Northern Snakehead by anglers without a key understanding of identifying characteristics of each species.

the problems. There have been a few signs of recovery. However, there are continued low points such as the *Columnaris* infection of Smallmouth Bass."[28]

Bleech fished in the river during the sojourn and caught and released several Smallmouth Bass. In one instance, "a 14-inch Smallmouth Bass took the stickbait on the first retrieve (and) true to its nature, it busted skyward before it tired enough for me to grasp its lower lip and remove the hook."[29] His experience demonstrated the skill and thrill of catching the marvelous fish—one that continues to be at severe risk, because the Susquehanna isn't as healthy as it was before the arrival of settlers in the New World, 400 years earlier, and as man-made pollution took its toll.

While shad fishing was up, boating fatalities were down. In 2010, seven deaths were recorded as compared to 12 one year earlier. PFBC claimed some of the credit that, staff said, resulted from its boating safety programs. There appeared several consistencies when it came to boating fatalities. First, alcohol was usually a factor. Second, the victims were seldom wearing a life jacket. Third, the month of May experienced the highest number of deaths as boaters were taking to the waterways with the coming of milder weather. Next, most fatalities occurred on Saturdays and, finally, the majority of victims were over the age of 50. In one effort to mitigate fatalities, PFBC established a new law that, as of November 1, 2012, required all boaters to wear a life jacket on boats less than 16 feet in length and all canoes and kayaks during cold weather months from November 1 through April 30.

When it came to fishing from a kayak, angler John Allen had a good deal of expertise and wrote that it required bodily adroitness and had its advantages and disadvantages:

"In general, using a kayak is pretty easy. Fishing out of a kayak takes a lot of coordination. If you can master the coordination of using a rod and paddles, you will never want to use a motorboat again. For those who cannot get that part down, they will never want to fish out of a kayak again. The biggest advantage is being able to paddle into the creeks of a lake (where) many Largemouth Bass will venture up the cooler creeks during the summer months, looking for baitfish that have moved up the creeks, as well. Some of my biggest summertime bass have come while fishing spots that a motorboat could never fish. The biggest disadvantage is not being able to move around very quickly. If one spot doesn't seem to hold bass, it is not very easy to just move to the other side of the lake."[30]

Financial Condition in the New Millennium

Fifteen years into the new millennium, PFBC was in good shape financially. In Fiscal Year 2014–2015 Fish Fund revenue exceeded $54 million, while Boat Fund income was more than $22.7 million. Moreover, PFBC stocked 2,150,000 pounds of fish at a $5 cost per pound; 887,000 fish licenses were sold; 333,000 boats were registered; more than 34,000 warnings were issued for law violations; and 6,000 convictions were secured.

Besides paying for salaries, propagation, education, maintenance, and the like, PFBC revenue went for other worthy causes, as well. For example, the Erie-Western Pennsylvania Port Authority received a grant of $150,000 to construct a fishing pier at Liberty Park on Lake Erie. PFBC acquired 27.1 acres along Clarks Valley Road in Middle Paxton Township, Dauphin County, for the purpose of providing a buffer zone and public access to Clark Creek. The agency also provided grants for construction of a fishway on Bald Eagle Creek, near Lock Haven, and for a habitat restoration project on Darby Creek, a Delaware River tributary.

Other significant accomplishments during this time period include . . .
- In 2012, a Pennsylvania Historical and Museum Commission State Historical Marker acknowledging Ralph W. Abele was dedicated at Commission headquarters on Elmerton Avenue in Harrisburg.
- Act 66 of 2012 granted PFBC permission to issue 3-year and 5-year licenses for the first time.
- In 2013, the popular Mentored Youth Trout Day was piloted in southeastern Pennsylvania. It was held on a Saturday, one week prior to the Regional Opening Day of trout season. Youth and their adult mentors were permitted to keep two trout. The pilot program was successful and was expanded statewide in 2014.
- On December 29, 2014, PFBC closed on the purchase of a former furniture factory and warehouse in Bellefonte, Centre County. When renovations are completed and staff have moved in, this facility (Centre Region Office) will consolidate the staff

and equipment currently housed in multiple buildings and facilities at PFBC's Pleasant Gap Complex and will also house PFBC's Law Enforcement Northcentral Region office. This building was purchased for $3.995 million and includes 104,000 square feet of space capable of sheltering boats, vehicles, heavy equipment, lab space, and 100 staff with all of the required modern safety lighting, accessibility, and security features expected of a modern office and field operations facility.

FishBoatPA mobile app

- In 2015, PFBC developed its first smartphone application called FishBoatPA to provide easily accessible information to anglers and boaters. It is available for Apple and Android devices and, in a matter of seconds, provides real time fish stocking and boat access information along with location services that can direct the user through maps and driving directions to waters and fishing and boating opportunities.

- In September of 2015, the Commission announced that it had reached a $2.5 million settlement with Murray Energy for civil damages resulting from a devastating 2009 pollution incident in which discharges from a coal mine entered Dunkard Creek, contributing to a massive fish kill spanning nearly 30 miles of stream in West Virginia and Pennsylvania. The devastation was astonishing. Commission biologists collected 40 species of fish and 14 species of mussels that were killed by the incident. Among the dead mussels was the Pennsylvania endangered Snuffbox Mussel. In 2011, PFBC initiated an action against Consol Energy in West Virginia state court.[31] Ohio-based Murray, which subsequently acquired the mine from Consol, agreed to pay the settlement in lieu of civil damages for the lost aquatic life and lost fishing opportunities for Pennsylvania anglers as a result of the pollution incident. The funds were placed in a restricted revenue account within the Fish Fund to be utilized for the primary purpose of developing and implementing projects that benefit recreational fishing and boating and the aquatic resources of the Dunkard Creek watershed. Once restoration is complete, the Commission may use the remaining funds for restoration projects in other southwestern Pennsylvania watersheds.

RALPH W. ABELE
(1921-1990)

Conservation leader and Pennsylvania Fish Commission executive director, 1972-87. Abele's "Resource First" philosophy strengthened the agency's mission to protect, conserve, and enhance water quality, improve fish passage, and increase youth conservation education. Notable achievements included modernizing the Fish and Boat Code, emphasizing conservation enforcement, and leading efforts to restore American shad to the Susquehanna River.

Ralph W. Abele State Historical Marker at PFBC Harrisburg Headquarters   photo-Spring Gearhart

    Clearly, **PFBC** has come a long way since its inception in 1866. PFBC provides outstanding angling and boating opportunities for the public. It is a regulatory and law enforcement agency, serves as an important educator when it comes to angling and boating safety, is the Commonwealth's lead agency with regard to propagation and protection of aquatic species, acts as a protector of reptiles and amphibians, and is a key conservation agency. Quite simply, the agency is second-to-none in carrying-out its philosophy of Resource First.

Conclusion: Into the Future

"The vast possibilities of our great future will become realities only if we make ourselves responsible for that future."
—*Governor Gifford Pinchot, 1924*

When the Pennsylvania Fish & Boat Commission was created in 1866, the American Civil War just ended, Tennessee was the first former Confederate state to be readmitted to the Union, the United States was less than 100 years old, work was underway on the first transcontinental railroad that would open in 1869, the extant dome on the United States Capitol Building in Washington, D.C., was completed, and just one other state had a fisheries agency.

Pennsylvania Governor Gifford Pinchot

In creating a fisheries agency, Pennsylvania was a leader as it has been in many instances in American history. In this case, it led the way to restore the American Shad, clean up polluted waters, and mitigate problems that resulted from overfishing and rapid industrialization. Throughout the history of PFBC, a great deal has been accomplished. The agency has remained a leader and, from its history of leadership, there are several important themes that emerge and remain constant.

Hatchery delivery truck in the 1920s.

WCO Richard Morder informs an angler during a sportshow. *A stream habitat improvement project.*

These include the professionalism and dedication of the staff, their work to protect and ensure the purity of the Commonwealth's waters, its innovative outreach and education programs, and the agency's embrace of technology. A final theme is that PFBC is a true public service agency serving anglers, boaters, and the common person. While there may be others to consider, these themes appear most consistently throughout the agency's history.

When it comes to the professionalism and dedication of the agency's staff, the record speaks for itself. PFBC grew from a single commissioner with virtually no budget or staff in 1866 to a present complement of 432 full-time and 90 seasonal employees with 10 Commissioners with Fish Fund and Boat Fund revenues exceeding $50 million and expenditures of nearly the same amount reported for Fiscal Year 2014–2015. The nature of the staff's work as well as their job titles, duties,

PFBC Biologists Jason Detar and Dave Kristine during a Fisheries survey.

PFBC Chief Herpetologist Chris Urban during a Timber Rattlesanke survey.

Into the Future

complexities, and responsibilities have grown and changed in countless ways. Consistent with most Pennsylvania state government agencies, with the advent and implementation of the modern science of Public Administration, PFBC has become much more professionalized and specialized, especially in the latter-half of the twentieth century.

For example, Fish Wardens are now Waterways Conservation Officers. Fish Culturists are Fisheries Biologists, jobs unknown in the nineteenth century now make-up the agency's professional ranks. Education and outreach is professionalized through the agency's employment of educators and parks and recreation professionals. There are also various trades, maintenance, equipment operations, fiscal, legal, personnel, and administrative posts all requiring specific skills and competencies.

Beyond the titles and formalities, the professionalism of PFBC's staff is reflected in their actions and accomplishments. Some of these stories are told herein, but there isn't space enough to account for nearly enough. And, *Pennsylvania Angler*, *Pennsylvania Angler & Boater*, and the Minutes of Commission Meetings are replete with such accounts. They could fill pages of volumes. Thanks to the consistent dedication of its staff, PFBC remains Pennsylvania's preeminent agency dedicated to "protect, conserve, and enhance" the Commonwealth's aquatic resources. Pennsylvanians are the beneficiaries.

Likewise, protection and ensuring the purity of Pennsylvania's waters is another consistent theme throughout PFBC's history. Water pollution is always a concern, but it was a growing problem in the

photos–Spring Gearhart, PFBC

nineteenth and twentieth centuries as a result of deforestation, rapid industrialization, acid mine drainage, inadequate municipal sewage treatment, and other causes and impacts on the environment. In 1925, for example, the Board of Fish Commissioners had the foresight and reported to Governor Gifford Pinchot that "the pollution of our streams is one of the greatest problems confronting the people of the Commonwealth today, not only from the standpoint of the conservation of fish, but also the health of its citizens."[1]

The struggle to maintain and enhance the purity of the Commonwealth's lakes and streams and efforts to clean up those that are impaired continues in the twenty-first century and will do so well into the future. The "Save Our Susquehanna" campaign makes this clear. Many once-polluted streams have been returned to their natural condition. Anti-water pollution laws, regulations, and policies, and the strict enforcement of them have resulted in healthier waters. Moreover, scientifically-based propagation programs have meant the return of historically important fish species to once polluted waters, American Shad, chief among them. And, the work continues. What Governor John S. Fine (1951–1955) said in 1951—"Fishing in Pennsylvania will expand and improve as we carry on our fight for clean streams"—certainly remains true in the present and for the future.[2]

Angler and boater education is another consistent theme that emerges from PFBC's history. Today the nomenclature is "outreach," which is much more encompassing. The agency's formal educational initiatives date at least to its participation in the London International

photo-Ted Walke, PFBC

photo-Art Michaels, PFBC

photo-Art Michaels, PFBC

Into the Future 319

Fisheries Exhibition of 1883 and the Columbian Exposition a decade later. Of course, the annual reports issued by the Board of Fish Commissioners were very educational, as they were chock-full of facts, data, and editorializing about fish and water quality. Teaching someone something about angling—whether showing an angler new fly-tying methods or educating a politician about a water quality issue—has always been high on the agency's agenda.

As the agency's work expanded and its staff expertise grew in the twentieth century, so did its programming. Many new educational programs were adopted in the early-to-mid twentieth century and included initiatives targeting schools, colleges, and community organizations. *Pennsylvania Angler* and, later, *Pennsylvania Angler & Boater* grew to become a key educational tool of PFBC, as did many of the agency's other publications. As the century progressed and recreational boating became more popular, PFBC staff took on direct responsibility for implementing related educational programs that emphasized boating safety. In addition, youth have been targeted in PFBC's outreach through initiatives such as the recent Mentored Youth Program.

In the twenty-first century, education and outreach takes innumerable forms. Outreach is central to PFBC's strategic planning and to the day-to-day functions of the staff. Initiatives such as the Fishing Tackle Loaner Program, PLAY, and family fishing programs encourage angling and getting outdoors as a way to recreate. In addition, PFBC's website features a "learning center" with excellent information on fishing fundamentals, boating basics, water and ice

320   Conclusion

photo courtesy of Tim Klinger, PFBC webmaster

safety, and aquatic creatures and their habitats, as well as specific pages for educators and students.

 Technology has greatly aided the Commission's ability to provide information and to educate. In fact, the agency's central outreach and educational tool is its website. The latter-decades of the twentieth century and these first 16 years of the twenty-first century are referred to as "the information age." It has been and continues to be an era of technological advancements unprecedented in human history. Humans live in a "T.G.I.F." world: Twitter, Google, the Internet, and Facebook. PFBC is fully on-board.

 Anglers and boaters, from Native Americans to the mid-twentieth century, could have hardly imagined that, one day, a hand held device called a "smartphone" could "log-on" to an "app" or "website." It would have been a stretch for them to think that desktop and laptop computers would become necessities of contemporary life. The needs of Native Americans and Colonial-era citizens were quite simple. Fish were a form of sustenance, as well as a foodstuff for sale and purchase in the marketplace. The implements of angling were rudimentary by today's standards. Fish hooks were carved from bone. Boats consisted of the famed birch-bark canoe and were made from wood harvested from Pennsylvania's rich forest resources.

 There were advances in technology of all facets in the nineteenth and twentieth centuries. But it wouldn't be until the post-World War II era that computer technology would play an increasingly critical role. Since then, there has been lightning progression, and PFBC has been progressive with using technology in its day-to-day operations. Today, PFBC's website (www.fishandboat.com), which was launched in

Into the Future **321**

1996, is populated with a myriad of data, reports, maps, references to laws and regulations, answers to frequently asked questions, online fish license applications, boating information, educational material, biology reports by region, past issues of *Pennsylvania Angler & Boater* magazine, and much more. To continue to provide up-to-the-minute communication and information, PFBC staff launched a Twitter account in 2010 and a Facebook page in 2012, and the main web page contains a "News and Notes" section with the latest information on many topics ranging from stocking reports to press releases.

The website also contains very useful resources for boaters with its water trails web page, featuring the recreational network titled Pennsylvania Water Trails. These are boat routes suitable for canoes, kayaks, and small motorized watercraft. Like conventional trails, water trails are recreational corridors between specific locations and are comprised of access points, boat launches, day use sites, and—in some cases—overnight camping areas. Each water trail is unique, a reflection of Pennsylvania's diverse geology, ecology, and communities. Water trail guides show "trail heads" (boat launch and take-out points) and provide background about the scenic, historic and geologic points of interest along the way. As the Commission's website states, "Throw in a little fishing, wildlife watching, and camping, and you can see how water works wonders in Pennsylvania." Web-based technology advanced with rapidity in the late twentieth and early twenty-first centuries and will certainly continue to do so in the decades to follow. As PFBC staff have done and are doing, they will continue to embrace technological advancements to inform and educate the public.

A final theme that is evident in the history of PFBC is its work in service to the common person in the Keystone State. Commission reports, *Pennsylvania Angler, Pennsylvania Angler & Boater,* and other agency historical records are replete with stories of ordinary people finding pleasure in catching fish, tying flies, rowing a canoe or boat, operating a motorboat, water-skiing, and otherwise recreating in the outdoors. Some of those stories are told in these pages. There is no extant socioeconomic or demographic study of precisely who the common person is, was, or will be. Historically speaking, there isn't a common archetype as to how they earned their living, what type of housing they occupied, or which type of vehicle they drove.

NEW FOR 2013

Carefree and Convenient Fishing at Your Fingertips!

The Pennsylvania Fish & Boat Commission is launching a new type of fishing license. For 2013, you'll be able to purchase a license for three years or five years with one purchase. That's right, no more remembering at the last minute to buy a license before opening day or before that weekend fishing opportunity with friends and family.

Five years of fishing in one purchase.

1 2 3 4 5

To order and for information on license products, go to:
www.GoneFishingPa.com

Pennsylvania's BEST Fishing Waters
PROTECT • CONSERVE • ENHANCE

Commonwealth waters have always provided outstanding fishing opportunities for a variety of popular fish species. Pennsylvania's Best Fishing Waters is a program established by PFBC, using the expertise and knowledge of its fisheries biologists, to highlight statewide locations for different categories of fish to assist anglers in knowing the prime fishing hotspots. Confirmed by survey catch rates and the availability of public access, the waters offered as a resource by the Commission are intended to increase anglers' success and convenient access to this information. You deserve the best!

www.PaBestFishing.com

Waters listing available December 1, 2012!

Mark your calendar for the
Pennsylvania Fish & Boat Commission's

Mentored Youth Trout Day
March 23, 2013

Take part in the Commission's first Mentored Youth Trout Day. Youth under the age of 16 can join a mentor angler, who has a current fishing license and trout permit, to fish this day on selected waters within the 18 southeastern regional counties for regional trout season.

www.FishandBoat.com

ad design-Jeff Decker, PFBC

As shown in this excerpt from **Pennsylvania Angler & Boater** *magazine in 2012, multiple-year fishing licenses, the Best Fishing Waters program, and Mentored Youth Days continue to be successful initiatives launched and promoted by PFBC.*

Into the Future

Yet, there are passing references to industrial and office workers, outdoorsmen (and women), campers, hunters, families, and youth, along with an occasional scout troop or community organization. For most, a fishing license was (and is) an investment in recreating; a boat registration was (and is) a privilege promising hours of fun and relaxation on the water. These were the individuals for whom recreational angling and boating remained and remains an important form of leisure. These are the people that former Governor George M. Leader and his secretary of Forests and Waters, Maurice Goddard, had in mind when they both agreed on a policy to place a state park within 25 miles of every Pennsylvanian in 1955. And, these are the people that Ralph Abele and John Arway had in mind when they editorialized about the "Common Man" in the Executive Director's columns in *Pennsylvania Angler* and *Pennsylvania Angler & Boater*. In summary, PFBC serves no one special interest. Rather, as it has in the past, it serves and will continue to serve the common person with its mission to protect, conserve, and enhance the Commonwealth's aquatic resources and provide fishing and boating opportunities. The Commonwealth's natural resources are common to all and for all.

It is hard to predict what the future will have in store for PFBC and for anglers and boaters in Pennsylvania and those nationally and internationally who frequent the state's waterways. Certainly, agency staff will continue improve accessibility to recreational opportunities and address water pollution problems when and where they occur, boating safety will be high on the agenda, and science will continue to play an important role in species propagation. The agency's public outreach programs will continue. Perhaps PFBC will morph into a configuration not imaginable at the present. In the years to come, technology will long outpace that which is available now. Smartphone applications or websites may well be obsolete, replaced by some yet undreamed-of technology that PFBC will no doubt employ.

What will remain a constant, however, are the many great fishing and boating opportunities available throughout the Keystone State. In 1928, then Commissioner of Fisheries N. R. Buller, put it this way: "I might say that you will find as good streams in one section of the Commonwealth as another. I do not think that the fishermen can make a mistake by going to any of the counties."[3] Few Pennsylvanians would disagree then, now, or tomorrow.

Notes

Introduction
1. John Arway, Interview by Kenneth C. Wolensky, *Pennsylvania Conservation Heritage Oral History Project Final Report*, April 9, 2015. 46.
2. Ibid.

Chapter One
1. Wallace Nutting, *Pennsylvania Beautiful*, (New York: Bonanza Books, 1924), 18.
2. Wallace, Paul A. W., *Indians in Pennsylvania*, (Harrisburg, PA: Pennsylvania Historical and Museum Commission, 1961), 37.
3. Daniel Richter, "The First Pennsylvanians," *Pennsylvania: A History of the Commonwealth*, (Harrisburg and University Park, PA: Pennsylvania Historical and Museum Commission and Pennsylvania State University Press, 2002), 3–4.
4. Pennsylvania Department of Fisheries, *Report of the Department of Fisheries from December 1, 1914 to November 30, 1915*, By Wm. Stanley Ray, Harrisburg, PA: State Printer, 1916, 140.
5. Dr. William C. Kendall, "The Status of Fish Culture in our Inland Public Waters and the Role of Investigation in the Maintenance of Fish Resources," *Roosevelt Wild Life Bulletin of the Roosevelt Wild Life Forest Experimentation Station of The New York College of Forestry at Syracuse University*, (Syracuse, NY: Roosevelt Wild Life Forest Experiment Station, March 1924), 211.

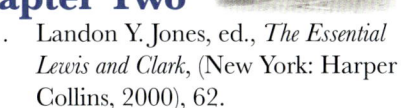

Chapter Two
1. Landon Y. Jones, ed., *The Essential Lewis and Clark*, (New York: Harper Collins, 2000), 62.
2. Pennsylvania Department of Agriculture Division of Forestry, *Annual Report of the Pennsylvania Department of Agriculture's Division of Forestry*, By Clarence Munsch, Harrisburg, PA: State Printer of Pennsylvania, 1896, 90.
3. Ibid., 43.
4. Richard Grifo and Anthony Noto, *Italian Presence in Pennsylvania*, (University Park, PA: The Pennsylvania Historical Association, 1990), 6.
5. State Commissioners of Fisheries, *Report of the State Commissioners of Fisheries for the years 1883–84*, By Lane S. Hart, Harrisburg, PA: State Printer, 1885, 4.
6. Ibid.
7. Ibid., 6.
8. State Commissioners of Fisheries, *Report of the State Commissioners of Fisheries for the years 1879 and 1880*, By Lane S. Hart, Harrisburg, PA: State Printer, 1881.
9. Ibid., 33–34.
10. Dr. William C. Kendall, "The Status of Fish Culture in our Inland Public Waters and the Role of Investigation in the Maintenance of Fish Resources," *Roosevelt Wild Life Bulletin of the Roosevelt Wild Life Forest Experimentation Station of The New York College of Forestry at Syracuse University*, (Syracuse, NY: Roosevelt Wild Life Forest Experiment Station, March 1924), 211.

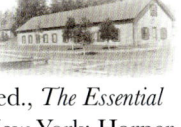

11. Ibid.
12. State Commissioners of Fisheries, *Report of the State Commissioners of Fisheries for the years 1879–80*, By Lane S. Hart, Harrisburg, PA: State Printer, 3–6.
13. State Commissioners of Fisheries, *Report of the State Commissioners of Fisheries for the years 1885 and 1886*, By Edwin K. Meyers, Harrisburg, PA, State Printer, 1887, 2.
14. State Commissioners of Fisheries, *Report of the State Commissioners of Fisheries for the years 1883–84*, By Edwin K. Meyers, Harrisburg, PA: State Printer, 1885, 6–8.
15. State Commissioners of Fisheries, *Report of the State Commissioners of Fisheries for the years 1885 and 1886*, By Edwin K. Meyers, Harrisburg, PA, State Printer, 1887, 10.
16. Board of Fish Commissioners, *Report of the Board of Fish Commissioners for the year 1894*, By W. E. Meehan, Harrisburg, PA, 8.
17. State Commissioners of Fisheries, *Report of the State Commissioners of Fisheries, 1898–99*, By W. E. Meehan, Harrisburg, PA, 3.

Chapter Three

1. Department of Fisheries of the Commonwealth of Pennsylvania, *Report of the Department of Fisheries of the Commonwealth of Pennsylvania, June 1, 1903, to November 20, 1904*, By Wm. Stanley Ray, Harrisburg, PA: State Printer of Pennsylvania, 1905, 3, 11.
2. Department of Fisheries, *Report of the Department of Fisheries from December 1, 1908 to November 30, 1909*, By C. E. Aughinbaugh, Harrisburg, PA: Printer to the State of Pennsylvania, 1910, 11.
3. Department of Fisheries, *Report of The Department of Fisheries*, By C. E. Aughinbaugh, Harrisburg, PA: Printer to the State of Pennsylvania, 1909, 8.
4. Department of Fisheries, *Report of the Department of Fisheries, December 1, 1908 to November 30, 1909*, By C. E. Aughinbaugh, Harrisburg, PA: Printer to the State of Pennsylvania, 8.
5. Department of Fisheries, *Report of the Department of Fisheries, December 1, 1910 to November 30, 1911*, By C. E. Aughinbaugh, Harrisburg, PA: Printer to the State of Pennsylvania, 1912, 6.
6. George M. Leader, interview by Kenneth C. Wolensky, April 17, 2009.
7. Department of Fisheries, *Report of the Department of Fisheries, 1912*, By C. E. Aughinbaugh, Harrisburg, PA: Printer to the State of Pennsylvania, 17.
8. Department of Fisheries, *Report of the Department of Fisheries, December 1, 1914 to November 30, 1915*, By Wm. Stanley Ray, Harrisburg, PA: State Printer, 1916, 135–38.
9. Commonwealth of Pennsylvania, Board of Fish Commissioners, *Bulletin No. 3*, 1927.
10. Ibid., 5.
11. Ibid., 5.
12. Commonwealth of Pennsylvania, Board of Fish Commissioners, *Bulletin No. 6*, 1928.
13. Ibid., 3.
14. Ibid., 13.

Chapter Four

1. Oliver M. Deibler, *Pennsylvania Angler* 1, no. 1 (December 1931): 3.

2. Lorraine Schock, Interview by Kenneth C. Wolensky, July 6, 2015.
3. Charles A. French. "Kill the Watersnake," *Pennsylvania Angler* 8, no. 9 (October 1939): Frontispiece.
4. Ibid., 1.
5. Ibid., 3.
6. Ibid., 2.
7. Nora Del Smith Gumble, "The Wallenpaupack," *Pennsylvania Angler* xix, no. 1 (January 1950): Frontispiece.
8. *Pennsylvania Angler*, 2, no. 1 (December 1931): 2.
9. Ibid., 6–7.
10. Ibid., 6–7.
11. Dick Fortney, "The Angler's Notebook: Selinsgrove Angler Invents Novel Rod," *Pennsylvania Angler* 9, no. 3 (March 1940): 24.
12. Board of Fish Commissioners, *Board of Fish Commissioners Report of 1933*, 1–3.
13. Board of Fish Commissioners, *Board of Fish Commissioners Report of 1934*, 6.
14. French, Charles A, "Junior Conservationists," *Pennsylvania Angler* 9, no. 2 (February 1940): Frontispiece.
15. *Pennsylvania Angler*, 9, no. 1 (January 1940): 12–13.
16. William Boyd, "America: Land of Opportunity," *Pennsylvania Angler* xix, no. 5 (May/June 1949): 10–11.

Chapter Five

1. Kenneth C. Wolensky and Governor George M. Leader, *The Life of Governor George M. Leader: Challenging Complacency* (Bethlehem, PA: Lehigh University Press, 2011), 71.
2. Keith Schuyler, "Why Not Take Her Along?" *Pennsylvania Angler* XVIII, no. 11 (November 1949): 6.
3. "So You've Retired," *Pennsylvania Angler* 27, no. 2 (February 1958): 9.
4. "Conservation Across the Nation: Family Fishing," *Pennsylvania Angler* 27, no. 8 (August 1958): 24.
5. Pennsylvania Fish Commission, *Minutes of the First Meeting of the Pennsylvania Fish Commission* 1, no. 4 (April 25, 1949).
6. Gordon. L. Trembly, "Pennsylvania's New Fish Management Program," *Pennsylvania Angler* xix, no. 2 (February 1950): 2–3.
7. Wolensky and Leader, *The Life of Governor George M. Leader: Challenging Complacency*. 70–71.
8. Ibid.
9. Al Clark, "There are three Bill Voigt's," *Pennsylvania Angler* 24, no. 10 (October 1955): 18.
10. Pennsylvania Fish Commission, "Comptroller's Report of Budget and Finances to the Commissioners of the Pennsylvania Fish Commission," *Minutes of the Eighty-Third Meeting of the Pennsylvania Fish Commission* 17 (March 29, 1965): 1.
11. Joint State Government Commission, *Observations and Recommendations of the Wildlife Management Institute Re; Pennsylvania Fish Commission and Pennsylvania Game Commission* (July 1962): 20.
12. Ibid., 23.
13. Ibid., 38.
14. Ibid., 40.
15. Pennsylvania Fish Commission, *Minutes of the Eighty-Third Meeting of the Pennsylvania Fish Commission* 17, no. 3 (March 29, 1965): 26.
16. Rachel Carson, *Silent Spring*, (New York: Houghton Mifflin, 1994), xv.
17. Ibid., 40.
18. Ibid., 41.
19. Wiliam O. Douglas, *My Wilderness* (New York: Doubleday, 1960).

20. Pennsylvania Fish Commission, *Minutes of the 100th meeting of the Pennsylvania Fish Commission*, Report of the Executive Director to the Commissioners (July 28, 1969): 4.

Chapter Six

1. Robert Bielo, "Observation Viewpoint: A Stronger Clean Streams Law," *Pennsylvania Angler* 39, no. 10 (October 1970): frontispiece.
2. Pennsylvania Fish Commission, "Report of the Executive Director to the Commissioners," *Minutes of the 108th meeting of the Pennsylvania Fish Commission* (July 26, 1971): 1–2.
3. Robert Bielo, "Conservation Viewpoint: Permanent Improvement?," *Pennsylvania Angler* 38, no. 7 (July 1969): frontispiece.
4. "Receives Governor's Award," *Pennsylvania Angler* 30, no. 1 (January, 1970): 25.
5. Robert Bielo, "Observation Viewpoint," *Pennsylvania Angler* 41, no.1 (January 1972): frontispiece.
6. Ralph Abele Jr., "Projects . . . Progress!" *Pennsylvania Angler* 41, no. 3 (March 1972): frontispiece.
7. Peter Duncan, Interviews by Kenneth C. Wolensky, *Ralph Abele Legacy Research Project: Final Report to the Ralph W. Abele Scholarship Fund Board*, August 1, 2012, 40–43.
8. Harry Bittle, Interview by Kenneth C. Wolensky, *Ralph Abele Legacy Research Project: Final Report to the Ralph W. Abele Scholarship Fund Board*, August 1, 2012, 38–39.
9. Thomas Qualters, Sr, Interview by Kenneth C. Wolensky, *Ralph Abele Legacy Research Project Final Report to the Ralph W. Abele Scholarship Fund Board*, August 1, 2012, 14–15.
10. John Arway, Interview by Kenneth C. Wolensky, *Ralph Abele Legacy Research Project Final Report to the Ralph W. Abele Scholarship Fund Board*, August 1, 2012, 3–5.
11. Ralph Abele, Jr., Interview by Kenneth C. Wolensky, *Ralph Abele Legacy Research Project Final Report to the Ralph W. Abele Scholarship Fund Board*, August 1, 2012, 12–13.
12. Jennifer, Smith, Interview by Kenneth C. Wolensky, *Ralph Abele Legacy Research Project Final Report to the Ralph W. Abele Scholarship Fund Board*, August 1, 2012, 28–29.
13. "Our Heritage: Our Future," *Pennsylvania Angler* 41, no. 2 (February, 1972): frontispiece.
14. Ralph Abele, "Aftermath," *Pennsylvania Angler* 41, no. 10, (October 1972): frontispiece.
15. Ralph Abele, "Fishing is Great!" *Pennsylvania Angler* 41, no. 11 (November 1972): frontispiece.
16. "Leaky Boots, Monthly Mail," *Pennsylvania Angler* 43, no. 10 (October 1974): 5.
17. *Pennsylvania Angler* 44, no. 10 (October 1975): frontispiece.
18. Ralph Abele, "Extortion," *Pennsylvania Angler* 46, no. 9 (September 1977): frontispiece.
19. Pennsylvania Fish Commission Division of Fisheries, *Minutes of the 118th Meeting of the Pennsylvania Fish Commission, January 11, 1974* 26, Cooperative Nursery Branch Statement of Policy (January 10, 1972); Division of Fisheries Cooperative Nursery Branch, *Approved Cooperative Nurseries* (January 1, 1974): Exhibit G.
20. Pennsylvania Fish Commission, *Minutes of the 132nd meeting of the Pennsylvania Fish Commission* (July 25, 1977): 54.

21. Ibid., 55.
22. Pennsylvania Fish Commission, *Minutes of the 144th Meeting of the Pennsylvania Fish Commission* (July 14, 1980): 59–61.
23. Joanne Haibach, "Through the Eyes of a Little Girl," *Pennsylvania Angler* 45, no. 9 (September 1976): 27.
24. Ralph Abele, "True Conservation," *Pennsylvania Angler* 43, no. 10 (October 1974): frontispiece.
25. Michael L. Hendricks, *American Shad Restoration* (Harrisburg, PA: Pennsylvania Fish & Boat Commission).
26. "Fish Commission Annual Report: Fiscal Year July 1, 1978 to June 30, 1979," *Pennsylvania Angler* 49, no. 1 (January 1980): 9–24.
27. Alan Mackay, "Drag Boat Weekend," *Pennsylvania Angler* 44, no. 8 (August 1975): 29–30.
28. Alan Mackay, "Noise—another pollution?" *Pennsylvania Angler* 44, no. 10 (October 1975): 28–29.
29. Ralph Abele, "A Special Time," *Pennsylvania Angler* 48, no. 4 (April 1979): frontispiece.
30. Pennsylvania Fish Commission, *Minutes of the 13th Meeting of the Pennsylvania Fish Commission*, "Report of the Executive Director," 31, no. 24, exhibit A.
31. Ralph Abele, "The Road Back," *Pennsylvania Angler* 48, no. 5 (May 1979): frontispiece.
32. Ralph Abele, "Straight Talk," *Pennsylvania Angler* 54, no. 1 (January 1985): frontispiece.
33. Robert Weber, Russell T. Greene, John Arway, R. Scott Carney and Leroy Young, *History of the Management of Trout Fisheries in Pennsylvania*, (Harrisburg, PA: Pennsylvania Fish & Boat Commission, 2010), 20.
34. John Arway, *Resource First: A Review*, (Harrisburg, PA: Pennsylvania Fish & Boat Commission, 2008).
35. Ibid., 1.
36. Edwin L. Cooper, *Fishes of Pennsylvania and the Northeastern United States by Edwin L. Cooper*, (University Park, PA: Pennsylvania State University Press, 1983).
37. Ralph Abele, "Welcome Aboard," *Boat Pennsylvania* 1, no.1 (May/June 1984): 2.
38. Leann R Diehl, "Paddling the Yough," *Boat Pennsylvania* 1, no. 1 (May/June 1984): 4–8.
39. "The Law and You," *Boat Pennsylvania* 1, no. 1 (May/June 1984): 20.
40. "Mail," *Boat Pennsylvania* 1, no. 1 (May/June 1984): 21.
41. Marcelline Burns, "Alcohol Effects on Skills Performance," *Boat Pennsylvania* 3, no. 4, (July/August 1986): 27.
42. "Mail," *Pennsylvania Angler & Boater* 76, no. 5 (September/October 2007): 6.
43. *Pennsylvania Angler* 56, no. 10 (October 1987): 4–5.
44. Ibid.
45. Steve Ulsh, "The Volunteer Education and Information Corps," *Pennsylvania Angler 56*, no. 2 (February 1987): 4–5.
46. Steve Ulsh, "First Aid for Anglers," *Pennsylvania Angler* 56, no. 9 (September 1987).
47. Ralph Abele, "Straight Talk," *Pennsylvania Angler* 56, no. 5 (May 1987): 2.
48. Pennsylvania Fish Commission, *Minutes of the 175th meeting of the Pennsylvania Fish Commission* (April 13, 1987): Exhibit A.

49. Edward Miller, "Straight Talk: A Special Group," *Pennsylvania Angler* 56, no. 7 (July 1987): frontispiece.
50. Jeff Mulhollem, "One hour from Altoona," *Pennsylvania Angler* 56, no. 8 (August 1987): 10–12.
51. Pennsylvania Fish Commission, *Minutes of the 189th meeting of the Pennsylvania Fish Commission*, Executive Director's Report (Oct, 23, 1989): Exhibit A, 8.
52. Pennsylvania Fish Commission, *Minutes of the 189th meeting of the Pennsylvania Fish Commission*, Bureau of Education and Information Report by Cheryl K. Riley, (Oct, 23, 1989): exhibit A.
53. Edward Miller, "Straight Talk: Reflections by Edward, R. Miller," *Pennsylvania Angler & Boater* 63, no. 4 (March 1994): frontispiece.
54. *Lehigh Falls Fishing Club v. Andrejewski*, 735 A.2d 718, 720 (Pa. Super, 1999), *petition for allowance of appeal denied*, 563 Pa. 702, 761 A.2d 550 (2000), *quoting Shrunk v. Schuylkill Navigation Co.*, 14 Serg. & Rawle 71 (1826).
55. Pennsylvania Fish Commission, *Minutes of the 193rd Meeting of the Pennsylvania Fish Commission*, "Rules and Regulations: Final Rulemaking—Property Regulations," (July 31, 1990): 23.
56. "Pennsylvania's 'Mr. Muskie,'" *Pennsylvania Game and Fish* (June 1997): 17–19.
57. David Ehrig, "Pennsylvania's New Shad River," *Pennsylvania Sportsman* XXXV, no. 3, 63 and 116.
58. Vic Attardo, "Pennsylvania's Best Family Fishing Vacations," *Pennsylvania Game and Fish* (June 2001) 20–22, 49.

Chapter Seven

1. John Arway, Interview by Kenneth C. Wolensky, *Ralph Abele Legacy Research Project Final Report to the Ralph W. Abele Scholarship Fund Board*, August 1, 2012, 3–4.
2. Alex Zidock Jr, "All about Engine Oil," *Pennsylvania Angler & Boater* 69, no. 1, (January/February 2000): 25–26.
3. David Kaneski, "Not bad for the 'slow' time of the year," *Pennsylvania Angler & Boater* 70, no. 1 (January/February 2001): 49.
4. Martha Mackey, "Notes from the Streams; Las Vegas, PA," *Pennsylvania Angler & Boater* 69, no. 5 (September/October 2000): 57.
5. Terry Brady, "Thank Goodness for Marlene, Gail, Vickie, Michele, Bonnie and Barb," *Pennsylvania Angler & Boater* 72 (May/June 2003): 36–38.
6. "Cast and Caught," *Pennsylvania Angler & Boater* 70, no. 5 (September/October 2001): 70.
7. *Commonwealth of Pennsylvania v. Espy*, Nos. 2003–781 and 2003–1297, C.P. Huntingdon, June 13, 2007, Order dated June 13, 2007.
8. Douglas Austen, "Protect, Conserve, Enhance: Common Themes of Conservation, Fishing and Boating Groups," *Pennsylvania Angler & Boater* 73, no. 4 (July/August 2004): 2.
9. Thomas Edwards, "WCO Diary: Ice Fishing Clinics," *Pennsylvania Angler & Boater* 75, no. 1 (January/February 2006): 49.
10. Alice Stitt, "Pennsylvania's Turtles," *Pennsylvania Angler & Boater* 57, no. 5 (September/October 2006): 50–56.

11. Art Michaels, "Angler Profiles: Misty's World—Leaping Over Boundaries," *Pennsylvania Angler & Boater* 75, no. 4 (July/August 2006): 20–21.
12. Linda Steiner, "Bowfishing," *Pennsylvania Angler & Boater* 80, no. 5 (September/October 2011): 32–35.
13. "Belly Boating Lake Erie," *Pennsylvania Angler* 63, no. 2 (February 1994): 10–11.
14. Douglas Austen, "Chesapeake Bay and the Susquehanna," *Pennsylvania Angler & Boater* 77, no. 1 (January/February 2008): 2–3.
15. Douglas Austen, "Protect, Conserve, Enhance," *Pennsylvania Angler & Boater* 74, no. 2 (March/April 2005): 1–2.
16. John Arway, Interview by Kenneth C. Wolensky, *Ralph Abele Legacy Research Project Final Report to the Ralph W. Abele Scholarship Fund Board*, August 1, 2012, 3–4.
17. Deborah Weisberg, "Meet John Arway," *Pennsylvania Angler & Boater* 79, no. 3, 25.
18. John Arway, Interview by Kenneth C. Wolensky, *Ralph Abele Legacy Research Project Final Report to the Ralph W. Abele Scholarship Fund Board*, August 1, 2012, 3–4.
19. Michael Hendricks, "Delaware Shad on the Drift," *Pennsylvania Angler & Boater* 8, no. 3 (May/June 2012): 46–47.
20. John Arway, Interview by Kenneth C. Wolensky, *Ralph Abele Legacy Research Project Final Report to the Ralph W. Abele Scholarship Fund Board*, August 1, 2012, 3–4.
21. John Arway, "Straight Talk," *Pennsylvania Angler & Boater* 81, no. 6 (November/December 2012): 2–3.
22. John Arway, "Straight Talk," *Pennsylvania Angler & Boater* 84, no. 4 (July/August 2015): 2–3.
23. Press Release, December 16, 2015. "PFBC Launched On-Line Fundraising Site.
24. "PFBC Launched On-Line Fundraising Site," *Pennsylvania Angler & Boater* 84, no. 4 (July/August 2015): 4–5.
25. John Arway, "Straight Talk: An Executive Decision," *Pennsylvania Angler & Boater* 80, no. 3 (May/June 2011): frontispiece and 4–5.
26. John Arway, "Highway Robbery," *Pennsylvania Angler & Boater* 80, no. 1 (January/February 2011): 4–5.
27. Deborah Weisberg, "Stop Aquatic Hitch Hikers," *Pennsylvania Angler & Boater* 78, no. 2 (March/April 2009): 14–15.
28. Bleech, Mike. "Susquehanna River Sojourn." *Pennsylvania Angler & Boater* 79, no. 3 (May/June 2010): 38.
29. Ibid.
30. John Allen, "Kayak Fishing for Largemouth Bass," *Pennsylvania Angler & Boater* 84, no. 4 (July/August 2015): 34–36.
31. *Commonwealth of Pennsylvania v. Consol Energy, Inc.*, Civil Case No. 11-C-556, Circuit Court of Monongalia County).

Conclusion

1. Board of Fish Commissioners, *Biennial Report for the Period Ending May 31, 1924*, (Harrisburg, PA: Board of Fish Commissioners, 1925), 18.
2. Governor John S. Fine, *Pennsylvania Angler* (October 1951).
3. Board of Fish Commissioners, *Biennial Report for the Period Ending May 31, 1928*.

Appendix

State Commissioners of Fisheries
Board of Fishery Commissioners
Board of Fish Commissioners
Pennsylvania Fish Commission
Pennsylvania Fish & Boat Commission
Boating Advisory Board and Executive Directors
1866–2016

Entries, names, and locations are as they appear in Commission reports.

Commissioner of Fisheries, 1866–1873
James Worrall

State Commissioners of Fisheries, 1873–1874
(board comprised of three members during this period)

J. Duffy, *Marietta*
B. L. Hewit, *Hollidaysburg*
H. J. Reeder, *Easton*

1875–1878 Reports unavailable

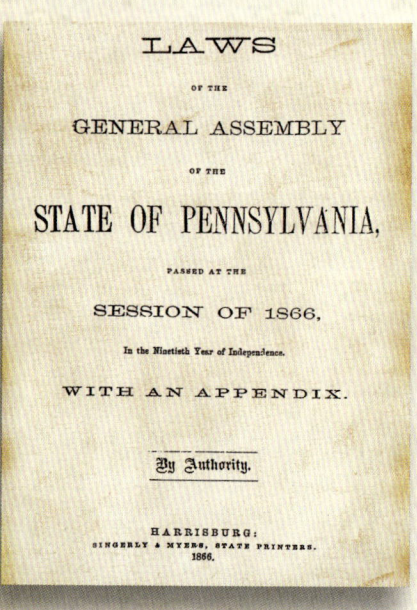

Board of Fishery Commissioners, 1879–1897
(board comprised of six members during this period with these individuals serving at various terms during these years)

Jas. W. Corrrell, *Easton*
D. P. Corwin, *Pittsburgh*
James A. Dale, *York*
Robert Dalzel, *Pittsburgh*
H. H. Derr, *Wilkes-Barre*
H. C. Demuth, *Lancaster*
James Duffy, *Marietta*
A. S. Dickson, *Meadville*
Augustus Duncan, *Chambersburg*
F. W. Ebel, *Harrisburg*
Henry C. Ford, *Philadelphia*
John Gay, *Greensburg*

Benjamin L. Hewit, *Hollidaysburg*
John Hummel, *Selinsgrove*
James V. Long, *Pittsburgh*
Arthur Maginnis, *Swift Water*
G. M. Miller, *Wilkes-Barre*
Charles Porter, *Erie*
W. L. Powell, *Harrisburg*
H. J. Reeder, *Easton*
A. M. Spangler, *Philadelphia*
S. B. Stillwell, *Scranton*
Louis Streuber, *Erie*
George H. Welsons, *Pittsburgh*

332 *Appendix*

Board of Fishery Commissioners, 1898–1902
(board comprised of five to six members during this period with these individuals serving at various terms during these years)

James W. Correll, *Easton*
D. P. Corwin, *Pittsburgh*
Harry C. Cox, *Wellsboro*
James A. Dale, *York*
H. C. Demuth, *Lancaster*
John Hamberger, *Erie*
Louis Streuber, *Erie*
S. B. Stillwell, *Scranton*

Board of Fishery Commissioners, 1903–1913
(board comprised of five members during this period)

Nathan R. Buller, *Harrisburg*
James W. Correll, *Easton*
Henry C. Cox, *Wellsboro*
H. C. Demuth, *Lancaster*
John Hamberger, *Erie*
W. A. Leisenring, *Mauch Chunk*
Charles R. Miller, *Altoona*
John C. Ogden, *Johnstown*
S. B. Stillwell, *Scranton*
Andrew R. Whitaker, *Phoenixville*

Board of Fishery Commissioners, 1914–1918
(board comprised of five to six members during this period with these individuals serving at various terms during these years)

Nathan R. Buller, *Harrisburg*
John Hamberger, *Erie*
W. A. Leisenring, *Mauch Chunk*
John C. Ogden, *Johnstown*
Charles H. Thompson, *Philadelphia*
John H. Wagner, *Carnegie*

1919–1921 Reports unavailable

Board of Fish Commissioners, 1922–1936
(board comprised of eight to nine members during this period with these individuals serving at various terms during these years)

C. R. Buller, *Pleasant Mount*
Nathan R. Buller, *Harrisburg*
O. M. Deibler, *Greensburg*
Charles A. French, *Ellwood City*
George E. Gilchrist, *Lake Como*
John Hamberger, *Erie*
T. H. Harter, *Bellefonte*
William Mann Irvine, *Mercersburg*
Edgar W. Nicholson, *Philadelphia*
Milton L. Peek, *Devon*
Kenneth A Reid, *Connellsville*
Charles Reitell, *Pittsburgh*
M. A. Riley, *Ellwood City*
Dan R. Schnabel, *Johnstown*
Leslie W. Seylar, *McConnellsburg*
Roy Smull, *Mackeyville*
H. R. Stackhouse, *Waterford*
Harry E. Weber, *Philipsburg*
F. J. Weckesser, *Wilkes-Barre*

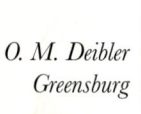

O. M. Deibler
Greensburg

Charles A. French
Ellwood City

Appendix 333

Board of Fish Commissioners, 1937–1948

(board comprised of seven to nine members during this period with these individuals serving at various terms during these years)

Paul F. Bittenbender, *Wilkes-Barre*
William D. Burk,
    Melrose Park, Philadelphia
Joseph Critchfield, *Confluence*
Oliver M. Deibler, *Greensburg*
Charles A. French, *Ellwood City*
John Hamberger, *Erie*
Bernard S. Horne, *Pittsburgh*
J. Fred McKean, *New Kensington*
C. A. Mensch, *Bellefonte*
John L. Neiger, *Scranton*
Edgar W. Nicholson, *Philadelphia*
Milton L. Peek, *Devon*
Frank J. Pentrack, *Johnstown*
Kenneth A. Reid, *Connellsville*
Dan R. Schnabel, *Johnstown*
H. R. Stackhouse, *Waterford*
Col. A. H. Stackpole, *Dauphin*
Samuel J. Truscott, *Dalton*
Harry E. Weber, *Philipsburg*
Clifford J. Welsh, *Erie*
Louis S. Winner, *Lock Haven*

Pennsylvania Fish Commission, 1949–1966

(board comprised of seven to eight members during this period with these individuals serving at various terms during these years)

Gerard Adams, *Hawley*
Philip E. Angle, *Sharon*
Paul F. Bittenbender, *Wilkes-Barre*
Maynard Bogart, *Danville*
William D. Burk,
    Melrose Park, Philadelphia
Joseph M. Critchfield, *Confluence*
Wallace C. Dean, *Meadville*
John W. Grenoble, *New Bloomfield*
Howard R. Heiny, *Williamsport*
Albert R. Hinkle, *Clearfield*
Bernard S. Horne, *Pittsburgh*
Charles C. Houser, *Allentown*
Douglas McWilliams, *Bear Gap*
Milton L. Peek, *Radnor*
Robert M. Rankin, *Galeton*
R. Stanley Smith, *Waynesburg*
Gen. A. H. Stackpole, *Dauphin*
Clifford J. Welsh, *Erie*
Raymond M. Williams, *East Bangor*
Louis S. Winner, *Lock Haven*

Pennsylvania Fish Commission, 1967–1982

(board comprised of nine members during this period with these individuals serving at various terms during these years)

Gerald J. Adams, *Hawley*
William Cox, *Elysburg*
Wallace C. Dean, *Meadville*
Clarence Dietz, *Bedford*
Walter F. Gibbs, *Reno*
Leonard A. Green, *Carlisle*
Sam Guaglianone, *Johnsonburg*
Howard R. Heiny, *Williamsport*
Ross J. Huhn, *Saltsburg*
William O. Hill, *Erie*
John A. Hugya, *Johnstown*
Calvin J. Kern, *Whitehall*
Robert L. Martin, *Bellefonte*
Frank E. Masland Jr., *Carlisle*
Douglas McWilliams, *Bear Gap*
Michael Mead, *Warren*
Garrett P. Mortensen, *Newville*
Robert M. Rankin, *Galeton*
R. Stanley Smith, *Waynesburg*
James J. Stumpf, *Laughlintown*
Jerome E. Southerton, *Honesdale*
Raymond M. Williams, *East Bangor*
J. Wayne Yorks, *Benton*

The Pennsylvania Board of Fish Commissioners shown in a meeting held on Friday, February 13, 1948. Seated, left to right: Charles A. French, Chairman, Ellwood City; Milton L. Peek, Radnor; and Clifford J. Welsh of Erie. Standing, left to right H. R. Stackhouse, Administrative Secretary, Waterford; William D. Burk, Melrose Park, Philadelphia; Paul F. Bittenbender, Wilkes-Barre; Bernard S. Home, Pittsburgh; Louis S. Winner, Lock Haven; and General A. H. Stackpole, Harrisburg and Dauphin.

Governor James H. Duff, surrounded by the Pennsylvania Fish Commission, signed House Bill No. 982 in 1949, creating the new Commission which supersedes the Pennsylvania Board of Fish Commissioners. From left to right are: General A. H. Stackpole; Bernard S. Horne; George Goodling, Member of the House of Representatives from York County; C. A. French, Executive Director of the Pennsylvania Fish Commission; J. Allen Barrett, Director of Publicity; Milton L. Peek; Louis S. Winner; George Shoemaker, Member of the House of Representatives, Clifford J. Welsh, Paul F. Bittenbender; ; C. R. Buller, Chief Fish Culturist; William D. Burk; and H. R. Stackhouse, Administrative Secretary.

Appendix **335**

On July 14, 1980, at the Commission meeting, three recently appointed members of the Pennsylvania Fish Commission were greeted by newly elected President Leonard A. Green, second from right, and Executive Director Ralph W. Abele, far right. The new Commissioners, left to right, are: Robert L. Martin, Bellefonte; Ross J. Huhn, Saltsburg; and J. Wayne Yorks, Benton.

Pennsylvania Fish Commission, 1983–1992

(board comprised of nine members during this period with these individuals serving at various terms during these years)

James S. Biery Jr., *Swatara*
Marilyn Black, *Meadville*
David Coe, *State College*
Mark Faulkner, *Boalsburg*
Walter F. Gibbs, *Titusville*
Leonard A. Green, *Carlisle*
John A. Hugya, *Johnstown*
Ross J. Huhn, *Saltsburg*
Calvin J. Kern, *Whitehall*

Robert L. Martin, *Bellefonte*
T. T. (Ted) Metzger Jr., *Johnstown*
Howard E. Pflugfelder, *New Cumberland*
Joan R. Plumly, *Jenkintown*
Leon Reed, *Honesdale*
William J. Sabatose, *Brockport*
Jerome E Southerton, *Honesdale*
J. Wayne Yorks, *Benton*

Pennsylvania Fish & Boat Commission, 1993–2000

(board comprised of nine to ten members during this period with these individuals serving at various terms during these years)

Donald K. Anderson, *Meyersdale*
James S. Biery Jr., *Swatara*
Marilyn A. Black, *Cochranton*
Samuel M. Concilla, *North East*
Ross J. Huhn, *Saltsburg*
Ted R. Keir, *Athens*
Donald N. Lacy, *Reading*

Paul J. Mahon, *Clarks Green*
T. T. (Ted) Metzger Jr., *Johnstown*
Enoch S. "Inky" Moore Jr., *Newville*
Howard E. Pflugfelder, *New Cumberland*
Leon Reed, *Honesdale*
William J. Sabatose, *Brockport*
J. Wayne Yorks, *Benton*

Pennsylvania Fish & Boat Commission, 2001–2010

(board comprised of six to ten members during this period with these individuals serving at various terms during these years)

Donald K. Anderson, *Meyersdale*	Leonard L. Lichvar, *Boswell*
Robert A. Bachman, *Denver*	Paul J. Mahon, *Clarks Green*
Samuel M. Concilla, *North East*	Fred Osifat, *Tresckow*
Richard W. Czop, *Collegeville*	Howard E. Pflugfelder, *New Cumberland*
G. Warren Elliott, *Chambersburg*	Leon Reed, *Honesdale*
Norman R. Gavlick, *Kingston*	William J. Sabatose, *Brockport*
Ross J. Huhn, *Saltsburg*	Thomas C. Shetterly, *North Charleroi*
Ted R. Keir, *Athens*	Rozell A. Stidd, *Huntingdon*
Donald N. Lacy, *Reading*	William R. Worobec, *Williamsport*

Pennsylvania Fish & Boat Commission, 2011–2016

(board comprised of ten members during this period with these individuals serving at various terms during these years)

Rocco S. Ali, *North Apollo*	Leonard L. Lichvar, *Boswell*
Robert A. Bachman, *Denver*	Edward P. Mascharka, III, *Erie*
G. Warren Elliott, *Chambersburg*	William J. Sabatose, *Brockport*
Norman R. Gavlick, *Kingston*	Thomas C. Shetterly, *North Charleroi*
Eric C. Hussar, *Lewisburg*	Glade E. Squires, *Downingtown*
Steven N. Ketterer, *Harrisburg*	William R. Worobec, *Williamsport*

photo–Spring Gearhart, PFBC

Shown in this presentation of the Commission receiving various proclamations touting PFBC's 150th anniversary in 2016 (see pages 349–352), are the Pennsylvania Fish & Boat Commissioners with PFBC Executive Director John Arway. From top row, left to right, are Glade E. Squires, Downingtown; Norman R. Gavlick, Kingston; Eric C. Hussar, Lewisburg; G. Warren Elliott, Chambersburg; and Leonard L. Lichvar, Boswell. Bottom row, left to right, are William J. Sabatose, Brockport; John A. Arway, Executive Director; Edward P. Mascharka III, Erie; Steven N. Ketterer, Harrisburg; and Rocco S. Ali, North Apollo. As this is a 10-member board, one Commissioner vacancy existed at the time of this photograph.

Members of the Boating Advisory Board, 1980–1992

(board comprised of four to five members during this period with these individuals serving at various terms during these years)

Nicholas Apfl, *Fairless Hills*
Clayton Buchanan, *Pittsburgh*
Charles Chattaqaway, *Monongahela*
David Coe, *State College*
Martin P. Eisert, *Erie*
Leroy Guccini, *Greentown*
Sherwood Krum, *Hawley*
Helen B. Lange, *Sharpsville*
Donald J. Little, *Philadelphia*
Leon Lyon, *Bellefonte*
Judy Obert, *Greentown*
Thaddeus Piotrowski, *Bloomsburg*
Edward J. Rogowski, *Holland*
Gerald Sedney, *Erie*

Shown in 1988, from left to right, are Bureau of Boating Director John Simmons and Boating Advisory Board Members Thaddeus Piotrowski, Clayton Buchanan, Judy Obert, and Helen B. Lange.

Members of the Boating Advisory Board, 1993–2000

(board comprised of five members during this period with these individuals serving at various terms during these years)

Gary Babbin, *Lancaster*
Clayton Buchanan, *Pittsburgh*
Richard W. Czop, *Collegeville*
Martin P. Eisert, *Erie*
Steven M. Ketterer, *Harrisburg*
Donald J. Little, *Philadelphia*
G. Edwin Matheny, *Greensburg*
Gary Miles, *North East*
Judy Obert, *Greentown*
Thaddeus Piotrowski, *Bloomsburg*
Vincent P. Riggi, *Clarks Summit*

Members of the Boating Advisory Board, 2001–2010

(board comprised of five to six members during this period with these individuals serving at various terms during these years)

Rex R. Beers, *Philadelphia*
Richard W. Czop, *Collegeville*
Henry Grilk, *Lakeview*
Steven M. Ketterer, *Harrisburg*
Michael LeMole, *Media*
Michael L. Lentine, *Langhorne*
Mary Liskow, *Marysville*
Loren W. Lustig, *Biglerville*
G. Edwin Matheny, *Greensburg*
Gary Miles, *North East*
Thaddeus Piotrowski, *Bloomsburg*
Andrew Talento, *Verona*
Damian Zampogna, *Harrisburg*

Members of the Boating Advisory Board, 2011–2016

(board comprised of five members during this period with these individuals serving at various terms during these years)

Mary Gibson, *Marysville*
Henry Grilk, *Lakeview*
Michael LeMole, *Media*
Loren W. Lustig, *Biglerville*
Andrew Talento, *Verona*

Pennsylvania Fish Commission and Pennsylvania Fish & Boat Commission Executive Directors

(date of appointment)

Charles A. French
April 25, 1949

William Voigt Jr.
September 12, 1955

Albert M. Day
July 18, 1960

Robert J. Bielo
January 11, 1965

Ralph W. Abele
January 3, 1972

Edward R. Miller
June 1, 1987

Lawrence W. Hoffman
March 1, 1994

Peter A. Colangelo
October 3, 1994

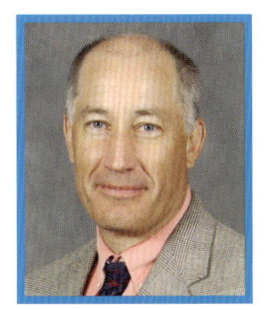

Douglas J. Austen Ph.D.
January 27, 2004

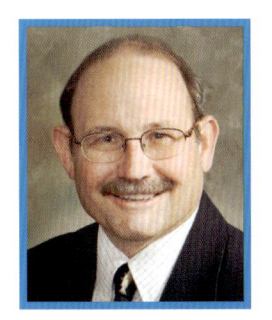

John A. Arway
March 2, 2010

Harrisburg Headquarters • *Harrisburg*

photo-Spring Gearhart, PFBC

Pennsylvania Fish & Boat Commission Locations:
Main Offices

Centre Region Office Complex • *Bellefonte*

Pleasant Gap Office Complex • *Pleasant Gap*

Appendix **341**

Pennsylvania Fish & Boat Commission Locations: State Fish Hatcheries

Oswayo State Fish Hatchery • *Coudersport*

Pleasant Mount State Fish Hatchery • *Pleasant Mount*

Tylersville State Fish Hatchery • *Loganton*

Van Dyke Research Station • *Thompsontown*

Benner Spring Research Station • *State College*

Pleasant Gap State Fish Hatchery • *Pleasant Gap*

Appendix

Bellefonte State Fish Hatchery • *Bellefonte*

Corry State Fish Hatchery • *Corry*

Union City State Fish Hatchery • *Union City*

Reynoldsdale State Fish Hatchery • *New Paris*

Fairview State Fish Hatchery • *Fairview*

Huntsdale State Fish Hatchery • *Carlisle*

Linesville State Fish Hatchery • *Linesville*

Tionesta State Fish Hatchery • *Tionesta*

Appendix **345**

Pennsylvania Fish & Boat Commission Locations: Bureau of Law Enforcement Region Offices

Northwest Region Office • *Meadville*

Northcentral Region Office • *Bellefonte*

Northeast Region Office • *Sweet Valley*

346 *Appendix*

Southwest Region Office • *Somerset*

photo-Captain Thomas Crist, PFBC

Southcentral Region Office • *Newville*

photo-Sergeant Craig Garman, PFBC

Southeast Region Office • *Elm*

photo-Captain Raymond Bednarchik Jr., PFBC

Appendix 347

2016

While its first use was in 1934 as a Fish Warden School, it wasn't officially opened until November 9, 1964, as a formal training facility for PFC and PFBC law enforcement officers.

photo-Dee Fisher, PFB

1954

1936

    The Commission's **H. R. Stackhouse School of Fishery Conservation and Watercraft Safety** is named after Commission employee H. R. Stackhouse. Also known as "Mr. Fish Commission," he came to the agency in 1917 and attained the position of Administrative Secretary in 1923. He maintained that role under every Executive Director of the Commission, except one, until his retirement after 43 years in 1960. At the beginning of 1960, he was appointed Acting Executive Director and was urged by friends to accept the position, but he declined. In 1954, he was honored with the Pennsylvania Fish and Game Associations' Gold Medal Award as the outstanding sportsman of the state.

150th Anniversary (1866–2016): Pennsylvania Fish & Boat Commission

This page and the following three pages contain national and state documents officially acknowledging the Commission's anniversary year and its contributions to both the United States and the Commonwealth of Pennsylvania.

COMMONWEALTH OF PENNSYLVANIA
OFFICE OF THE GOVERNOR
HARRISBURG

THE GOVERNOR

GREETINGS:

I am delighted to commemorate the 150th anniversary of the Pennsylvania Fish and Boat Commission.

Established in 1866 after a convention held in Harrisburg to investigate water pollution and the halting of American Shad runs by dams on the Susquehanna River, the Commission has evolved from a one-man operation supported solely by the general fund to a professional agency funded primarily by anglers and boaters through license and registration fees and the federal excise taxes on fishing and boating equipment.

Now in its 150th year, the agency protects, conserves, and enhances the commonwealth's aquatic resources while providing some of the best fishing and boating opportunities in the United States. An estimated 1.1 million anglers and over 3 million boaters enjoy Pennsylvania's waters each year, generating $1.2 billion in annual fishing-related expenditures. With more than 86,000 miles of streams and nearly 4,000 lakes, ponds, and reservoirs in the state, the commonwealth's aquatic resources are extensive, rich, and diverse.

As outlined in the Pennsylvania Constitution, the people have a right to clean air, pure water, and to the preservation of the natural, scenic, and historic values of the environment. Pennsylvania's public natural resources are the common property of all the people, including generations yet to come. As trustee of these resources, the commonwealth shall conserve and maintain them for the benefit of all people, and the Pennsylvania Fish and Boat Commission is essential in this mission.

As Governor, and on behalf of all citizens of the Commonwealth of Pennsylvania, it is my pleasure to congratulate the Pennsylvania Fish and Boat Commission on its 150th anniversary. Please accept my best wishes for continued success.

TOM WOLF
Governor
March 30, 2016

Appendix **349**

THE GENERAL ASSEMBLY OF PENNSYLVANIA

SENATE RESOLUTION
No. 314
Session of 2015

PRINTER'S NO. 1651

INTRODUCED BY SCAVELLO, BREWSTER, BAKER, TEPLITZ, SABATINA, DINNIMAN, FONTANA, EICHELBERGER, BARTOLOTTA, GREENLEAF, COSTA, RESCHENTHALER, ARGALL, TARTAGLIONE, RAFFERTY, KITCHEN, VULAKOVICH, FOLMER, BROWNE, McILHINNEY, YUDICHAK AND HUGHES, MARCH 22, 2016

INTRODUCED AND ADOPTED, MARCH 22, 2016

A RESOLUTION

1 Congratulating the Pennsylvania Fish and Boat Commission on 150
2   years of service to the Commonwealth.
3 WHEREAS, A convention held in Harrisburg to investigate water
4 pollution and the halting of American Shad runs by dams on the
5 Susquehanna River resulted in Governor Andrew Curtin signing the
6 act of March 30, 1866, establishing what is known today as the
7 Pennsylvania Fish and Boat Commission; and
8   WHEREAS, Over the last 150 years, the commission has evolved
9 from a one-man operation supported solely by the General Fund to
10 a professional agency funded primarily by anglers and boaters
11 through license and registration fees and the Federal excise
12 taxes on fishing and boating equipment; and
13   WHEREAS, With the guiding philosophy of "Resource First," the
14 commission protects, conserves and enhances this Commonwealth's
15 aquatic resources while provide fishing and boating
16 opportunities; and

---

1   WHEREAS, The commission provides the public with some of the
2 best recreational fishing and boating in the United States; and
3   WHEREAS, An estimated 1.1 million anglers and more than 3
4 million boaters enjoy Pennsylvania's waters each year,
5 generating $1.2 billion in annual fishing-related expenditures;
6 and
7   WHEREAS, Section 27 of Article I of the Constitution of
8 Pennsylvania provides:
9   The people have a right to clean air, pure water, and to
10   the preservation of the natural, scenic, historic and
11   esthetic values of the environment. Pennsylvania's public
12   natural resources are the common property of all the
13   people, including generations yet to come. As trustee of
14   these resources, the Commonwealth shall conserve and
15   maintain them for the benefit of all the people;
16 and
17   WHEREAS, With more than 86,000 miles of streams and nearly
18 4,000 lakes, ponds and reservoirs in the state, this
19 Commonwealth's aquatic resources are extensive, rich and
20 diverse; and
21   WHEREAS, The commission is responsible for managing and
22 safeguarding both aquatic habitat and species resources;
23 therefore be it
24   RESOLVED, That the Senate congratulate the Pennsylvania Fish
25 and Boat Commission on 150 years of service to the Commonwealth
26 and wish the agency well as it embarks on another 150 years of
27 service to the Commonwealth, its aquatic resources and our rich
28 recreational fishing and boating heritage.

20160SR0314PN1651   - 2 -

350   *Appendix*

PRINTER'S NO. 2955

THE GENERAL ASSEMBLY OF PENNSYLVANIA

HOUSE RESOLUTION
No. 737 Session of 2015

INTRODUCED BY GILLESPIE, HARHAI, TOOHIL, PEIFER, BENNINGHOFF, BOBACK, KIRKLAND, MURT, KOTIK, KNOWLES, V. BROWN, BAKER, SACCONE, PASHINSKI, BURNS, WATSON, MILLARD, CALTAGIRONE, MACKENZIE, THOMAS, VEREB, ELLIS, WHEELAND, D. COSTA, GODSHALL, NEILSON, WARD, HARHART, HENNESSEY, MALONEY, MARSICO, ROSS, PICKETT, SAINATO, KINSEY, O'NEILL, SONNEY, DUSH, PAYNE, GOODMAN AND READSHAW, MARCH 15, 2016

INTRODUCED AS NONCONTROVERSIAL RESOLUTION UNDER RULE 35, MARCH 15, 2016

A RESOLUTION

1 Celebrating the 150th anniversary of the Pennsylvania Fish and
2 Boat Commission.
3   WHEREAS, A convention held in Harrisburg to investigate water
4 pollution and the halting of American shad runs in the
5 Susquehanna River resulted in Governor Andrew Curtin signing Act
6 336 of 1866, which eventually led to what is known today as the
7 Pennsylvania Fish and Boat Commission; and
8   WHEREAS, Over the last 150 years, the commission has evolved
9 from a one-person operation funded solely by the money allocated
10 from the General Fund to a professional agency funded primarily
11 by anglers and boaters through license and registration fees and
12 Federal excise taxes on fishing and boating equipment; and
13 WHEREAS, With the guiding philosophy of "Resource First," the
14 commission protects, conserves and enhances this Commonwealth's
15 aquatic resources while providing fishing and boating

1 opportunities; and
2   WHEREAS, The commission provides the public with some of the
3 best recreational fishing and boating in the United States; and
4   WHEREAS, An estimated 1.1 million anglers and more than 3
5 million boaters enjoy this Commonwealth's waters each year,
6 generating $1.2 billion in annual fishing-related expenditures;
7 and
8   WHEREAS, Section 27 of Article I of the Constitution of
9 Pennsylvania states the following:
10   "The people have a right to clean air, pure water, and to
11   the preservation of the natural, scenic, historic and
12   esthetic values of the environment. Pennsylvania's public
13   natural resources are the common property of all the
14   people, including generations yet to come. As trustee of
15   these resources, the Commonwealth shall conserve and
16   maintain them for the benefit of all the people";
17 and
18 WHEREAS, With more than 86,000 miles of streams and nearly
19 4,000 lakes, ponds and reservoirs, this Commonwealth's aquatic
20 resources are extensive, rich and diverse; and
21 WHEREAS, The commission is responsible for managing and
22 safeguarding both aquatic habitats and species resources;
23 therefore be it
24 RESOLVED, That the House of Representatives celebrate the
25 Pennsylvania Fish and Boat Commission for 150 years of service
26 to this Commonwealth and wish the commission well as it embarks
27 on another 150 years of service to this Commonwealth, its
28 aquatic resources and rich recreational fishing and boating
29 heritage.

2016HR0737PN2955   - 2 -

Appendix   351

In a historic moment during PFBC's 150th anniversary commemoration at The State Museum of Pennsylvania on March 30, 2016, PFBC Executive Directors (left to right) Edward R. Miller, Peter A. Colangelo, Douglas J. Austen, and John A. Arway are gathered for a group photo.

photo–Spring Gearhart, PFBC

H1622   CONGRESSIONAL RECORD — HOUSE   April 12, 2016

150TH ANNIVERSARY OF THE PENNSYLVANIA FISH AND BOAT COMMISSION

(Mr. THOMPSON of Pennsylvania asked and was given permission to address the House for 1 minute and to revise and extend his remarks.)

Mr. THOMPSON of Pennsylvania. Mr. Speaker, I rise today to congratulate the Pennsylvania Fish and Boat Commission, or the PFBC, on their 150th anniversary.

The PFBC was founded on March 30, 1866, following a convention in Harrisburg that was held to investigate water pollution caused by the effect logging in the Commonwealth was having on mountain lakes and streams. The discussion at that meeting prompted the current Governor, Andrew Curtin, to sign a law naming James Worrall as the State's first Commissioner of Fisheries, creating what would become the Nation's second oldest fish or wildlife agency.

Since its founding 150 years ago, the PFBC has grown to employ more than 400 people and operates on an annual budget of nearly $60 million funded by anglers and boaters through license and registration fees, among other methods. The PFBC is responsible for policing 86,000 miles of Pennsylvania streams, nearly 4,000 lakes, more than 60 miles of Lake Erie's shoreline, and around 400,000 acres of wetlands.

As an avid fisherman, I am proud of the work done by the Pennsylvania Fish and Boat Commission in keeping our lakes and streams healthy.

logo design–Ted Walke, PFBC

352   Appendix

Total Boating Accidents & Fatalities Per Year 1998-2015

1990s Boating Safety billboard

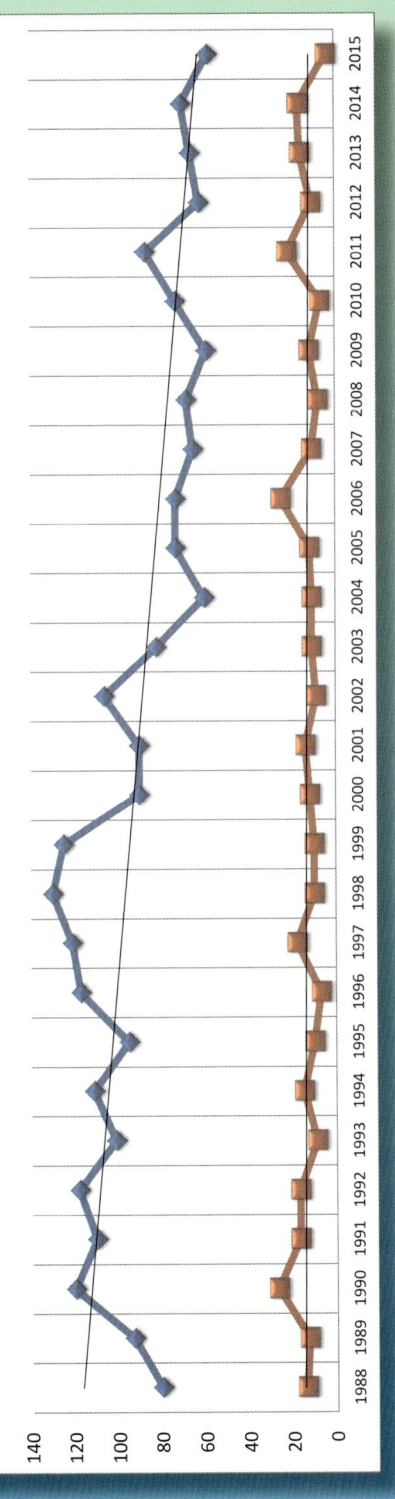

1980s Boating Safety billboard

Appendix 353

Editors of
Pennsylvania Angler/
Pennsylvania Angler & Boater
(dateline of first or renewed credit in magazine)

Alex P. Sweigart, *December 1931*

J. Allen Barrett, *March 1945*

Richard F. Williamson, *August 1946*

Fred E. Stone, *January 1948*

J. Allen Barrett, *September 1949*

George W. Forrest, *January 1951*

J. Allen Barrett, *October 1956*

George W. Forrest, *July 1960*

D. Thomas Eggler, *January 1968*

James F. Yoder, *January 1972*

Lou Hoffman, *August 1981*

Dave Wolf, *December 1981*

Art Michaels*, *August 1982*

Spring Gearhart, *September/October 2008***

*Concurrently editor of Boat Pennsylvania *magazine from datelines May/June 1984 through Fall 1995.*

**Pennsylvania Angler was retitled as Pennsylvania Angler & Boater with a bimonthly dateline, beginning with the January/February 1997 edition.

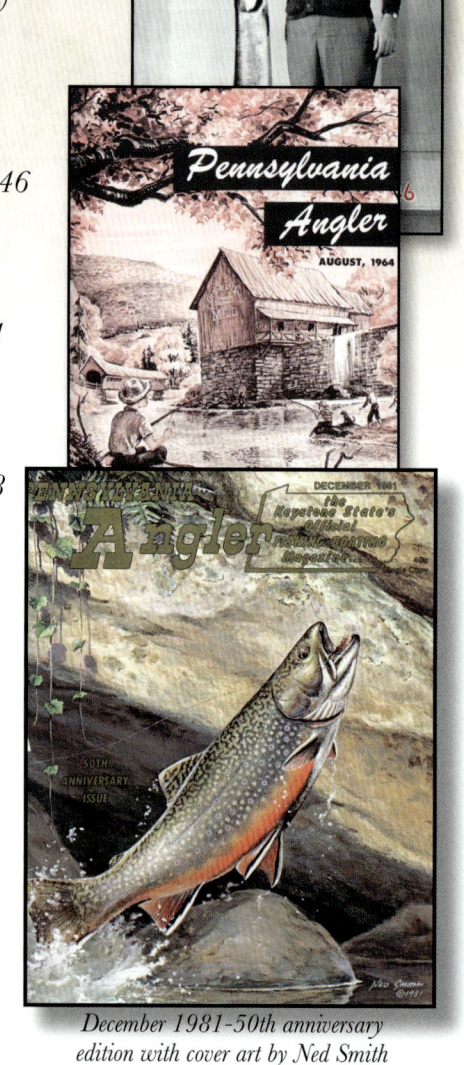

December 1981-50th anniversary edition with cover art by Ned Smith

354   *Appendix*

Pennsylvania Species by Watersheds

updated June 1, 2016, by Douglas Fischer, PFBC Ichthyologist

This table lists most Pennsylvania fishes occurring naturally in or introduced into Pennsylvania's major watershed systems. Listings denote any known occurrence.

Status
- **EN** = Endangered
- **TH** = Threatened
- **C** = Candidate
- **EX** = Believed extirpated
- ***** = Aquatic Invasive Species
- **DL** = Delisted

(removed from the endangered, threatened, or candidate species list due to significant expansion of range and abundance)

Watersheds
- **E** = Lake Erie
- **O** = Ohio River
- **G** = Genesee River
- **P** = Potomac River
- **S** = Susquehanna River
- **D** = Delaware River

Watershed Status
- **I** = Introduced
- **N** = Native
- **X** = Present in drainage, status uncertain at this time

For up-to-date species status and regulations, visit the Commission's website at **www.fishandboat.com**.

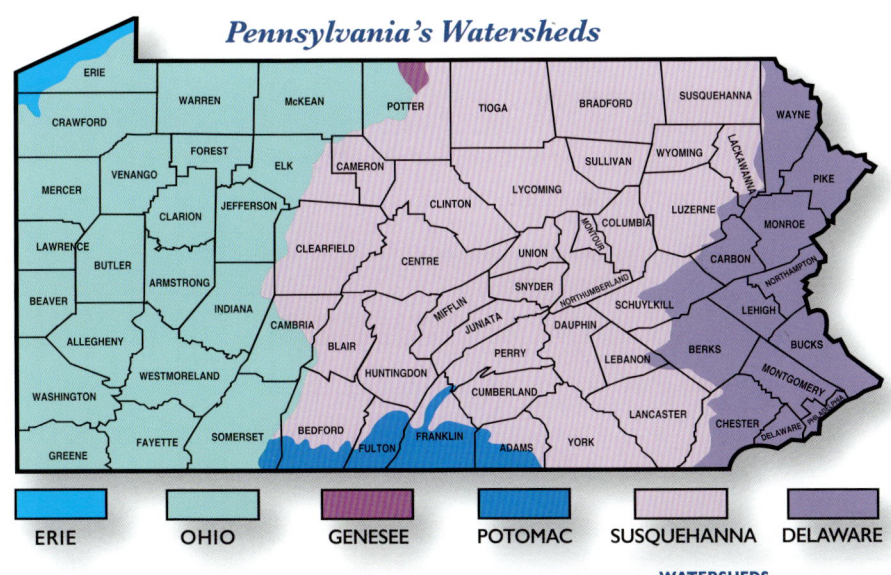

Pennsylvania's Watersheds

ERIE	OHIO	GENESEE	POTOMAC	SUSQUEHANNA	DELAWARE	

		WATERSHEDS					
SPECIES	**STATUS**	**E**	**O**	**G**	**P**	**S**	**D**
Lampreys (Family Petromyzontidae)							
Ohio Lamprey (*Ichthyomyzon bdellium*)	C		N				
Northern Brook Lamprey (*Ichthyomyzon fossor*)	EN	N	N				
Mountain Brook Lamprey (*Ichthyomyzon greeleyi*)	TH		N				
Silver Lamprey (*Ichthyomyzon unicuspis*)		N					
Least Brook Lamprey (*Lampetra aepyptera*)	C		N			N	
American Brook Lamprey (*Lethenteron appendix*)	DL	N	N	N			N
Sea Lamprey (*Petromyzon marinus*)		I*				N	N

Appendix 355

SPECIES	STATUS	E	O	G	P	S	D
Sturgeons (Family Acipenseridae)							
Shortnose Sturgeon (*Acipenser brevirostrum*)	EN						N
Lake Sturgeon (*Acipenser fulvescens*)	EN	N	N				
Atlantic Sturgeon (*Acipenser oxyrhynchus*)	EN					N	N
Shovelnose Sturgeon (*Scaphirhynchus platorynchus*)	EX		N				
Paddlefishes (Family Polyodontidae)							
Paddlefish (*Polyodon spathula*)	EX	N	N				
Gars (Family Lepisosteidae)							
Spotted Gar (*Lepisosteus oculatus*)	EN	N					
Longnose Gar (*Lepisosteus osseus*)	DL	N	N			N	N
Shortnose Gar (*Lepisosteus platostomus*)	EX		N				
Bowfins (Family Amiidae)							
Bowfin (*Amia calva*)	C	N	N			I	I
Mooneyes (Family Hiodontidae)							
Goldeye (*Hiodon alosoides*)	EX		N				
Mooneye (*Hiodon tergisus*)	DL	N	N				
Tenpounders (Family Elopidae)							
Lady Fish (*Elops saurus*)							N
Freshwater Eels (Family Anguillidae)							
American Eel (*Anguilla rostrata*)			N		N	N	N
Anchovies (Family Engraulidae)							
Bay Anchovy (*Anchoa mitchilli*)							N
Herrings (Family Clupeidae)							
Blueback Herring (*Alosa aestivalis*)							N
Skipjack Herring (*Alosa chrysochloris*)	DL		N				
Hickory Shad (*Alosa mediocris*)	EN					N	N
Alewife (*Alosa pseudoharengus*)		I	I		I	N	N
American Shad (*Alosa sapidissima*)						N	N
Atlantic Menhaden (*Brevoortia tyrannus*)							N
Gizzard Shad (*Dorosoma cepedianum*)		N	N			N	N
Carps and Minnows (Family Cyprinidae)							
Central Stoneroller (*Campostoma anomalum*)		N	N	N	N	N	X
Goldfish (*Carassius auratus*)		I	I		I	I	I
Northern Redbelly Dace (*Chrosomus eos*)	EN		N			N	
Southern Redbelly Dace (*Chrosomus erythrogaster*)	TH	N	N				
Mountain Redbelly Dace (*Chrosomus oreas*)						I	
Redside Dace (*Clinostomus elongatus*)		N	N	N		N	
Rosyside Dace (*Clinostomus funduloides*)					N	N	N
Grass Carp (*Ctenopharyngodon idella*)		I	I	I	I	I	I
Satinfin Shiner (*Cyprinella analostana*)					N	N	N
Spotfin Shiner (*Cyprinella spiloptera*)		N	N		N	N	N
Steelcolor Shiner (*Cyprinella whipplei*)			N				
Common Carp (*Cyprinus carpio*)		I			I	I	I
Streamline Chub (*Erimystax dissimilis*)			N				
Gravel Chub (*Erimystax x-punctatus*)	EN		N				
Tonguetied Minnow (*Exoglossum laurae*)			N	N			
Cutlips Minnow (*Exoglossum maxillingua*)						N	N	N
Brassy Minnow (*Hybognathus hankinsoni*)			N				
Eastern Silvery Minnow (*Hybognathus regius*)					N	N	N
Bigeye Chub (*Hybopsis amblops*)		N	N				
Bigmouth Shiner (*Hybopsis dorsalis*)	TH		N				
Ide (*Leuciscus idus*)						I	I
Striped Shiner (*Luxilus chrysocephalus*)		N	N				
Common Shiner (*Luxilus cornutus*)		N	N	N	N	N	N

SPECIES	STATUS	E	O	G	P	S	D
Redfin Shiner (Lythrurus umbratilis)	EN	N	N				
Silver Chub (Macrhybopsis storeriana)	DL	N	N				
Allegheny Pearl Dace (Margariscus margarita)		N	N	N	N	N	N
Hornyhead Chub (Nocomis biguttatus)	C	N	N				
River Chub (Nocomis micropogon)		N	N		N	N	I
Golden Shiner (Notemigonus crysoleucas)		N	N		N	N	N
Comely Shiner (Notropis amoenus)					N	N	N
Popeye Shiner (Notropis ariommus)	EX		N				
Emerald Shiner (Notropis atherinoides)		N	N				
Bridle Shiner (Notropis bifrenatus)	EN						N
River Shiner (Notropis blennius)	EN		N				
Silverjaw Minnow (Notropis buccatus)		N	N		N	N	
Ghost Shiner (Notropis buchanani)	EN		N				
Ironcolor Shiner (Notropis chalybaeus)	EN						N
Blackchin Shiner (Notropis heterodon)	EN	N	N				
Blacknose Shiner (Notropis heterolepis)		N	N				
Spottail Shiner (Notropis hudsonius)		N	I		N	N	N
Silver Shiner (Notropis photogenis)		N	N				
Swallowtail Shiner (Notropis procne)						N	N
Rosyface Shiner (Notropis rubellus)		N	N		N	N	
Sand Shiner (Notropis stramineus)		N	N				
Mimic Shiner (Notropis volucellus)		N	N	N		I	
Channel Shiner (Notropis wickliffi)			N				
Pugnose Minnow (Opsopoeodus emiliae)			N				
Bluntnose Minnow (Pimephales notatus)		N	N	N	I	N	N
Fathead Minnow (Pimephales promelas)		N	N	N	I	I	I
Bullhead Minnow (Pimephales vigilax)	EX		N				
Blacknose Dace (Rhinichthys atratulus)		N	N	N	N	N	N
Longnose Dace (Rhinichthys cataractae)		N	N	N	N	N	N
Rudd* (Scardinius erythrophthalmus)		I			I	I	
Creek Chub (Semotilus atromaculatus)		N	N	N	N	N	N
Fallfish (Semotilus corporalis)			I		N	N	N
Suckers (Family Catostomidae)							
River Carpsucker (Carpiodes carpio)			N				
Quillback (Carpiodes cyprinus)		N	N			N	N
Highfin Carpsucker (Carpiodes velifer)	EX		N				
Longnose Sucker (Catostomus catostomus)	EN	N	N				
White Sucker (Catostomus commersonii)		N	N	N	N	N	N
Blue Sucker (Cycleptus elongatus)	EX		N				
Eastern Creek Chubsucker (Erimyzon oblongus)					N	N	N
Lake Chubsucker (Erimyzon sucetta)	EX	N					
Northern Hogsucker (Hypentelium nigricans)		N	N	N	N	N	I
Smallmouth Buffalo (Ictiobus bubalus)	DL	X	N				
Bigmouth Buffalo (Ictiobus cyprinellus)	EN	N	N				
Black Buffalo (Ictiobus niger)			N				
Spotted Sucker (Minytrema melanops)	TH	N	N				
Silver Redhorse (Moxostoma anisurum)		N	N				
Smallmouth Redhorse (Moxostoma breviceps)			N				
River Redhorse (Moxostoma carinatum)	DL		N				
Black Redhorse (Moxostoma duquesnii)		N	N				
Golden Redhorse (Moxostoma erythrurum)		N	N		X		
Shorthead Redhorse (Moxostoma macrolepidotum)		N			N	N	
North American Catfishes (Family Ictaluridae)							
White Catfish (Ameiurus catus)			I			N	N
Black Bullhead (Ameiurus melas)	EN	N	N				X
Yellow Bullhead (Ameiurus natalis)		N	N		N	N	N
Brown Bullhead (Ameiurus nebulosus)		N	N		N	N	N
Blue Catfish (Ictalurus furcatus)	EX		N				

Appendix 357

SPECIES	STATUS	E	O	G	P	S	D
Channel Catfish (*Ictalurus punctatus*)		N	N		I	I	I
Mountain Madtom (*Noturus eleutherus*)	EN		N				
Stonecat (*Noturus flavus*)		N	N	N			
Tadpole Madtom (*Noturus gyrinus*)	EN	N	N	N		N	N
Margined Madtom (*Noturus insignis*)					N	N	N
Brindled Madtom (*Noturus miurus*)	TH	N	N				
Northern Madtom (*Noturus stigmosus*)	EN		N				
Flathead Catfish (*Pylodictis olivaris*)		N	N			I	I

Smelts (Family Osmeridae)
SPECIES	STATUS	E	O	G	P	S	D
Rainbow Smelt (*Osmerus mordax*)			I	I		I	N

Trouts and Salmons (Family Salmonidae)
SPECIES	STATUS	E	O	G	P	S	D
Longjaw Cisco (*Coregonus alpenae*)	EX	N					
Cisco (*Coregonus artedi*)	EN	N				I	
Lake Whitefish (*Coregonus clupeaformis*)		N					
Pink Salmon (*Oncorhynchus gorbuscha*)		I					
Coho Salmon (*Oncorhynchus kisutch*)		I	I			I	I
Rainbow Trout (*Oncorhynchus mykiss*)		I	I	I	I	I	I
Golden Rainbow Trout (*Oncorhynchus mykiss*)		I	I	I	I	I	I
Chinook Salmon (*Oncorhynchus tshawytscha*)		I				I	I
Sockeye Salmon (Kokanee) (*Oncorhynchus nerka*)						I	I
Atlantic Salmon (*Salmo salar*)		I				I	I
Brown Trout (*Salmo trutta*)		I	I	I	I	I	I
Brook Trout (*Salvelinus fontinalis*)		N	N	N	N	N	N
Lake Trout (*Salvelinus namaycush*)		N	I			N	I

Pikes and Mudminnows (Family Esocidae)
SPECIES	STATUS	E	O	G	P	S	D
Redfin Pickerel (*Esox americanus americanus*)						I	N
Grass Pickerel (*Esox americanus vermiculatus*)		N	N				
Northern Pike (*Esox lucius*)		N	N		I	I	I
Tiger Muskellunge (*Esox lucius x Esox masquinongy*)			I			I	I
Muskellunge (*Esox masquinongy*)		N	N		I	I	I
Chain Pickerel (*Esox niger*)			I		N	N	N
Amur Pike (*Esox reichertii*)						I	
Central Mudminnow (*Umbra limi*)	C	N	N				
Eastern Mudminnow (*Umbra pygmaea*)	C						N

Trout-Perches (Family Percopsidae)
SPECIES	STATUS	E	O	G	P	S	D
Trout Perch (*Percopsis omiscomaycus*)		N	N				

Pirate Perches (Family Aphredoderidae)
SPECIES	STATUS	E	O	G	P	S	D
Pirate Perch (*Aphredoderus sayanus*)	EX						N

Cods (Family Gadidae)
SPECIES	STATUS	E	O	G	P	S	D
Burbot (*Lota lota*) (endangered-inland populations only)	EN	N	N		N		

Toadfishes (Family Batrachoididae)
SPECIES	STATUS	E	O	G	P	S	D
Oyster Toadfish (*Opsanus tau*)							N

Mullets (Family Mugilidae)
SPECIES	STATUS	E	O	G	P	S	D
Striped Mullet (*Mugil cephalus*)							N

New World Silversides (Family Atherinopsidae)
SPECIES	STATUS	E	O	G	P	S	D
Brook Silverside (*Labidesthes sicculus*)	DL	N	N				
Rough Silverside (*Membras martinica*)							N
Inland Silverside (*Menidia beryllina*)							N
Atlantic Silverside (*Menidia menidia*)							N

Needlefishes (Family Belonidae)
SPECIES	STATUS	E	O	G	P	S	D
Atlantic Needlefish (*Strongylura marina*)							N
Agujon (*Tylosurus acus*)							N

SPECIES	STATUS	E	O	G	P	S	D
Topminnows (Family Fundulidae)							
Banded Killifish (*Fundulus diaphanus*)		N	N		N	N	N
Mummichog (*Fundulus heteroclitus*)			I			I	N
Striped Killifish (*Fundulus majalis*)							N
Pupfishes (Family Cyprinodontidae)							
Sheepshead Minnow (*Cyprinodon variegatus*)							N
Livebearers (Family Poeciliidae)							
Eastern Mosquitofish (*Gambusia holbrooki*)			I		I	I	I
Sticklebacks (Family Gasterosteidae)							
Fourspine Stickleback (*Apeltes quadracus*)						I	N
Brook Stickleback (*Culaea inconstans*)	C	N	N			I	
Threespine Stickleback (*Gasterosteus aculeatus*)	EN						N
Pipefishes and Seahorses (Family Syngnathidae)							
Northern Pipefish (*Syngnathus fuscus*)							N
Sculpins (Family Cottidae)							
Mottled Sculpin (*Cottus bairdii*)		N	N	N	N	N	
Blue Ridge Sculpin (*Cottus caeruleomentum*)					N	N	
Slimy Sculpin (*Cottus cognatus*)						N	N
Potomac Sculpin (*Cottus girardi*)					N	N	
Spoonhead Sculpin (*Cottus ricei*)	EX	N					
Checkered Sculpin (*Cottus sp. cognatus*)					N		
Deepwater Sculpin (*Myoxocephalus thompsoni*)	EX	N					
Temperate Basses (Family Moronidae)							
White Perch (*Morone americana*)			I	I		N	N
White Bass (*Morone chrysops*)			N	N		I	
Striped Bass (*Morone saxatilis*)					I	N	N
Striped Bass Hybrid (*Morone chrysops x Morone saxatilis*)				X		X	X
Sunfishes (Family Centrarchidae)							
Mud Sunfish (*Acantharchus pomotis*)	EX						N
Rock Bass (*Ambloplites rupestris*)		N	N		I	I	I
Blackbanded Sunfish (*Enneacanthus chaetodon*)	EX						N
Bluespotted Sunfish (*Enneacanthus gloriosus*)						N	N
Banded Sunfish (*Enneacanthus obesus*)	EN						N
Redbreast Sunfish (*Lepomis auritus*)					N	N	N
Green Sunfish (*Lepomis cyanellus*)		N	N		I	I	I
Pumpkinseed (*Lepomis gibbosus*)		N	N	N	N	N	N
Warmouth (*Lepomis gulosus*)	EN	N	N			I	I
Orangespotted Sunfish (*Lepomis humilis*)			X				
Bluegill (*Lepomis macrochirus*)		N	N		I	I	I
Longear Sunfish (*Lepomis megalotis*)	EN		N			I	
Redear Sunfish (*Lepomis microlophus*)			I			I	I
Smallmouth Bass (*Micropterus dolomieu*)		N	N	N	I	I	I
Spotted Bass (*Micropterus punctulatus*)			N				
Largemouth Bass (*Micropterus salmoides*)		N	N		I	I	I
White Crappie (*Pomoxis annularis*)		N	N		I	I	I
Black Crappie (*Pomoxis nigromaculatus*)		N	N		N	N	N
Perches and Darters (Family Percidae)							
Eastern Sand Darter (*Ammocrypta pellucida*)	EN	N	N				
Greenside Darter (*Etheostoma blennioides*)		N	N	N	I	I	I
Rainbow Darter (*Etheostoma caeruleum*)		N	N		I		
Bluebreast Darter (*Etheostoma camurum*)	DL		N				
Iowa Darter (*Etheostoma exile*)	EN	N	N				

Appendix 359

SPECIES	STATUS	E	O	G	P	S	D
Fantail Darter *(Etheostoma flabellare)*		N	N	N	N	N	
Swamp Darter *(Etheostoma fusiforme)*	EX						N
Spotted Darter *(Etheostoma maculatum)*	DL		N				
Johnny Darter *(Etheostoma nigrum)*		N	N	N			
Tessellated Darter *(Etheostoma olmstedi)*					N	N	N
Tippecanoe Darter *(Etheostoma tippecanoe)*	DL		N				
Variegate Darter *(Etheostoma variatum)*			N				
Banded Darter *(Etheostoma zonale)*			N			I	
Yellow Perch *(Perca flavescens)*		N	N		N	N	N
Chesapeake Logperch *(Percina bimaculata)*	TH					N	
Logperch *(Percina caprodes)*		N	N				
Channel Darter *(Percina copelandi)*	DL	N	N				
Gilt Darter *(Percina evides)*	DL		N				
Longhead Darter *(Percina macrocephala)*	DL		N				
Blackside Darter *(Percina maculata)*		N	N	N			
Sharpnose Darter *(Percina oxyrhyncha)*	EX		N				
Shield Darter *(Percina peltata)*					N	N	N
River Darter *(Percina shumardi)*			N				
Sauger *(Sander canadensis)*		N	N				
Walleye *(Sander vitreus)*		N	N		I	X	I
Blue Pike *(Sander vitreus glaucus)*	EX	N					
Bluefishes (Family Pomatomidae)							
Bluefish *(Pomatomus saltatrix)*							N
Jacks (Family Carangidae)							
Florida Pompano *(Trachinotus carolinus)*							N
Snappers (Family Lutjanidae)							
Gray Snapper *(Lutjanus griseus)*							N
Drums and Croakers (Family Sciaenidae)							
Freshwater Drum *(Aplodinotus grunniens)*		N	N				
Silver Perch *(Bairdiella chrysoura)*							N
Weakfish *(Cynoscion regalis)*							N
Spot *(Leiostomus xanthurus)*							N
Atlantic Croaker *(Micropogonias undulatus)*							N
Cichlids and Tilapias (Family Cichlidae)							
Blue Tilapia *(Oreochromis aureus)*						I	
Gobies (Family Gobiidae)							
Round Goby* *(Neogobius melanostomus)*		I	I				
Naked Goby *(Gobiosoma bosc)*							N
Tubenose Goby* *(Proterorhinus semilunaris)*		I					
Snakeheads (Family Channidae)							
Northern Snakehead* *(Channa argus)*							I
Turbots (Family Scophthalmidae)							
Windowpane *(Scophthalmus aquosus)*							N
Sand Flounders (Family Paralichthyidae)							
Smallmouth Flounder *(Etropus microstomus)*							N
Summer Flounder *(Paralichthys dentatus)*							N
Righteye Flounders (Family Pleuronectidae)							
Winter Flounder *(Pseudopleuronectes americanus)*							N
American Soles (Family Achiridae)							
Hogchoker *(Trinectes maculatus)*							N

Index

A

Abele Memorial Glen, Ralph. W. 225
Abele, Ralph, Jr. 168, 169, 328
Abele, Ralph W. vi, xxvii, xxviii, xxxii, 156, 165, 166, 167, 168, 169, 170, 176, 183, 190, 201, 204, 205, 206, 210, 213, 222, 223, 224, 225, 240, 242, 254, 288, 289, 293, 300, 303, 304, 313, 315, 324, 328, 329, 330, 331, 336, 339
Academy of Natural Sciences 211
acid precipitation 206
acid rain 206, 207
Acre Lake 283
Act 39 of 1991, Act of December 12, 1991 248
Act 50 of 1993, Keystone Recreation Park and Conservation Fund 249
Act 66 of 1984, Waterways Conservation Officer xvii, 217
Act 66 of 2012, license flexibility, multi-year licenses 313
Act 86 of 1937, Sunday fishing lawful xv
Act 101 of 1988, Municipal Waste Planning Recycling and Waste Reduction 163
Act 180 of 1949, Pennsylvania Fish Commission iv
Act 195 of 1970, Public Employee Relations 174
Act 256 of 1955, Oil and Gas Lease Fund 127
Act 263 of 1925, Board of Fish Commissioners iv
Act 330 of 1957, fishing license fees 108
Act 400 of 1963, boat numbering and boat registration fees 137, 193
Act 442 of 1967, Project 500 148, 179
Act, 1910 Federal Insecticide, Federal Environmental Pesticide Control Act 147
Act, 1955 Federal Air Pollution Control Act 152
Act of 1937, Pittman-Robertson 113, 137
Act of 1940, Motorboat Act 88
Act of 1948, Federal Water Pollution Control 164
Act of 1950, Federal Aid in Sport Fish Restoration Act, Dingell-Johnson Act 113
Act of 1958, Federal Boating Act 134
Act of 1963, Clean Air Act 152, 208
Act of 1964, Wilderness Act 152
Act of 1967, Air Quality Act 152
Act of 1968, Wild and Scenic Rivers Act of 1968 152
Act of 1971, Boat Safety Act 136
Act of 1977, Clean Water Act 164
Act of 1987, Water Quality Act 164
Act of April 22, 1905, Sanitary Water Act 50
Act of April 28, 1873, Board of Fishery Commissioners 18
Act of June 3, 1878, Sunday fishing illegal xv
Act of June 22, 1964, Project 70 Land Acquisition and Borrowing 139, 147, 148
Act of March 30, 1866, Fishery Commissioner iv, 18
Act of May 25, 1901, prohibition of poisonous substances xvi
algae xx, 302, 309
algae, wooly green 309
Allen, John 312, 331
Amendment, Environmental Rights, Article 1, Section 27 xxiii, 156, 158, 293
American Red Cross 172
American Revolution 11
American Viscose Corporation 158, 159
American Water Company 297
amphibians xv, xviii, xxvii, xxix, 174, 196, 207, 209, 211, 263, 277, 281, 315
Andrejewski, John 255
anniversary, 100th 145
anniversary, 125th 249
anniversary, 150th iv, xxxii, 337, 349, 352
Aquatic Resource Program Specialist 280
Arthur, Chester A. 27
Arway, John A. iv, xxvii, xxviii, xxxi, xxxii, 168, 208, 209, 252, 264, 292, 293, 294, 295, 296, 300, 301, 302, 303, 305, 307, 308, 324, 325, 328, 329, 330, 331, 337, 339, 352
Association, American Sportfishing 254
Association, Blooming Grove Park Fish 37, 39
association, Boating Association of Southeast Pennsylvania 281
Association, Delaware River Shad Fishermen's 205, 262
Association, Enola Sportsmen's 302
Association, Fishing Creek Sportsmen's 303
Association, Fish Protective Association of Eastern Pennsylvania 32, 37, 39
Association, National Parks 176
Association, Norristown Fish and Game Protective 39
Association, Pennsylvania Fish Protective 37, 39
Association, Pohoqualine Fish 39
Austen, Douglas J. 269, 270, 281, 287, 288, 289, 330, 331, 339, 352
Avau, Susan 268
Award, American Motors Conservation 170
Award, Angler 189, 286
Award, Ralph W. Abele Conservation Heritage Award 225

B

Baird, Spencer Fullerton 26
Bald Eagle Creek 16, 20, 242, 313
Barrett, J. Allen 335, 354
baseball, Baltimore Orioles 55
baseball, Chicago White Stockings 55
baseball, Pittsburgh Pirates 55
bass vi, vii, xiii, xviii, 11, 20, 25, 53, 59, 64, 67, 69, 71, 82, 83, 112, 160, 183, 219, 262, 268, 286, 293, 300, 302, 312, 313
bass, black vii, 25, 53, 83
Bass, Largemouth 72, 110, 138, 160, 231, 267, 280, 312, 331, 359

Index   **361**

Bass, Smallmouth xii, xviii, xix, xxxi, 67, 71, 72, 160, 207, 231, 280, 300, 301, 302, 312, 359
Bass, Spotted 160, 359
Bass, Striped 228, 232, 262, 280, 287, 359
Beltzville Lake 179
Benner Township 296
Bertram, Joseph 82
Bethlehem Steel 176, 177
Bielo, Robert J. xx, 143, 144, 146, 149, 158, 159, 160, 161, 165, 166, 176, 328, 339
Bigelow Lake 44
Big Fill Run 286
Big Spring vii, 148, 248
biologists, fish culturists 115, 128, 200
Bittle, Harry 167, 328
Black, Marilyn 224, 336
black spot xviii, xix
Blackwell, Oliver P. 47
Bleech, Mike 310, 312, 331
Blooming Grove Creek 20
Blue Coal Corporation 136
Bluegill 83, 110, 234, 292, 359
Board, Great Lakes Water Quality 151
boating ii, iv, v, xvii, xx, xxi, xxiii, xxiv, xxviii, xxxi, 88, 108, 119, 127, 131, 136, 137, 139, 149, 165, 166, 170, 187, 191, 193, 195, 200, 211, 212, 213, 215, 216, 219, 221, 242, 246, 248, 249, 251, 254, 255, 264, 265, 269, 271, 273, 281, 282, 283, 284, 294, 296, 301, 312, 314, 315, 320, 322, 324
boating safety xvii, 119, 166, 187, 195, 211, 221, 247, 254, 264, 265, 312, 315, 320, 324, 353
Boating Safety Education 195, 265

Boating Safety Education Certificate xvii, 265
Boating Under the Influence (BUI) xvii, 215, 216, 219, 283, 329
book, *Fishes of Pennsylvania and the Northeastern United States* 211, 329
book, *Guns of Autumn, The* 176
book, *History of the Management of Trout Fisheries in Pennsylvania* 208, 329
book, *My Wilderness* 147, 327
book, *Pennsylvania Angler's Cookbook* 179
book, *Pennsylvania Fishing Summary* xiii
book, *Silent Spring* 143, 144, 327
Boughter, Steven 261
Bowfin xxvii, 233, 311, 356
bowfishing 285
Boyden, Horace 64
Briggs, Frank P. 137
British Common Law 8
Brown, Dave 182
Brumbaugh, Martin 8, 40, 55
Buck, John 141
Buckman, Walter 297
Buller, C. R. 60, 333, 335
Buller, Nathan 51
Buller, William vii, 27
Burbot 233, 311, 358
Bureau of Boating 221, 247, 338
Bureau of Education and Information 218, 220, 240, 243, 246, 330
Bureau of Fisheries 145, 178, 179, 247, 248, 265
Bureau of Hatcheries 309
Bureau of Law Enforcement xxviii, 228, 271, 292, 346, 347
Bureau of Property and Facilities Management 247

Bureau of Research xi, 59
Bureau of Waterways 178, 195, 204, 212, 213
Burkholder, Gail 267
Burns, Marcelline 216, 329
Buss, Keen 143

C

cadets, law enforcement 209, 254
Canada-United States Great Lakes Quality Agreements 151
Canoe Creek 242
carp vii, xvii, 53, 118, 262, 280, 285, 310
Carp, Asian 310
Carson, Rachel 143, 152, 327
Carter, Jimmy 190
Casey, Robert P. 240, 243, 248, 249, 260, 310
Casselman River 20
catfish 83, 110
Catfish, Bullhead xxvii, 71, 233
Chambers, Virgil 209, 211, 212
Chesapeake Bay v, vi, xviii, xix, xx, xxx, 26, 286, 287, 300, 310, 331
Civil War, American xxi, 13, 126, 316
Clark Creek 313
Clark's Ferry 29
Clark, William 14
Clean Streams Month 144
club, Fly Fishers' Club of Harrisburg 90
Club, Helping Hands for Habitat 276
Club, Lehigh Falls Fishing 255, 330
Club, Pine Creek Conservation 175
Club, Pittsburgh Sportsmen's Luncheon 87
club, Schuylkill Fishing Company of the State in Schuylkill 10
Clubs, Federation of Sportsmen's 204, 255, 281

Club, Spruce Creek Rod and Gun 165
Coalition of Concerned Anglers 281
Code, Fish and Boat xvii, 204
code, Vehicle Code, Title 75 255
codification 181, 201, 204, 208
Colangelo, Peter 250, 261, 269, 352
College, Gettysburg 250
college, The New York College of Forestry 13, 325
Colonial Assembly 8, 10, 11
Columnaris 312
Commission, Atlantic States Marine Fisheries xxx, 142
Commission, Chesapeake Bay xxx
Commission, Civil Service 112
Commission, Delaware River Basin xxx, 205, 305
Commissioner of Fisheries iv, xxix, 18, 44, 45, 51, 56, 60, 324
Commissioners, Board of Fish iv, xv, 59, 60, 66, 87, 88, 111, 319, 320, 326, 327, 331, 333, 334, 335
Commission, Federal Energy Regulatory 204, 247
Commission, Great Lakes Fisheries xxx
Commission, Joint State Government 140, 327
Commission, New Jersey Fish 47
Commission, Nuclear Regulatory (NRC) 196
Commission, Oregon Fish 134
Commission (PGC), Pennsylvania Game xxx, xxxi, 59, 140, 163, 166, 295, 296, 327

362 *Index*

Commission (PHMC), Pennsylvania Historical and Museum 148, 249, 313, 325
Commonwealth Court of Pennsylvania 269
Conneaut Lake 46, 261
Conservation Acquisition Partnership (CAP) 251
Consol Energy 314, 331
Constitution of the United States 11
Corbett, Tom 301, 302
Corl, Sally A. xvii
Corps, Civilian Conservation 64, 110
Corps of Discovery, The 14
Corps, Pennsylvania's Youth Conservation 183
Corps, Volunteer E & I 220, 221
Court of Common Pleas of Dauphin County 159
Court of Common Pleas of Huntingdon County, 268
Court of Common Pleas of Luzerne County 255
Court, Pennsylvania Superior 254, 255
CPR 195, 213, 282
Cranberry Glade Lake 292
crappies 210, 219, 234, 262
Creveling, John P. vi, 30
Cronkite, Walter 176
Crystal Spring Brook Trout Company 53
Curtin, Andrew G. iv, 18

D

Dailey, James 48
Dam, Columbia 12, 20, 29
Dam, Conowingo vi, 59, 174, 188, 189, 191, 204, 262
Dam, Dock Street 287

Dam, Fairmount Park 191
Dam, Holtwood v, vi, 13, 191
dam, low-head 212, 287
Dam, North Island 13
Dam, Safe Harbor 64, 86, 263
Dam, York Haven vi, 191, 267
Darby Creek 313
Davis, Art 310
Davis, E. W. 70
Day, Albert M. 134, 137, 143, 339
Day at a Hatchery 246
Day at the River 221
DDT 139, 144, 147, 161
Deibler, Oliver M. 62, 63, 73, 326, 334
Deibler, Terence 261
Delaware River vi, xiii, xxii, xxiv, xxix, 10, 11, 12, 13, 20, 21, 32, 35, 37, 47, 150, 191, 205, 262, 294, 305, 313, 355
Department of Agriculture 16, 325
Department of Conservation and Natural Resources (DCNR) xxx, 254, 255, 262, 268, 275, 295
Department of Corrections 295, 296
Department of Environmental Protection (DEP) xv, xviii, xxx, 255, 262, 268, 286, 300, 301, 302, 305, 306, 307, 308, 310
Department of Environmental Resources (DER) 162, 163, 165, 166, 167, 168, 173, 195, 210, 246, 247, 249, 310
Department of Fisheries 44, 45, 56, 325, 326
Department of Forests and Waters 64, 118, 127, 148, 158
Department of Health 50, 52, 163, 196

Department of Labor and Industry 40
Department of Mines and Mineral Industries 148, 163
Didymosphenia 308
Diehl, Leann R. 214, 215, 329
Dietz, Clarence 146, 334
Diez, Tom 278, 279
Division, Boating Safety and Education 247
Division, Law Enforcement 195, 219
Division of Engineering 195
Division of Fisheries 177, 194, 210, 218, 252, 328
Division of Fisheries Environmental Services 210, 218
Donegal Springs vi
Douglas, William O. 144
Driscoll, Jeremiah 48
Duff, James 110, 332
Duncan, Peter 166, 167, 328
Dunkard Creek 314
Duran Jr., Tom 9, 61, 203, 229, 230, 231, 232, 233, 234, 235, 236, 237, 238, 239
Durkin, James 137

E

Earle, George 77, 111
Earth Day 108, 156, 161, 162
East and West Basin Ponds 277
Easton vi, 20, 262
Edwards Jr., Thomas 277, 330, 346
Eel, American 232, 262, 356
Eggler, D. Thomas 354
electric, Metropolitan Edison Company 196, 200
electric, Pennsylvania Power and Light Company 59, 69, 204
electric, Philadelphia Electric Company 191, 204

electric, Safe Harbor Water Power Company 64, 205
electroshocking 147, 161
endocrine disrupting chemicals (EDCs) 302
Enhancing Fishing and Boating in Pennsylvania: Strategies for the 21st Century 264
Environmental Movement 152
Environmental Planning Designs Inc. 296
Erie-Western Pennsylvania Port Authority 313
Everett, Fred 90, 91, 92, 93, 94, 95, 96, 97, 98, 99, 100, 101, 102, 103, 104, 105, 106
Evitts Creek Water Company 86
exhibits, portable backwall 273
extinction 279

F

Facebook xii, xxviii, 321, 322
Family Fishing Festivals 298, 299
Fine, John S. 319, 331
fingerlings vii, xi, 172, 189, 220, 265, 272
Finnegan, James 128
Fischer, Douglas 355
fish, anadromous v, 188
Fisheries Management Research 139
Fisherman's Paradise xiii, xv, 66, 118, 120, 121, 122, 123, 124, 125, 133, 137, 140, 141, 296
Fish-for-Free Day-Days xii, 216, 217, 298
Fish-for-Fun area xiii, 129
fishing ii, iv, v, xii, xiii, xv, xvi, xvii, xx, xxi, xxiii, xxiv, xxvii, xxviii, xxxi, 2, 5, 6, 7, 8, 9, 10, 11, 12, 13, 21, 30, 32, 34, 36, 40, 46, 48, 52, 57, 59, 63, 64, 66, 67, 70, 71, 72, 73, 86, 87, 88, 89,

Index   363

fishing (continued)
90, 108, 109, 110, 112, 113, 118, 120, 124, 125, 127, 129, 137, 138, 149, 165, 170, 175, 180, 181, 182, 183, 190, 193, 195, 200, 205, 210, 212, 216, 217, 219, 220, 221, 242, 246, 248, 249, 250, 251, 254, 255, 261, 262, 264, 267, 268, 269, 270, 271, 273, 276, 277, 280, 281, 282, 284, 285, 287, 288, 292, 293, 294, 296, 297, 298, 299, 300, 301, 302, 308, 312, 313, 314, 320, 322, 323, 324

fishway v, vi, 20, 26, 29, 313
flood control 59, 69
Flood, Dan 171
fly-tying classes 81, 116
Fondoski, Wayne 276
Fords Lake 70
Forest, Bridger National 147
Forked Springs 82
Forrest, George W. 354
fracking xix, 304
Frankstown Branch of the Juniata River 242
French, Charles A. iv, 111, 118, 327, 333, 334, 335, 339
French Creek 158, 262
Frog, Bullfrog 60, 61, 237
Frog, Northern Green 60, 237, 279
Frog, Northern Leopard 237, 279
Frog, Pickerel 60, 237
frogs, propagating 61
Fund, Boat 174, 178, 194, 218, 313, 317
Fund, Fish 174, 175, 178, 194, 218, 246, 251, 313, 314, 317
Fund, Ralph W. Abele Conservation Scholarship xxviii, xxxii, 303, 304
Fund, State Land and Water Conservation and Reclamation 148

G

Gearhart, Spring xix, xxxii, 58, 135, 225, 265, 272, 273, 282, 287, 289, 291, 292, 295, 296, 297, 299, 307, 315, 317, 318, 320, 337, 340, 352, 354, 368
Geographic Information System (GIS) 289
Germany vii, 27, 51, 89
Gettig, Russ 190, 199, 210, 213, 214, 215, 217, 218, 219, 220, 221, 226, 240, 252
Gilmore-Luben, Marlene 267
Ginsberg, Allen 162
Glade Run 297
Glen Alden Mining Corporation 136, 137
Glendale Lake xi, xv
Goddard, Maurice K. 127, 128, 163, 165, 324
Google 321
Gore Jr., Al 143
Graff, Delano R. 145, 252
Grasso, Vincent 16
Graybill, J. Carl 252
Great Depression, The 63, 89
Greiner, Gerald 242
Growing Greener 275
Guise, Dennis T. 181, 204, 250, 252, 261, 269
Gutermuth, C. R. 137

H

habitat improvement xxx, 80, 247, 263, 275, 281, 285, 317
Haibach, Joanne 181, 329
Hall, Samuel 164
Harmon Creek 148
Hartman, Philip 50
Hatchery, Bellefonte State Fish vii, 43, 44, 53, 67, 82, 83, 84, 122, 140, 141, 309, 313, 333, 334, 336, 338, 341, 344, 346

hatchery, Benner Spring Research Station vii, 66, 118, 119, 139, 174, 195, 241, 295, 296, 309, 343
Hatchery, Bristol State Fish xiii, 35, 37
Hatchery, Corry (Western) State Fish vii, 21, 22, 23, 24, 25, 26, 27, 36, 53, 84, 248, 344
Hatchery, Crawford State Fish 46
Hatchery, Eastern State Fish 24, 26, 36
Hatchery, Fairview State Fish vii, 179, 345
Hatchery, Huntsdale State Fish vii, 73, 85, 179, 248, 309, 345
Hatchery, Linesville State Fish vii, 147, 149, 229, 246, 345
Hatchery, Oswayo State Fish vii, 149, 179, 342
Hatchery, Pleasant Gap State Fish vii, 240, 248, 309, 343
Hatchery, Pleasant Mount (Wayne) State Fish vii, xi, 41, 42, 44, 53, 56, 60, 82, 85, 342
Hatchery, Reynoldsdale State Fish vii, 59, 83, 84, 183, 344
Hatchery, Spruce Creek 44
Hatchery, Tionesta State Fish vii, 59, 83, 87, 248, 345
Hatchery, Torresdale State Fish 44, 45, 53, 85
Hatchery, Trexler State Fish 89
Hatchery, Tylersville State Fish vii, 309, 310, 342
Hatchery, Union City State Fish vii, xi, 60, 344
hatchery, Van Dyke Research Station vi, 188, 189, 343
hatch house 119, 188
Havre de Grace 26, 37

Hendricks, Michael L. 188, 189, 294, 295, 329, 331
herring vi, 6, 35, 150, 191
Hewitt, Charles A. 47
Highway Robbery 305, 306, 307, 331
Hille, Ernie 89
Hoffa, James R. "Jimmy" 137
Hoffman, Lawrence W. 250, 339
Hoffman, Lou 354
Hoover, Raymond 182
Hoover's Spring vi
Hornicak, Jake 216
Houser, Cecil 276

I

illegal trafficking 263
Illinois Department of Natural Resources 270
Industrial Revolution, American xxi
Ingram Springs 148
Internet xii, 321

J

Jackson and Sharp of Wilmington 35
Jackson, Larry 228
jet skis, Personal Watercraft (PWC) xvii, 266
Johnson, J. Albert 64
Johnson, Lyndon B. 152
Johnstown Flood 176
Johns, Will 210
Joint House-Senate Conservation Committee 166
Juniata River vi, 13, 29, 242, 268, 269
Junior Citation Winners 150
Junior Conservationists of Pennsylvania 67, 87, 88

K

Kahle Lake 183
Kamerzel, Thomas 228, 248
Kaneski, David 261, 266, 267, 330
Kauffman, M. M. 86
Kaufmann, Michael 217

364 *Index*

Keller, John 267
Kennedy, John F. 152
Kettle Creek 172
Kilbuck Access 265
King Charles II 6
King's College 306
Kokanee Salmon xi, 230, 358
Kray, Robert 252, 256
Kriesock, Billy 72
Kury, Franklin 156

L

Lackawaxen Creek xi
Lafayette, General 11
Lake Ariel 69
Lake Erie xiii, xv, xviii, 26, 30, 32, 34, 35, 48, 50, 51, 61, 88, 150, 179, 181, 182, 251, 265, 272, 296, 308, 313, 331, 355
Lake Gordon 86
Lake Somerset 118
Lake Wallenpaupack 59, 69, 70, 150
Land and Water Management 139
Lane, Carol 110
Larsen, Howard 223
Laudadio, John 165
Laurel Highlands 297
Lauver, Donald L. 292
Lavanish, George 252
Law, Clean Streams 66, 158, 328
law enforcement, Deputy Waterways Conservation Officers (DWCOs) xv, xvi, xvii, 179, 282
law enforcement, Fish Wardens xv, xvi, xvii, 18, 30, 39, 44, 52, 53, 57, 59, 112, 115, 138, 142, 318
law enforcement, Special Wardens xv
law enforcement, Special Waterways Patrolmen 179, 180
law enforcement, Thin Green Line xxviii, 150, 168, 218, 271
law enforcement, Waterways Conservation Officers (WCOs) xv, xvii, xxxi, 59, 179, 218, 228, 248, 250, 252, 266, 267, 282, 292, 297, 318, 330

law enforcement, Waterways Patrolmen xvii, 150, 162, 163, 164, 165, 168, 172, 178, 179, 180, 181, 182, 195, 216, 217
Lawrence, David L. xiii
Law, Resident Fish License xvi
Leader, George M. 52, 108, 126, 127, 128, 324, 326, 327
legislation, House Bill 296 175
legislation, House Bill 2155 281
legislation, Pennsylvania General Assembly xxx, 21, 26, 32, 44, 48, 127, 140, 156, 162, 166, 167, 168, 174, 175, 210, 281
Lehigh River 26, 71, 255, 262, 265, 296
Lehigh River Preservation, Protection and Improvement Foundation 262
Lenapes 2
Leopold, Aldo xix, xx
Let's Go Fishing in Pennsylvania Week 146
Lewis and Clark Expedition 14
Lewis, Meriwether 14
Leyendecker, J. C. 90
Liberty Bell 59
license button, fishing xii, xvi, 57, 116, 302
license, fishing xii, xvi, xxi, xxvii, 57, 59, 89, 108, 129, 137, 149, 175, 190, 246, 281, 294, 302, 323, 324
license, multiple-year fishing 313, 323
license, voluntary youth xii
Little Juniata River 268, 269
Little Lehigh River 26, 71
London International Fisheries Exhibition 27, 319
Long, Stanley 150
Lord of the Fish 201
Louis XIV 53

Loyalsock Creek 172
Lyman Lake 284

M

Mackay, Alan 192, 329
Mackey, Martha 267, 330
magazine, *Boat Pennsylvania* xii, 213, 214, 215, 216, 249, 329, 354
magazine, *Pennsylvania Angler* xii, xxi, xxviii, xxxii, 67, 68, 69, 70, 73, 88, 90, 91, 92, 93, 94, 95, 96, 97, 98, 99, 100, 101, 102, 103, 104, 105, 106, 107, 109, 119, 139, 145, 150, 160, 166, 170, 177, 178, 179, 181, 193, 201, 205, 226, 229, 242, 244, 245, 248, 249, 256, 258, 259, 266, 274, 277, 280, 285, 290, 293, 307, 318, 320, 322, 323, 324, 326, 327, 328, 329, 330, 331
magazine, *Pennsylvania Angler & Boater* xxviii, xxxii, 229, 248, 258, 259, 266, 274, 277, 280, 285, 290, 293, 307, 318, 320, 322, 323, 324, 329, 330, 331
magazine, *Pennsylvania Game and Fish* 262
magazine, *Saturday Evening Post* 90
magazine, *The New Yorker* 144
Magna Carta 8
Mahon, Paul J. 252, 336, 337
Manning, Leroy "Shortie" 175
maps, region 273
Marcellus Shale 294, 301, 304, 305, 306, 308
Marsh Creek Lake 283
Martin, Dan 247, 281
Mayhew, Allison J. 252
McNaughton, Mark 260
Meehan, W. E. 45, 326
Mentored Youth Program xii, xxviii, 313, 320, 323

Michaels, Art ii, xvii, xxi, xxiv, 5, 7, 13, 220, 248, 250, 252, 259, 260, 261, 268, 269, 270, 271, 275, 276, 277, 280, 281, 286, 319, 331, 354
migratory fish restoration v, vi, xxix, 13, 113, 174, 183, 188, 189, 191, 204, 205, 264
Miller, Edward R. 223, 224, 252, 339, 352
Mingle, Walter 72
mining, anthracite, anthracite coal mine 15, 17, 20, 63, 126, 137
mining, bituminous, bituminous coal mine 15, 17, 63, 160
Misery Bay xiii
Mix Run 284
mobile application, FishBoatPA xii, 314
Mock, Johnny 87
Monongahela River 20, 37, 159, 243
Monongahelas 2
Moore, Enoch "Inky" 261, 336
Motor Boat Law, Pennsylvania's 193
Muddy Creek 228
mudminnows xxvii
Mulhollem, Jeff 242, 330
Murray Energy 314
Muskellunge xi, xiii, 59, 118, 138, 219, 231, 261, 262, 272, 358
Mussel, Snuffbox 314
Mussels, Pearl xi
Mussels, Quagga 308
Mussels, Zebra 308

N

Nader, Ralph 162
National Association of Engine and Boat Manufacturers 136
National Humane Education Center 176
National Pollutant Elimination System Permit 306
National Safety Council 212
National Water Safety Congress (NWSC) 195

Index **365**

Native Americans xxxi, 2, 3, 4, 5, 6, 7, 14, 150, 285, 321
Natural Resources and the Public Estate xxiii, 156
Neeper, Murray 276
Nelson, Gaylord 161
newspaper, *Clarion Democrat* 86
newspaper, *Clarion Republican* 86
newspaper, *Oil City Derrick* 86
newspaper, *Philadelphia Inquirer* 201
newspaper, *Pittsburgh Press, The* 87
newspaper, *Sun-Telegraph* 86
New York Harbor 27
New York State Conservation Department 90
Nixon, Richard M. 147, 152
Norfolk Southern 286
Norris, Thad vi, 20
North Branch Susquehanna River 273
Norvelt 64
Nutting, Wallace 2, 325

O

office, Centre Region Office Complex 313, 341
office, Harrisburg Headquarters, PFBC 267, 315, 340
office, Northcentral Region Office 346
office, Northeast Region Office 346
office, Northwest Region Office 346
Office of Information 179, 195, 210
office, Pleasant Gap Office Complex 314, 341
office, Southcentral Region Office 347
office, Southeast Region Office 347
office, Southwest Region Office 347
oil, Ashland Oil Company 243
oil, Shell Oil Company 110
oil, Sun Oil Company 52
Old Bastards, The 165 xv, 208, 209, 210, 288

P

Paasch Brothers 48
Paradise Brook Trout Company 53
Parrish, Don 216
Payne, John 261
Pearl Harbor 88
PennDOT 149
Penn's Charter 6
Penns Creek 225
Penn's Woods xviii, 2
Pennsylvania Department of Forests and Waters 118
Pennsylvania Farm Show, Pennsylvania Farm Show Complex 179, 260, 281
Pennsylvania League of Angling Youth (PLAY) xxix, 206, 220, 274, 277, 284, 320
Pennsylvania State Police 168, 195, 260, 283
Pennsylvania Women Outdoors Inc. 214
Penn, William xxxi, 2
Pennypacker, Samuel 44
Perch, Yellow xxvii, 46, 71, 83, 150, 219, 234, 283, 360
Perry, Oliver Hazard 48
Personal Flotation Devices, PFDs, life jackets 136, 221
Phillipe, Samuel 6
Piccola, Jeff 260
pickerel xi, xiii, 46, 53, 59, 69, 70, 72, 83, 118, 262
Pickerel, Chain vii, 46, 231, 358
pike xxvii, 35, 53, 83, 150
Pike, Amur xi, xv, 358
Pike, Blue 88, 360
Pike, Northern xi, 138, 231, 262, 280, 358
pike perch 83
Pinchot, Gifford 316, 319
Pine Creek 16, 64, 175, 182
Piney Creek Springs 148
Pisko, Mark 261
Plan, State Wildlife Action xviii
plan, Strategic Planning 251, 272
Policy for the Conservation and Management of Fishery Resources 208
Pollution Strike Force 158, 159, 160, 163
porcupine crib 285
post-World War II era xxxi, 150, 321
Potomac River vi, 355
Presque Isle Bay 286
Pritts, K. Derek 213, 209
program, Adopt-a-Lake 247
program, Adopt-a-Stream 247, 248
Program, Best Fishing Waters 323
Program, Boating Facility Grant 273
Program, Cooperative Nursery xi, 276, 328
Program, Fishing Tackle Loaner 284, 320
program, Keystone Aquatic Resource Education (KARE) 218, 248, 276
Program, Miller Brewing Company's Friends of the Field 297
program, Pennsylvania Water Trails 254, 277, 322
program, Rails-to-Trails 254
Program, Wild Resource Conservation 210, 275
Progressive Era 40, 53, 63
Pymatuning Reservoir 86, 118, 210

Q

Qualters, Tom, Sr. 168
Queen Victoria 30
Quinn, Martin and Thomas 16

R

Raccoon Lake 110
rail car vii, 35, 39
railroad, Pennsylvania Railroad 27, 35, 39, 48, 52
Ranck, Paul A. 134
Raystown Lake 219, 228
Reading Fire Department 213
Ready, Set, Inflate! 296
Real Estate Division 139
Recreational Boating and Fishing Foundation (RBFF) 127
Recreational Demonstration Area 110
Reed, Leon H. 252
registration, boat 149, 194
Rendell, Edward G. 281, 301
report, *Aquatic Life Maintained at the Wayne Fish Hatchery for Educational Purposes* 60
report, *Methods Employed in Producing the Bullfrog (Rana Catesbiana) Tadpoles at the Pennsylvania State Hatcheries* 60
report, *Roosevelt Wild Life Bulletin, The* 13
reptiles xv, xviii, xxvii, xxix, 174, 196, 207, 209, 211, 263, 277, 281, 315
Resource First xv, xxvii, 208, 209, 210, 240, 242, 293, 294, 329
Richardson, Carl xxxii, 299
Ridge, Tom 251, 261
Riley, Cheryl K. 220, 240, 243, 330
river rescue, River Rescue Conference 212, 213
rock snot 308
Rockview Penitentiary 82, 296
Rockwell, Norman 90

Roosevelt, Eleanor 64
Roosevelt, Franklin D. 88
Rosato, Nicholas 198
Rosato, Peg 175
Rotigel, Misty 280
R. S. Kemmerer Company 53
rules of the road 179
Rush, Benjamin 14

S

salmon x, xi, xiv, xv, 11, 26, 37, 38, 179, 219, 230, 242, 358
Salmon, Coho xi, 230, 358
Sandy Creek 284
Sanitary Water Board 66, 136, 142, 144, 158, 159, 160
Sapp, Dawn 269
Save Our Susquehanna (S.O.S.) xii, 302, 304, 319
Saylor, John 162
Schadt, John A. 69
Schilling, Frank 163
school, Greenwood School District 166
School, St. Mary's Area Middle 276
school, Youth Bass Anglers School (YBAS) 275
Schrader Creek 284
Schroll, Raymond L., Jr. xvi, 134, 135
Schuyler, Keith 109, 327
Schuylkill River 8, 10, 118, 163, 191, 213
Scouts, Boy 169
Scranton 70, 206
Scudders Falls 47
Scully, Lawrence 48
Section, Educational Media 254
Section, Graphic Services 243, 246, 252
Sevareid, Eric 176
Shad Advisory Committee (SSAC) 174
Shad, American iv, v, vi, xx, xxi, xxiv, xxix, 6, 8, 9, 20, 174, 183, 189, 191, 232, 262, 316, 319, 329, 356

Shad, Gizzard 220, 232, 356
Shafer, Raymond P. 146, 158
Shaffer, Larry 220
Shapp, Milton 159, 172
Shelley, Carl 159
Shetterley, Tom 293
Shiels, Andrew 278, 308
ship, Commodore Perry xiii, 48, 49, 50
ship, *Niagara* xiii
ship, *Perca* xiii, 151
ship, *U.S.S. Midway* 134
Shoemaker, William E. xvi, 58, 59
Shriner, Charles A. 47, 70
Sink, Kenneth L. 165, 225
Sinnemahoning-Portage Creek 286
Skink, Broadhead 236, 278
Slaymaker, Samuel 146
Slutter, Gary 252
Smith, Bruce 261
Smith, Captain John 287
Smith, Jennifer 169
Smith, Ned xxxii, 107, 354
Snake, Earth 239, 279
Snakehead, Northern 311, 360
snake, rattlesnakes 174, 239, 275, 279
snake, watersnakes 66, 67, 327
Snyder, Richard 164
Society, American Fisheries 270
Society, American Philosophical 14
Society, Bass Anglers Sportsman's Society (B.A.S.S.) 183
Society of Automotive Engineers and Boating Industry Association 194
Society of Fort St. David's 10
Society, Pennsylvania Audubon 87
sojourns 310
Sorenson, Dewey 240
Soviet Union xi

species (AIS), aquatic invasive xix, 308, 310, 311, 355
species, candidate 279
species, endangered 279
species management 211, 263
species, threatened 279
speedboats 192
Speedwell Forge 164
Spring Creek 66, 73, 82, 120, 179, 195, 240, 295, 296
Spring Creek Canyon 66, 295
Spruce Creek 44, 53, 165, 269
Stackhouse, H. R. 67, 140, 141, 282, 333, 334, 335, 348
Stackhouse (H. R. Stackhouse) School of Fishery Conservation and Watercraft Safety 122, 140, 282, 348
State Capitol Building 52, 55, 164, 292
State College High School 87
State Employees' Retirement System 112
State Federation of Bass Anglers 167
State Historical Marker 313, 315
State Park, Black Moshannon 284
State Park, French Creek 262
State Park, Gifford Pinchot 262
State Park, Keystone 127, 284
State Park, Lackawanna 128
State Park, Ohiopyle 214, 262
State Park, Presque Isle 128, 277
State Park, Raccoon Creek 110
State Park, Ricketts Glen 284
state parks 127, 163, 214, 249, 262, 284, 324

Steiner, Linda 285, 331
Stitt, Alice 277, 330
stocking fleet 114
stocking, Great White Fleet 194
stocking, tank truck 114
stocking truck, refrigerated 114
Stone, Fred E. 354
Stone Valley Recreation Area Civil Engineering Lodge 275
Stony Creek 20
Stout, James 261
Straight Talk xxviii, 201, 222, 293, 329, 330, 331
Stranahan, Susan 201
Stuart, Edward 277
Stuart, Edwin S. 48
sturgeon 6, 35
sturgeon fishing camp 36
suckers xxvii, 83
Sunbury xii, 48, 136, 301
sunfish 53, 83, 234, 262, 359
Susinno, Mark 274
Susquehanna flats, Maryland iv, 12
Susquehanna rail car 35
Susquehanna River iv, v, vi, vii, xii, xviii, xix, xx, xxix, xxx, xxxi, 8, 12, 20, 26, 27, 29, 48, 63, 65, 116, 131, 134, 136, 172, 183, 188, 196, 200, 204, 215, 218, 223, 254, 262, 263, 267, 272, 273, 286, 287, 300, 301, 302, 303, 304, 305, 310, 331, 355
Susquehanna River Anadromous Fish Restoration Committee (SRAFRC)-1976 vi, 183, 188, 223
Susquehanna River Anadromous Fish Restoration Cooperative (SRAFRC)-1995 vi
Susquehanna River Basin Commission xxx, 188, 305

Index **367**

Susquehanna
 Shad Advisory
 Committee-1969 174,
 188
Svetahor, Emil 214
Swanson, Paul 149, 209,
 217
Sweigart, Alex P. 354
Sweppenhiser, Mark
 283, 284
Swift, Tom 180
syndrome, blotchy bass
 xviii, 302

T

Take Me Fishing in PA
 298
tax, excise iv, 113
Tax, Oil Company
 Franchise 294
Tenner, John K. xvi
Third Pennsylvania
 Welfare, Efficiency,
 and Engineering
 Conference 55
Thornburgh, Dick 196,
 250
Three Mile Island 196,
 200
Three Rivers Regatta
 242
Tide Water Canal
 Company 12
Tioga Creek 172
Treasure Lake 191
Trembly, Gordon 112
Trenton Water Power
 Company 47, 48
Tropical Storm Agnes
 171, 172, 173, 174
trout vii, xiii, xv, xxvii, 6,
 14, 24, 35, 53, 59, 62,
 64, 66, 67, 71, 72, 73,
 82, 83, 85, 88, 118,
 125, 129, 137, 138,
 139, 147, 160, 165,
 172, 175, 177, 178,
 180, 194, 197, 207,
 209, 219, 228, 229,
 247, 248, 252, 262,
 265, 270, 271, 276,
 281, 284, 288, 293,
 306, 307, 308, 313
Trout, Brook xi, xv, xix,
 37, 39, 53, 59, 67,
 178, 203, 230, 252,
 297, 358
Trout, Brown vii, 27,
 64, 69, 71, 73, 83,
 150, 178, 203, 230,
 242, 268, 286, 296,
 358
Trout, Golden Rainbow
 202, 230, 358
Trout, Lake 83, 230,
 358
Trout Perch xxvii
Trout, Rainbow vii, 27,
 64, 178, 202, 230,
 242, 358
trout stamp competition
 252
trout, steelhead vii, 179,
 230, 265, 280, 286,
 293
Trout Unlimited (TU)
 87, 165, 167, 173,
 182, 225, 273, 297
Troxel, Rueben 26
Tulpehocken Creek 284
Tunnel, Butler Mine
 218
Turtle, Blanding's 236,
 279
Turtle, Bog 236, 279
Turtle, Redbellied 236,
 278, 279
Turtle, Wood 236, 267
Twitter xii, xxviii, 289,
 321, 322

U

Ulsh, Stephen B. 160,
 220, 221, 252, 329
Unassessed Waters
 Initiative 307
Unified Sportsmen of
 Pennsylvania 281
United States Bureau of
 Fisheries xi
University, Iowa State
 270
University of Illinois
 270
University of Pittsburgh
 250, 292
University, Pennsylvania
 State 127, 143, 162,
 240, 242, 275, 295,
 296, 325, 329
U.S. Air Force 250
U.S. Army 143, 166,
 242, 250
U.S. Army Corps of
 Engineers xxx, 179,
 219, 242, 250
U.S. Coast Guard 88,
 140, 215, 296
U.S. Commission on
 Fish and Fisheries
 vii, 26, 35, 37
U.S. Department of
 Labor 40
U.S. Department of the
 Interior 137, 174,
 204
U.S. Environmental
 Protection Agency
 xxx, 147, 164, 208
U.S. Fish and Wildlife
 Service xxx, 134,
 138, 143, 144, 188,
 191, 224, 275
U.S. House of
 Representatives 172
U.S. Navy 134
U.S. Public Health
 Service 152

V

Van Gordon, Moses 32
viral hemorrhagic
 septicemias (VHS)
 308
Virgin Run Lake 113
Voigt Jr., William 128,
 339

W

Wagner, Honus 55
Wagner, Howard 261
Wagner, James 214
Walke, Ted i, xxiii, xxv,
 xxxii, 1, 157, 212,
 220, 240, 241, 243,
 249, 252, 263, 274,
 277, 287, 295, 296,
 299, 307, 311, 319,
 352
Wallenpaupack Creek
 69
walleyed pike 37
Walleyes xiii, 59, 138,
 219, 262, 280, 293
Walt, Ryan 282
War, Korean 108
water rescue 212, 213,
 247
Wear It Pennsylvania!
 296
Weber, Bob xx, 268
Weirich, Blake C. 218
Western Pennsylvania
 Coalition for
 Abandoned Mine
 Reclamation 297
Western Pennsylvania
 Conservancy 168,
 306
Wharton, Thomas 11
Whitefish, Lake 26, 30,
 31, 35, 53, 150, 358
Wilderness Trout
 Stream xiii
Wildlands Conservancy
 296
Wild Life Forest
 Experimentation
 Station 13, 325
Wildlife Management
 Institute 137, 140,
 327
Williamson, Richard
 F. 354
Williamsport 16, 89,
 134
Williams, Raymond
 143
Wolf, Dave 220, 240,
 354
Wood, Lloyd 126
World's Fair, Chicago,
 1893 xii, 36
World's Fair, St. Louis,
 1904 xii, 36, 45, 47
World War II xxxi, 88,
 89, 108, 110, 134,
 150, 166, 321
Worrall, James iv, xxix,
 18, 332
W.P.A. 65, 80
Wyrich, Douglas 180

Y

Yellow Breeches Creek
 283
Yellow Creek 242
Yoder, James F. 354
York County
 Democratic Party
 126
York, Duke of 6
Youghiogheny River
 168, 214, 262, 297
Young, C. Joel 71

Z

Ziddock, Alex, Jr. 266

*inside back cover photograph
by Spring Gearhart, PFBC*